THE WORD OF ISLAM

Cover and title page calligraphy by Mohamed Zakariya: the Islamic profession of faith, "There is no god but God, and Muhammad is the Messenger of God."

THE WORD OF ISLAM

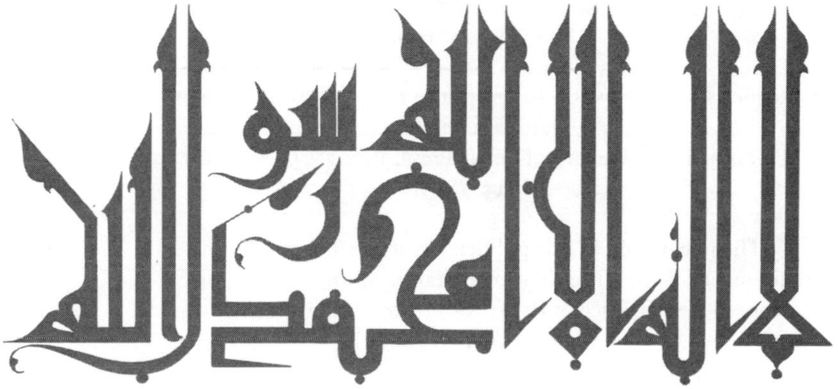

Edited by John Alden Williams

UNIVERSITY OF TEXAS PRESS

AUSTIN

Printed in the United States of America
First edition, 1994

∞ The paper used in this publication meets the minimum requirements of American National Standard for Information Sciences—Permanence of Paper for Printed Library Materials, ANSI Z39.48-1984.

Library of Congress Cataloging-in-Publication Data

The Word of Islam / edited by John Alden Williams. — 1st ed.
p. cm.
Includes index.
ISBN 0-292-79075-9 (alk. paper). — ISBN 0-292-79076-7 (pbk.)
1. Islam. I. Williams, John Alden.
BP161.2.W67 1994
297—dc20 93-4676

For Emily, Hilary, and Felicity

THE OPENER

In the Name of God, the Merciful, the Compassionate.
Praise be to God,
The Lord of the Worlds,
The Merciful One, the Compassionate One,
The Master of the Day of Doom.
You alone we worship, to You alone we call for help.
Guide us in the straight path,
The path of those You have blessed,
Not of those with whom You are angry,
Nor of those who go astray.

The *Fātiḥa*, the opening *sūra* of the Qur'ān, the *Sūra* of Praise, is recited every time Muslims begin their prayer and when any new thing is to be undertaken. It properly begins *The Word of Islam*.

CONTENTS

INTRODUCTION

Nearly a generation ago, I edited a book with an approach similar to this one, named simply *Islam*. It will be clear to anyone who has seen them both that this is not that book, but both try to let Islam speak for itself, and this book stands on the other's shoulders. There have been many sound attempts at objective books on Islam: "Islam is *X*, Muslims believe *Y*, Muslims perform *Z*." My discontent with the limitations of an approach that turns faith into an object, and thus is inevitably perceived as violence by people who hold that faith, has led me to believe that it is truer to let a tradition speak for itself, insofar as it is possible. It is when the people of a tradition tell each other what they are about that we may come most authentically to perceive it; when they discourse on a common enterprise, we may hope to catch the genuine accents of their tradition, to the extent that materials in translation will permit us to do so.

A book about a religion which does not allow its adherents to say, "Yes, it is like that," has a necessarily limited value. Moreover, every great religion is an ocean, with many bays, inlets, and unplumbed areas; we cannot pour it into a bottle and hold it up to the light. We can only come to it, smell it, taste it, touch it, observe what thrives there, and listen to its many moods. Our apprehension of it will be incomplete, but we will not falsify it by reducing it to an image or a model.

This new book tries, with a bit more confidence than I felt with the first one, to let Islam's word come through. After all, I have been listening to this particular ocean for an additional thirty years. Yet I am well aware that the ocean, ever itself, is also in a process of changing its boundaries and its colors, even that living people have the power to pollute it. It will be there when they are gone, but it may not be quite the same.

In the meantime, Muslims and non-Muslims are concerned about how one may most effectively and practically study Islam. My answer will always be the same: read the texts which convey its tradition in as wide a range as one can. An original text is worth more than many words of explanation. Go to the sources and listen to voices that have rung with authority for generations, that Muslims have recognized, and use only enough introductory material to set the voice in its context. When one has done that, one begins to be able to discriminate clearly among the modern voices.

It is because Muslims have been appreciative of this approach in the past that I am using it again. Necessarily, some of the same authoritative texts used earlier are used here, but in cases of prose I have usually made new translations of my own or revised my earlier translations, so that the original comes through more clearly. (All translations are mine, unless otherwise noted.) One change that I have often made, at the urging of Muslim friends, is to try to use gender-inclusive language even where the traditional language is almost entirely male. It was considered more appropriate in the past not to address women, even though the Qur'ān often does. Women were to live a sheltered and cherished private existence, but Islam is the religion of women as well as men, and translated texts should not give the impression that it is only intended for males.

I have also frequently translated the word *kāfir* as "rejecter," as well as "infidel." The word means one who deliberately and ungratefully rejects God's goodness; *kufr* is an action, rather than a quality of belief.

I have only rarely tried to produce new translations in the case of Ṣūfī poems translated by writers such as Edward Fitzgerald, R. A. Nicholson, and A. J. Arberry, who were themselves able poets. Occasionally, with permission, I have changed archaic diction (e.g., "thou sayest" to "you say").

Translations are ephemeral, particularly in the swiftly changing English language. By far the best English interpretation of the Qur'ān (Muslims do not consider that it can be translated, only interpreted) is that of A. J. Arberry— or it was in 1955.[1] No English interpretation done earlier or later approached Arberry's in its ability to suggest something of the beauty, profundity, and grandeur of the original. Yet in the 1990s its language strikes even college students as outdated and difficult to comprehend. Other interpretations have all been simply attempts to convey some of the meaning as faithfully as possible.

The problem is that the Arabic of the Qur'ān is much more than meaning. Any interpretation that does not at least suggest some of its remarkable qualities cannot be adequate, however faithful to literal meaning it may be. Two other English interpretations, those of Mohammed Marmaduke Pickthall (in 1930) and A. Yusuf Ali (in 1938), have won a measure of approval from Muslim scholars.[2] No one has taken exception to Pickthall's rendition of meaning, but from the first it was a poor literary product, apparently designed to sound somewhat like the King James Version of the Bible read at that time in churches. By this time, it is seriously misleading as an interpretation of what the Qur'ān is like. Ali's rendition has similar disadvantages.

For this book, I have had no choice but to make a new, contemporary interpretation directly from the Arabic for the sections I wanted to cite. It is a task both demanding and rewarding, and something I have done in other contexts over past years.

The transliteration system throughout this book is that found in the new *Encyclopaedia of Islam,* but uses *q* for *qāf* and *j* for *jīm* and omits a second *y* or *w* in diphthongs formed with *i* and *u*. Since "Allāh" is simply the Arabic word for God whether one is a Muslim or an Arab Christian or Jew, I have used the English word throughout. Non-Muslims should not be given the misleading impression so many have received in the past that Muslims do not worship God, but something else called "Allāh."

Common Era dates have been used throughout, and where it seems helpful Hijra dates (A.H.) have been added in parentheses.

GUIDE TO PRONUNCIATION OF ARABIC TERMS

The spelling of Arabic and Persian words in Latin letters in this volume closely follows current standard international practice. The sounds may be approximated in English as follows:

Consonants

Most of these are pronounced much the same as in English, with the following consonants which English does not offer:

Hamza, the glottal stop, represented by (’). This is found in English dialect pronunciations of words like “bo”l” for “bottle.” It also occurs in “uh-oh.”

‘Ayn, represented by (‘). A voiced pharyngeal fricative very characteristic of Arabic but difficult for English speakers. The throat muscles are constricted, with a twang of the vocal chords approximating a gagging sound.

Ḥa’, represented by (**ḥ**): a voiceless pharyngeal fricative, made like /h/ but further up in the throat.

Qāf, represented by (**q**): articulated like a /k/, but articulated against the soft palate, in a uvular plosive. Note that when followed by /u/, it is never pronounced /kw/ as in “quaint.”

Ghayn, represented by (**gh**): pronounced like the gargled /r/ in Parisian French: a voiced velar fricative.

Khā’, represented by (**kh**): pronounced like a strong /ch/ in German *Nacht* or the Greek *chi:* a voiceless velar fricative.

Ḍād, represented by (**ḍ**): the most distinctive consonant in Arabic, pronounced like /d/, but with the tongue raised up against the velar ridge behind the upper front teeth. It is accompanied by constriction in the back of the throat, and like all the velarized consonants darkens the sound of any vowel following it.

Ṭā', represented by (**ṭ**): the velarized /t/, made like ḍ/.

Ṣād, represented by (**ṣ**): a velarized /s/, with the tongue raised as much as possible toward the velar ridge.

Ẓā', represented by (**ẓ**): a velarized /z/.

Vowels

There are only three vowels in Arabic, /a/, /i/, and /u/, but each has a short and a long form. The long forms, but not the short, are letters of the Arabic alphabet.

Short /a/ is pronounced much like /a/ in "fat cat in hat."

Long /a/, *represented by* **ā:** an /a/ that is held, as in "cab," or when with a velarized letter as in "hard."

Short /i/, as in "bit" or "hit."

Long /i/, *represented by* **ī:** like the /ee/ in "feet."

Short /u/, as in "put," or the double /o/ in "foot."

Long /u/, *represented by* **ū:** like the double /o/ in "loot," prolonged.

I
THE WORD OF GOD: THE QUR'ĀN

The central point of Islam from which all flows, the point of departure, may be paraphrased as follows: the God of Abraham (the only God: Allāh in Arabic, Khudā in Persian, Tanrı in Turkish, ho Theos in Greek, God in plain English) has spoken to man in the Qur'ān. This divine Word is seen as the culmination of a long series of divine communications which began when God created humankind, because He is eternally the One who guides. Adam was the first prophet, the first with whom God communicated.

The kernel of the message was always the same in every generation and for every people: the Creator is good, He deserves the praises of humankind, and in worship of Him lies their happiness. They are responsible to Him for what they do, and the consequences of their actions are tremendous. In every case, the message was deformed by perverse and deceitful people. In His great mercy, God finally sent His definitive revelation in clear Arabic, through a prophet who confirmed all previous prophets: Muḥammad, the much-praised. Now it could not be changed or perverted. Muḥammad was also charged with forming a central community who would guarantee its truth: the Community of Muslims.

Muslims have argued about the sense *in which it is true that the Qur'ān is God's Word; whether it is created or uncreated, whether it is true of the Arabic letters or of the message as a whole, whether it is as true of a copy of it as it of the recitation of it. But they have never questioned that it* is truly *God's Word.*

The Qur'ān is in Arabic, and it is inimitable. This means that translation in any real sense is impossible: it may be interpreted in other languages, but only the Arabic original is Qur'ān. Arabic expertly used is remarkably tense, rich, and forceful. The Arabic of the Qur'ān is unique: as H.A.R. Gibb stated, "No man in fifteen hundred years has played on that deep-toned instrument with such power, such boldness, and such range of emotional effect."[1]

God Speaks to Humankind

Using the We of Majesty, God addresses men and women and His messenger and prophet Muḥammad directly in the Qur'ān. This contains words addressed to His messenger, as well as the full sending down to earth of the eternal message addressed to the Children of Adam. The first verses of the Sūra *(chapter) of the Clot are the first words revealed to Muḥammad.*

In the Name of God, the Merciful, the Compassionate

1. Recite: In the Name of your Lord who created,
2. Created Man of a blood-clot.
3. Recite: And your Lord is the Most Generous,
4. Who taught by the Pen.
5. Taught Man what he knew not.
6. And yet indeed Man is rebellious,
7. For he thinks him self-sufficient.
8. Surely your returning is unto your Lord.
9. Have you seen him who restrains
10. A servant when he prays—
11. Have you seen that he was on guidance,
12. Or ordered to piety?
13. Have you seen that if he cries lies and turns away—
14. Did he not know that God sees?
15. And yet indeed if he desists not We shall seize him by the forelock;
16. The lying, sinful forelock.
17. So let him call upon his concourse!
18. We shall call upon the guards of Hell.
19. No indeed: do not obey him, but prostrate yourself, and draw nigh [your Lord].
    (*Sūra* 96:1–19)

The section here following is the beginning of the second and longest chapter, the Sūra *of the Cow. It serves as a sort of introduction to the Book as a whole.*

In the Name of God, the Merciful, the Compassionate

1. *Ālif Lām Mīm*
2. This is the Book, wherein there is no doubt, guidance to the Godfearing,
3. Who have faith in the Unseen and perform the ritual prayer, and expend of what We have provided them;
4. Who have faith in what has been sent down on you, and what was sent down before you, and are certain of the Hereafter.
5. Those are upon guidance from their Lord; those are they who will succeed.
6. As for the rejecters, alike is it to them whether you have warned them or have not warned them; they do not have faith.
7. God has set a seal on their hearts and hearing, on their eyes a covering. For them is mighty punishment.
8. Some there are of humankind who say, "We believe in God and the Last Day," and they have not faith.
9. They would trick God and the Faithful; only themselves they trick, and are not aware.
10. In their hearts there is sickness, and God has increased their sickness. For them is painful chastisement, for that they called lies.
11. When it is said to them, "Do not do corruption in the land," they say, "We are only putting things right."
12. Truly, they are working corruption, but are not aware.
13. When it is said to them, "Have faith, as others do," they say, "Shall we believe as fools believe?" Truly they are the foolish ones, and they do not know.
14. When they meet the faithful they say, "We have faith"; but when they enter in with their Satans, they say, "We are with you; we were only mocking."
15. God shall mock them, and lead them on, blindly wandering in their opposition.
16. Those are they who have bought error at the price of guidance, and their commerce has not profited them, nor are they well-guided.
17. The likeness of them is the likeness of a man who kindled a fire, and when it lit all about him, God took away their light, leaving them in darkness unseeing;
18. Deaf, dumb, blind—they shall not return.
19. Or like a cloudburst out of heaven, in which is darkness, and thunder, and lightning: they thrust their fingers in their ears

against the thunderclaps, fearing death; but God surrounds the unfaithful on all sides.

20. Well-nigh the lightning snatches away their eyesight; when it flashes, they walk in it, and when darkness is over them, they stand still. Had God willed, He would have taken their hearing and their sight; surely God is powerful over every thing.
21. O People, worship your Lord who created you, and those who were before you—haply you will be Godfearing—
22. Who assigned the earth to you as a couch, and the heavens as an edifice, and sent forth from heaven water, bringing forth therewith fruits as provision to you; set up no peers for God wittingly.
23. And if you are in doubt about what We have sent down upon Our servant, then bring one *sūra* like it, and call as witnesses whom you will, apart from God, if you speak the truth.
24. But if you do not—and you never will— then fear the Fire whose fuel is humans and stones, prepared for the unbelievers.
25. Give good tidings to those who have faith and do good deeds, that for them await gardens underneath which rivers flow; whenever they are provided with the fruits therefrom, they shall say, "This is that from which we were nourished previously!" It shall be given them in full similitude, and for them there shall be pure spouses; there shall they dwell forever.

(*Sūra* 2:1–25)

The story of the Garden of Eden is very like that contained in the Book of Genesis, but there is no doctrine of original sin in Islam. The fall of Adam and Eve is seen as an error in judgment, not as a taint in their descendants. From Adam's creation, humankind has made a contract to serve God—a unique glory and burden, for which it is weak, but not impotent.

10. We established you upon the earth, and provided means of livelihood for you in it; little are the thanks you give.
11. We created you, then We shaped you, then We said to the angels, "Bow down to Adam"; so they bowed down, except Iblīs—he was not of those who bowed.
12. Said God, "What prevented you from bowing down, when I commanded you?" He replied, "I am better than he; You created me from fire, but him from clay."

13. Said God, "Get down from it; it is not for you to be insolent here; go forth: you are among the humbled."
14. Said he, "Give me respite, until the day they shall be raised."
15. Said God, "You are of those respited."
16. Said he, "Now for undoing me, I shall surely sit in wait for them along Your straight path.
17. And I shall come upon them from before and from behind, right and left. You shall not find most of them thankful."
18. Said God, "Go forth from it, despised and banished. As to those of them who follow you, I shall surely fill up Hell with all of you.
19. And you, O Adam, and your spouse, inhabit the Garden and eat from whence you wish, but come not near this tree, lest you be of the evildoers."
20. Yet the adversary whispered to them, to reveal what was hidden from them of their shameful parts. He said, "Your Lord only kept you from this tree lest you become angels, or immortals."
21. And he swore, "Truly, to you both I am a sincere adviser!"
22. So he led them on by deceit. And when they tasted the tree, their shame was revealed to them, so they took to patching on themselves the leaves of the Garden. And their Lord called unto them, "Did I not keep you from this tree? And tell you that Satan is for you an open enemy?"
23. They said, "Our Lord, we have wronged ourselves. If You do not forgive us and have mercy upon us, then surely we are among the lost."
24. Said He, "Go down, each the enemy of the other. In the earth a sojourn shall be yours, and provision for a while.
25. Therein you shall live and therein die, and therefrom shall you be brought forth."
26. Children of Adam, We revealed to you raiment to cover your shame, and adornment, yet the raiment of piety is best. That is one of God's signs: perhaps you will reflect.
27. Children of Adam, let not Satan beguile you, as when he brought your parents out of the Garden, stripping from them their covering, to expose to them their shame. Surely he sees you, he and his tribe, from whence you see them not. We have made the devils the intimates of those who have not faith.
28. Whenever they commit lewdness, they say, "We found our ancestors doing it, and God orders us to do it." Say, "God does not order indecent acts. Do you impute to God what you know not?"

29. Say, "My Lord orders justice. Set your faces in every place of worship and call on Him pure in service to Him. As He brought you forth, so you will return."
(*Sūra* 7:10–29)

172. When your Lord took from the Children of Adam, from their loins their seed, and made them bear witness as to themselves: "Am I not your Lord?" They said, "Yes, we bear witness!"—lest you should say on the Day of Resurrection, "Really, we were ignorant of this,"
173. Or lest you say, "It was only our ancestors who were idolators before us, and we are seed after them; what, will You destroy us for the deeds of vain-doers?"
174. Thus We distinguish the Signs; perhaps they will come back.
175. Relate to them the plight of one to whom we gave Our Signs, yet he turned aside from them, and Satan followed after him, and he became one of the perverted.
176. Had We willed, We would have exalted him thereby, but he inclined to the earth, and followed his lust. So his likeness is the likeness of a dog; if you attack it, it lolls its tongue out, or if you leave it, it lolls its tongue out. Such is the likeness of people who cry lies to Our Signs. Relate the story: perhaps they will reflect.
177. Evil is the likeness of people who cried lies to Our Signs; themselves they were wronging.
178. Whomsoever God guides, such are rightly guided; and whom He leads astray, such are the losers.
179. We have created for Hell many jinn and humans; they have hearts, but understand not with them; they have eyes, but perceive not with them; they have ears, but they hear not with them. They are like cattle, but further astray. Such are people unconcerned.
180. God's are the names most beautiful, so call Him by them. Leave those who blaspheme His names—they will be recompensed for what they have done.
181. Yet among those We have created are a community who guide by Truth, and by it act straightly.
(*Sūra* 7:172–181)

The Qur'ān repeatedly reminds humankind that it is surrounded by the evidences of divine handiwork and expresses astonishment that it is too blind to recognize the Creator.

In the Name of God, the Merciful, the Compassionate

1. God's command comes; seek not to hasten it. High exalted is He above what they associate with Him!
2. He sends down the angels with the Spirit of His command on whom He wills of His servants, saying, "Give warning that there is no God but I, so fear you Me!"
3. He created the heavens and the earth in truth; high be He exalted above all that they associate with Him!
4. He created humankind from a sperm-drop; yet behold, it is an open adversary.
5. And the cattle He created for you, whence you have warm clothing and other uses, and from them you eat.
6. In them is beauty for you, when you bring them home for rest and when you pasture them.
7. They bear your loads unto a land that you would never reach except with hardship for yourselves. Surely your Lord is Kind, Compassionate.
8. And the horses, the mules, the donkeys, for you to ride and as an adornment; and others He creates which you know not.
9. Unto God leads the right way, and some do deviate from it. Had He willed, He would have guided you all together.
10. He it is who sends down to you water out of heaven, of which you drink, of which come bushes to pasture herds.
11. Thereby He brings forth crops, and olives, palms, and grapes, and all kinds of fruit. Surely in that is a sign for people who reflect.
12. He subjected to you the night and the day, and the sun and moon, and the stars are subjected by His command. Surely in that are signs for people who use intelligence.
13. And other things He multiplied in the earth for you of diverse hues. Surely in that is a sign for people who remember.
14. He it is who subdued the sea, that you may eat fresh flesh from it and bring forth ornaments for you to wear. You may see the ships cleaving through it, and thus you may seek His bounty; so may you be grateful.
15. And He cast in the earth mountains, that it hold firm with you, and rivers and ways; so may you be guided.
16. And waymarks, and by the stars are people guided.
17. Is One who creates like one who does not create? Will you not remember?
18. If you count God's favor, you cannot reckon it; surely God is Forgiving, Compassionate.

19. God knows what you keep secret and what you publish.
20. And those they call on apart from God created nothing and are themselves created,
21. Dead, not alive, and they know not when they will be raised.
22. Your God is one God. As for those who have not faith in the world to come, their hearts deny, and they are puffed up with pride.
23. Without a doubt, God knows what they keep secret and what they disclose: He loves not those who wax proud.
(*Sūra* 16:1–23)

In the Name of God, the Merciful, the Compassionate

1. Blessed be He in whose hand is the Kingdom— He is powerful over everything—
2. Who created death and life that He might try you, which of you is fairest of deed; and He is All-Mighty, All-Forgiving,
3. Who created seven heavens one above the other. You see not in the creation of the All-Merciful any disproportion. Return your gaze; do you see any fissure?
4. Return your gaze again and again and it comes back to you dazed, aweary.
5. And We adorned the lower heaven with lamps, and made them things to stone Satans; and We prepared for them the torment of the Blaze.
6. For those who hold not faith in their Lord there await the torments of Hell; an evil homecoming!
(*Sūra* 67:1–6)

He Speaks through the Prophets

Abraham:

The Patriarch Abraham, ancestor of the Semites, is seen as the father and prototype of the Committed, the Muslim; it is suggested that he arrived at knowledge of God by right use of his intelligence even before God gave him the revelation and made him His friend. With his first-born son Ishmael or Ismāʿīl he built the first temple of the Kaʿba at Bakka (Mecca) and set up the rites of the Pilgrimage. Although he has been claimed as father by Jews and Christians, he did not belong to either of those religions; he was simply a man committed to God: a Muslim. Since Islam is the religion of Abraham, such matters as dietary prohibitions later adopted by Jews did not apply to his religion.

41. And mention in the Book Abraham; surely he was righteous, a prophet.
42. Remember when he said to his father, "Father, why do you worship what neither sees nor hears, nor avails you in any way?
43. Father, to me has come such knowledge as never came to you, so follow me; I will guide you to a level way.
44. Father, serve not Satan; surely Satan was a rebel to the All-Merciful.
45. Father, I fear lest torment from the All-Merciful befall you, and you become a friend of Satan."
46. Said he, "What, do you shrink from my gods, Abraham? Surely if you desist not, I shall stone you, so go away from me for some time."
47. He answered, "Peace be upon you! I will ask my Lord to forgive you; He has surely been ever gracious to me.
48. Now I will withdraw from you and those you call on apart from God, and I will call on my Lord. Perhaps in calling on my Lord I shall not be unprosperous."
49. So, when he withdrew from them and what they worshiped apart from God, We gave him Isaac and Jacob, and each We made a prophet;
50. And We gave them of our mercy and appointed for them a righteous tongue, exalted.

(*Sūra* 19:41–50)

93. All food was lawful to the Children of Israel, save that Israel forbade for himself, before the Torah was revealed. Say, "Bring the Torah and recite it, if you be truthful."
94. Whoever forges falsehood about God after that, they are oppressors.
95. Say, "God has spoken truth, so follow the way of Abraham, pure in faith; he was no idolator."
96. The first House of God to be established for the people was that at Bakka, a holy place, and a guidance for all beings.
97. In it are clear signs, and the place where Abraham stood. All who enter it are in security. It is a duty to God for all humankind to come to that House as pilgrims, whoever can make their way there. As for the rejecter, God is All-Sufficient; He needs no one.
98. Say, "People of the Book, why do you reject God's signs, when He is witness to all that you do?"

(*Sūra* 3:93–98)

135. They say, "Be Jews or Christians and you shall be guided." Say, "Nay, rather the way of Abraham, a man of pure faith; he was not an idolator."
136. Say, "We have faith in God, and what has been sent down on us, and sent down on Abraham, Ishmael, Isaac and Jacob and the tribes, and that which was given to Moses and Jesus and the prophets, by their Lord; we make no division between any of them, and we are committed unto Him."
137. If they have faith in the like of what you have faith in, then they have been guided, but if they turn away, then they are in schism; God will suffice you for them; He is All-Hearing, All-Knowing; the baptism [or: dye] of God; and who baptizes fairer than God? Him are we worshiping.
(*Sūra* 2:135–137)

Moses

Moses is one of the prophets most frequently mentioned; he was sent as God's chosen messenger to rescue the descendants of Ishmael's nephew Israel from Egypt. However, the Children of Israel became proud and disobeyed God; they regarded themselves as a chosen people in the wrong sense, oppressed their brethren, and associated other gods with God. When He sent prophets to warn them, they refused to listen and put His messengers to death. They are People of the Book, because God gave them the scriptures, but their revelation has been tampered with.

29. When Moses had fulfilled the term and was travelling with his family, he noticed on the side of Mount Tūr a fire. He said to them "Stay here; I observe a fire. Perhaps I may bring news of it, or a brand from the fire, that you may warm yourselves."
30. When he came near, a voice called to him from the tree on the right side of the watercourse, in the hallowed valley: "Moses, I am God, the Lord of all worlds.
31. Cast down your staff." Then when he saw it wriggling like a serpent, he turned his back and fled without turning back. "Moses, draw nigh, and fear not: surely you are in security.
32. Place your hand in your bosom, and it will come forth white without harm, and brace yourself against fear: these shall be

two proofs from your Lord to Pharaoh and the Council; they are indeed a wicked folk."

33. He said, "My Lord, I have taken a life from them, and I fear that they will slay me.
34. Moreover, my brother Aaron is more eloquent than I, so send him with me as a helper to confirm that I speak truly. I fear they will call me a liar."
35. God said, "We shall strengthen your arm by your brother, and give you both authority so they cannot reach you because of Our signs. You, and those who follow you, shall be the victors."
36. Yet when Moses came to them with Our clear signs, they said, "This is nothing but contrived sorcery: we never heard of this among our ancestors, the ancients."
37. But Moses said, "My Lord is more knowing of who comes with guidance from Him, and who shall possess the reward of the Abode. Surely oppressors will not prosper."
38. Pharaoh said, "Council, I know not that you have any god but me. Kindle me, Haman, fire upon brick, and build me a tower, that I may mount up to Moses' god, for I think that he is one of the liars."
39. And he waxed proud in the land with his hosts without right, thinking they would not be returned to Us.
40. So We seized him with his hosts and cast them into the sea; behold what was the end of the oppressors!
41. And We made them leaders inviting to the Fire, and on the Day of Resurrection they will not be helped.

(*Sūra* 28:29–41)

47. O Children of Israel, remember My favor wherewith I favored you, and that I have preferred you above all beings;
48. And guard against a day when no soul shall avail another in anything, and no intercession will be accepted from it, nor any ransom be taken, nor will they be assisted.
49. Recall when We delivered you from Pharaoh's folk, who were wronging you with an evil chastisement, slaughtering your sons and sparing your womenfolk; in that was a mighty trial from your Lord.
50. And when We parted the sea for you and delivered you, and drowned Pharaoh's people while you were looking on.
51. And when We appointed with Moses for forty nights, and then you took to yourselves the Calf after him, and did evil.

52. Even after that We pardoned you, that you might be grateful.
53. And when We gave Moses the scripture, and the discernment of good and evil, that you might perhaps be guided.
(*Sūra* 2:47–53)

61. And when you said, "Moses, we cannot endure one sort of food; call on your Lord for us, that He may bring forth for us what the earth produces: its greens, and cucumbers, grain, lentils, and onions!" He said, "Would you exchange the baser for the better? Then go down to Egypt; there you may have what you demanded." Abasement and misery were stamped upon them, and they were laden with God's anger; that, because they had rejected God's signs and slain the prophets without right; that, because they had rebelled and were transgressors.
62. Surely they who have faith, and those that guide by Judaism, and Christians, and Ṣābi'ans, who have faith in God and the Last Day and do righteousness—their reward is with their Lord; no fear shall be on them, nor shall they sorrow.
(*Sūra* 2:61–62)

Jesus

John and Jesus are seen as members of the righteous family of 'Imrān, among the Children of Israel. Jesus holds a particular place among the prophets of Islam. He is the promised Messiah and born of a virgin "purified above all women." He is "Word of God and Spirit from Him," who spoke from birth and worked great miracles by the power of God. However, central articles of Christian faith are set aside. The idea that God would beget a son is sternly rejected; Christians are in grave danger of worshipping three gods; and, since Jesus did not die upon the cross and there was no collective guilt of hu mankind for which the innocent Messiah should suffer, there was no atonement and no resurrection.

While they are also People of the Book, Christians are accused of having tampered with their revelation, and their worshipping of the Messiah as God is seriously wrong, if not blasphemous. While the Apostles were Muslims, later generations have been misguided, so that a new dispensation through Muḥammad became necessary. As for Jesus, God took him to Himself when the Jews rejected him and will justify him before the end of the world.

38. Then Zachariah prayed unto his Lord, saying, "Lord, of Your bounty give me goodly offspring. Truly, You hear all prayer."
39. The angels called to him, as he stood in the Sanctuary at worship, "God sends you good tidings of John [Yaḥyā], who will confirm a Word from God; a chief, continent, a prophet."
40. He said, "Lord, how shall I have a son, seeing that old age has reached me and my wife is barren?" "Even so," God said, "God does what He will."
41. "Lord," said Zachariah, "appoint for me a sign." He replied, "Your sign shall be that you shall not speak to people for three days, except in symbol. And remember your Lord often, and give glory at evening and at the dawn."

(*Sūra* 3:38–41)

45. When the angels said "O Mary, God gives you good news of a Word from Him whose name shall be the Messiah, Jesus, Son of Mary; illustrious in this world and the next, near stationed [to God].
46. He shall speak to people in the cradle and when of age, and be among the righteous."
47. "O Lord," said Mary, "how shall I have a son, seeing no man has touched me?" He replied, "Even thus God creates what He wills. When He decrees a matter, He but says to it 'Be,' and it is.
48. God will teach him the Book and the Wisdom, Torah and the Good News."

(*Sūra* 3:45–48)

22. So she conceived him, and withdrew with him to a far place.
23. Then the birthpangs overtook her at the trunk of a date-palm. She said "Oh would I had died before this, and become a thing forgotten!"
24. But he called to her from below her, "No, do not sorrow: your Lord has set a stream just below you.
25. Shake also the palm trunk, and there will tumble on you dates fresh and ripe.
26. Eat and drink, and be comforted. If you see any mortal, say, 'I have vowed a fast to the All-Merciful, and will not speak this day to any.'"
27. She brought the child to her people, carrying him, and they said, "Mary, you have surely done an astonishing thing!

28. Sister of Aaron, your father was not an evil man, and your mother was not an unchaste woman."
29. But she pointed to the child. They said, "How shall we speak to one who is only a child in a cradle?"
30. "I am a servant of God," he answered. "He has given me the Book, and appointed me a prophet.
31. Blessed has He made me, wherever I may be, and enjoined on me prayer and to give alms so long as I live,
32. And also to cherish my mother. He has not made me arrogant, a rebel.
33. Peace be upon me the day I was born, the day I shall die, and the day I shall be raised alive!"
34. That is Jesus, Son of Mary; the account of truth in what they contend about.
35. It is not for God to take a son unto Him. Glory be to Him! When He decrees a thing, He but says to it, "Be," and it is.
36. Jesus said, "Surely God is my Lord and your Lord, so worship Him; this is a straight path."

(*Sūra* 19:22–36)

52. And when Jesus perceived their rejection, he said, "Who will be my helpers unto God?" The Disciples said, "We will be God's helpers; we have faith in God. Bear witness that we are Muslims.
53. Lord, we have faith in what You sent down, and we follow the messenger. Enroll us with the witnesses of truth."
54. Then [his enemies] contrived against him, and God contrived; and God is the best of contrivers!

(*Sūra* 3:52–54)

156. And for their rejection and uttering great calumnies of Mary,
157. And for their saying, "We killed the Messiah Jesus, the Son of Mary," the messenger of God—yet they did not kill him nor did they crucify him, but it appeared so to them—those who differed in this are in doubt concerning him; they have no knowledge of it but the following of opinion. Of certainty they slew him not.
158. Rather God raised him to Himself; God is All-Mighty, All-Wise.
159. There is not one of the People of the Book but will be assured of this before their death, and on the Resurrection Day he will be a witness against them.

(*Sūra* 4:156–159)

171. People of the Book, be not extreme in your faith, and say nothing about God but the truth. The Messiah Jesus, the Son of Mary, is only a messenger of God and His Word that He conveyed unto Mary, and a Spirit from Him. So believe in God and His messengers, and do not say, "Three." Refrain; it is better for you. God is only One God. Glory be to Him—that He should beget a son! His is all that is in the heavens and in the earth, and God suffices as a guardian.
172. The Messiah will never disdain to be a servant of God, nor will the angels who are close to Him. And whoever disdains to serve Him and is proud He will surely muster to Him altogether.
(*Sūra* 4:171–172)

Muḥammad

Muḥammad is the chosen instrument by whom God sent the eternal message in its definitive form, the prophet who confirms all prophets. The Qur'ān addresses him directly, to affirm his place, to tell him how to address doubters, and even to assure him that he is not losing his mind. It points out that the truth of his message may be seen in the faith of his followers.

In the Name of God, the Merciful, the Compassionate
1. *Nūn*. By the pen, and what they inscribe,
2. You are not, by the grace of your Lord, a man possessed.
3. Surely yours is a reward unending.
4. Surely you are of a mighty nature.
5. So you shall see, and they will see,
6. Which of you is demented.
7. Surely your Lord knows best those who strayed from His way; He knows best those guided.
8. Obey not those who deny,
9. They only wish that you would compromise; then they would compromise.
(*Sūra* 68:1–9)

In the Name of God, the Merciful, the Compassionate
1. *Qāf*. By the Glorious Qur'ān,
2. Nay, but they marvel that a warner has come to them from

among themselves. The rejecters say, "This is an astonishing thing!

3. What, when we are dead and turned to dust? That would be a remote return!"
4. We know what the earth diminishes of them; with Us is a Book preserving all.
5. But no! They called reality lies when it came to them, so they are in a troubled case.
6. Have they not beheld the sky above them, how We built it and adorned it, and it has no flaws?
7. And the earth We spread out, and cast on it firm hills, and caused to grow thereon of every lovely kind;
8. A vision and a reminder to each penitent servant.
9. And We sent down from heaven blessed water, whereby We give growth to gardens and to grain for harvest,
10. And lofty date-palms with spathes compact,
11. Provision for Our servants; and thus We revived the dead land. Even so is the coming forth.
12. Thus before them denied the folk of Noah, the people of al-Rass, and Thamūd,
13. And 'Ād and Pharaoh, and the brethren of Lot,
14. And the dwellers of the Thicket and the folk of Tubba'; all denied the messengers, and My threat came true.
15. Were We wearied by the first creation? Yet they are in doubt about a new creation.
16. We indeed created humankind, and We know what the self whispers within them. We are closer to them than the jugular vein. (*Sūra* 50:1–16)

21. Hasten to the forgiveness of your Lord, and a Paradise broad as the heavens and the earth, prepared for those who have faith in God and in His messengers. That is the favor of God; He bestows it on whom He will, and God is He of mighty favor.
22. No affliction on earth or in yourselves befalls but is in a Book before We create it; that is easy for God.
23. That you may not grieve for what missed you, or revel in what comes to you; God loves no boastful braggart,
24. Such as are miserly, and order people to be miserly. Whoever turns away, God is All-Sufficient, All-Praised.
25. Surely We sent Our messengers with the clear proofs, and sent down with them the Scripture and the Balance, that people may

uphold justice. And We sent down iron, wherein is great harm, and many uses for the people, that God may know who helps Him and the messengers, though unseen. Surely God is Strong, Almighty.

26. We sent Noah and Abraham, and made prophecy and the Book to be among their seed; and some among them are guided, but many of them transgress.
27. Then in their footsteps We sent Our messengers, and We sent Jesus, Son of Mary, and gave him the Good News. We set in the hearts of those who followed him tenderness and mercy. And monasticism they invented—We did not prescribe it for them—seeking God's good pleasure, yet they observed it not with right observance.
28. O you who believe, fear God and believe in His messenger. He will give you a double portion of His favor, and appoint a light for you to walk in; God is All-Forgiving, All-Compassionate.
29. So that the People of the Book may know they have no power over any of God's favor; that favor is in God's hand; He bestows it on whom He will, and God is He of mighty favor.
(*Sūra* 57:21–29)

29. Muḥammad is the Messenger of God, and those who are with him are hard against rejecters, merciful one to another. You may see them bowing, prostrating, seeking favor of God and good pleasure. Their mark is on their faces, the trace of prostration. That is their likeness in the Torah, and their likeness in the Gospel; like a seed that puts forth its shoot, and makes it strong, so it grows stout and rises straight upon its stem, gladdening the sowers, that through them He may enrage the rejecters. God has promised those among them who have faith and do righteous deeds forgiveness and a mighty wage.
(*Sūra* 48:29)

God Reveals Himself

Because the Qur'ān is God's Word, the most certain knowledge that humankind may have of Him is there. It is by pondering on the Book as a whole rather than by paraphrasing it or abstracting from it that Muslims seek to know their Lord. In themselves, verses may seem contradictory. God may be seen as utterly transcending any knowledge, yet He is "nearer than the jugular vein"; both statements about Him are equally true. Similarly, he is the Tender, the Compassionate, the Guide, teaching and sustaining humankind, but if they reject His guidance, He "leads them further astray." Those who argue for predestination as well as those who hold that people are given freedom to choose their acts are both able to find support in the Qur'ān for their views. And while God has personal qualities, Muslims would not refer to Him as personal (shakhṣī)*; they regard that as an unacceptable limitation of the Reality. Humankind is invited and even commanded to have faith in God and serve Him, but in the end He is unknowable, except insofar as He chooses to reveal Himself. The way to Him lies through His Book and commitment to Him and His commands, and the reward is sure, but He enlightens and guides whom He will.*

255. God—there is no god but He, the Living, the Self-subsisting. Slumber seizes Him not, neither sleep; His is all that is in the heavens and on earth. Who is there that shall intercede with Him, except by His leave? He knows what lies before them and behind them, and they comprehend nothing of His knowledge, except as He wills. His throne comprises the heavens and the earth; the preservation of them wearies Him not; He is the Sublime, the Almighty.
256. There is no compulsion in religion. Rectitude has been made clear from error. Whoever rejects false deities and has faith in God has grasped the firm handhold unbreaking; God is All-Hearing, All-Knowing.
257. God is the Friend of the faithful; He brings them from the shadows into light. As for those who reject, their friends are false deities, who bring them from the light into darkness. Such are possessors of the Fire; therein shall they abide.

(*Sūra* 2:255–257)

35. God is the Light of the heavens and the earth. The likeness of His Light is as a niche in which is a lamp; the lamp in a glass, the glass as it were a shining star; kindled from a blessed tree, an olive neither of the East nor of the West, whose oil would wellnigh shine though no fire touched it. Light upon Light; God guides to His Light whom He will. And God speaks to humankind in similitudes, for God is Knower of all things.
36. In houses God has allowed to be raised up that His name be

commemorated within them, therein praising Him at morn and evening,

37. Are people whom neither commerce nor sale diverts from remembrance of God, or establishing prayer, or paying out alms, fearing a Day when hearts and eyes shall be overturned.
38. So may God requite them for their fairest deeds, and give them increase of His favor; for God provides for whom He will, without reckoning.
39. As for the rejecters, their works are like a mirage in a desert plain. The thirsty one supposes it to be water, until he comes to it and finds it is nothing. In the place thereof he finds God, who pays him his account in full—and God is swift at the reckoning.
40. Or they are like shadows on a vast uncharted sea, billow surging over billow, above which are clouds, shadows piled one upon another. When one stretches out his hand, he can scarcely see it, and they to whom God gives no light, no light have they.
41. Have you not seen how all that is in heaven or in earth, and the birds in flight, give praise to God? All: He knows their prayer and their praise.
42. For God's is the Kingdom of the heavens and the earth, and unto God is the journeying.

(*Sūra* 24:35–42)

38. Surely God knows the unseen in the heavens and the earth; surely He knows the thoughts within the breasts.
39. He it is that made you trustees on the earth, so whoever rejects, his rejection is charged against him; their rejection increases the rejecters only in God's disgust; their rejection increases rejecters only in loss.

(*Sūra* 35:38–39)

48. God is He that looses winds, that stirs up clouds, and spreads them in the heavens as He will, then shatters them, so you see the rain pouring down from within them. When He strikes with it whom He will of His creatures, they rejoice,
49. Though before it was sent down on them from Him they were in despair.
50. So consider the marks of God's mercy, how He enlivens the earth after it was dead. Surely He is Enlivener of the dead; He is over all things Powerful.

51. Yet if We loosed a wind, and they beheld it yellow [destroying], they would remain even then rejecting.
52. You shall not make the dead hear, nor shall you make the deaf listen to the call when they turn their backs.
53. You are not the guide of the blind from their straying, when you can make none hear except those who have faith in Our signs, and are committed.
(*Sūra* 30:48–53)

100. Yet they ascribe the elemental spirits [jinn] to God as partners, though He created them, and they assign to Him sons and daughters, without knowledge. Glory be to Him! High exalted is He above what they describe!
101. Creator of the heavens and the earth—how should He beget offspring, when He has no consort? He created all things, and is of all things All-Knowing.
102. That then is God your Lord; there is no god but He, the Creator of all things, so worship Him, for He is Guardian over all things.
103. Eyes attain Him not, but He attains eyes; He is the Subtle, the Aware.
(*Sūra* 6:100–103)

He Commands

It is characteristic of Islam to see religion as a Law sent down from Heaven. In the revelation, God makes known what He has chosen for humankind and what He has forbidden. The idea of a divine Law can be clearly grasped from the Qur'ān.

172. O you who have faith, eat of the good things We have provided for you, and give thanks to God, if it be Him you serve.
173. These things only has He forbidden you: carrion, blood, the flesh of swine, and what has been dedicated to other than God. Yet one who is constrained without desiring it or acting deliberately does not sin; God is Forgiving, Compassionate.
174. Those who conceal what God has revealed to them of the Book, selling it for a petty price, shall eat nothing but fire into their bellies; God will not speak to them on the Day of Resurrection or let them thrive; for them is painful torment.
175. Such are they who purchase error at the price of guidance, and

torment at the price of forgiveness: how constantly they seek the Fire!

176. That is because God has sent down the Book with the truth; those disputing about the Book are in wide schism.

177. It is not piety that you turn your faces to the East or to the West: piety is to have faith in God and the Last Day, and in the angels, the Book, and the prophets; to give one's wealth for love of God to the near of kin and orphans, to the needy, the traveler, the beggar, and to ransom slaves; to perform the ritual prayer and pay the poor-tax. Those who fulfill their covenant when they have made a covenant, who endure patiently sorrows, adversity, and times of peril, such are true in faith, such are the Godfearing.

178. O you who have faith, prescribed for you is retaliation for the slain, freeman for freeman, slave for slave, female for female. Yet for one who is pardoned somewhat by a brother, then pursuit in honor and payment in kindness. That is an alleviation from your Lord, and a mercy. One who transgresses after that shall have a painful torment.

179. In retaliation is life for you, O people of sense; so may you be Godfearing.

180. It is prescribed for any whom death nears, who has goods, to bequeath them equitably to parents and next of kin; it is a charge upon the Godfearing.

(*Sūra* 2:172–180)

183. O you who have faith, fasting is prescribed for you, even as it was for those before you—so may you be Godfearing.

184. Fast for days numbered; yet if any of you is sick or on a journey, then the same number of other days, and, for those able to afford it, a ransom: feeding one who is poor. Yet it is better for one who does good voluntarily, and fasting is a good for you, if you but knew.

185. The month of Ramaḍān, in which the Qur'ān was sent down, a guidance to the people, and clear proofs of Guidance and the Criterion [of truth and falsehood]. Let those of you who are present fast the month, but if anyone be sick or on a journey, then a like number of other days. God desires ease for you, not hardship for you, that you may complete the number and magnify God that He guided you—so may you be thankful.

(*Sūra* 2:183–185)

187. It is permitted to you on the night of the Fast to go unto your wives: they are raiment for you as you are raiment for them. God knows that you have been betraying yourselves, and has turned to you and pardoned you. So now lie with them and seek what God has ordained for you. And eat and drink, until the white thread is distinct to you from the black thread at dawn, then fulfill the Fast until the evening, and do not lie with them while you apply yourself to the places of prayer. These are God's bounds, so stay well within them. Thus God makes clear His signs to the people; so may they be guided.
188. Do not consume each other's wealth in vain, nor offer it to those in authority, to consume a part of people's wealth sinfully, acting knowingly.
(*Sūra* 2:187–188)

216. Fighting is prescribed for you, although you hate it. Yet it may be that you hate a thing that is better for you, or you may love a thing that is worse for you: God knows, and you do not know.
217. They will ask you about the holy month, and fighting in it. Say, "Fighting in it is a great fault, but to bar from God's way, and reject Him and the Holy Mosque, and expel its people from it is a greater fault in God's sight; that discord is worse than slaying." They will not cease to fight with you until they turn you from your faith, if they are able; whoever of you turns from the faith and dies rejecting—such have deeds worthless in this world and in the next; such are possessors of the Fire: they will abide in it.
218. But those who have faith and those who emigrate and strive in God's way—such may hope for God's mercy, and God is Forgiving, Compassionate.
219. They will ask you about wine, and games of chance. Say, "There is great sin in each of them, and some uses for people, yet the sin is greater than the usefulness." They will ask you what they should give. Say, "What you can spare." Thus does God make clear His signs to you; so may you reflect
220. On this world and on the world to come. They will ask you about the orphans. Say, "To improve their lot is the best. If you mingle your affairs with theirs, then they are your brethren. God knows well the corrupt from the improver, and had He willed, He would have surely have worked hardship on you; God is All-Mighty, All-Wise."

221. Marry not idolatrous women, until they have faith. A slave-girl who has faith is better than an idolatress, even though she pleases you. Do not marry your daughters to idolators, until they have faith; a slave who has faith is better than an idolator, even though he pleases you. Such invite you to the Fire, but God invites you to Paradise and pardon in His grace, and He makes clear His signs to people; so may they remember.

222. They will question you about menstruation. Say, "It is a hurt; so keep away from menstruating women and do not be intimate with them until they are purified. When they have cleansed themselves, then come to them as God ordains for you. Truly God loves the repentant, and loves those who cleanse themselves."

223. Your wives are a tillage for you, so come unto your tillage as you wish, but look forward for yourselves; and fear God, and know that you shall meet Him. Give the good tidings to the faithful.

(*Sūra* 2:216–223)

15. If any of your women commit indecency, then call four of you to witness against them, and if they testify, then detain the women in their houses until death visits them, or God appoints for them a way.

16. And if any two of you commit indecency, punish them both, but if they repent and reform, then let them be. Surely God accepts repentance and is Merciful.

(*Sūra* 4:15–16)

34. Men are in charge of women, because God has given some bounty over others, and because men shall expend of their wealth on them. So righteous women obey God, guarding unseen what God has guarded. As for women whose rebellion you fear, admonish them or banish them to their own beds or beat them. If they then obey, then seek not a way against them; God is Sublime, Great.

(*Sūra* 4:34)

43. O you who have faith, draw not near the ritual prayer when you are intoxicated, until you know what you are saying; nor when you are polluted, except when you are traveling, until you have

bathed. But if you are sick, or on a journey, or one of you comes from the privy, or you have touched women, and find no water, then have recourse to wholesome dust, and wipe your faces and hands; God is Forgiving, Pardoning.
(*Sūra* 4:43)

33. The recompense of those who wage war against God and His prophet, and haste about the land doing corruption shall only be to be slain, or crucified, or their hands or feet shall be cut off on opposite sides, or they shall be driven from the land: that shall be a degradation for them in this world, and in the world to come is a mighty torment,
34. Except for those who repent before you overpower them; know that God is Forgiving, Compassionate.
35. O you who have faith, fear God, seek the means to come to Him, and strive in His way: so you may prosper.
(*Sūra* 5:33–35)

2. The fornicatress and the fornicator: scourge each of them with a hundred lashes, and let no pity for them seize you in God's service, if you have faith in God and in the Last Day; and let a party of the faithful witness their punishment.
3. The fornicator shall marry none save a fornicatress or an idolatress, and the fornicatress none shall marry but a fornicator or an idolator; that is forbidden for the faithful.
4. Those who defame chaste married women and do not bring four witnesses, scourge with eighty lashes, and accept no testimony from them ever; such are evildoers,
5. Except those who repent thereafter and reform; God is Forgiving, Compassionate.
6. And those who cast accusations upon their wives, and have no witnesses but themselves, should each testify four times that he is of the truthful,
7. And a fifth time that the curse of God shall be on him if he is of the lying.
8. It will avert from her the punishment if she testifies four times that he is of the lying,
9. And a fifth that God's wrath shall be upon her if he is of the truthful.
(*Sūra* 24:2–9)

3. Forbidden food to you are carrion, blood, swine's flesh, what has been offered to other than God, the beast strangled, or beaten to death, or fallen to death, or gored, or mauled by wild beasts—except what you duly slaughter while still living—and animals sacrificed on altars, and meat portioned by divining arrows; that is ungodliness. Today despair the rejecters of your faith; so fear them not, fear Me! Today I have perfected your religion for you and completed My blessing upon you, and have accepted commitment [Islam] as your religion. Yet whoever is constrained in hunger, not inclining to sin—God is Forgiving, Compassionate.
4. They will ask you what is lawful. Say, "Pure food is permitted, and the hunting animals you teach, training them like hounds, teaching them as God has taught you. Eat of what they seize for you, and mention God's name over it, but fear God, for God is swift at the reckoning."
5. Today all clean things are made lawful for you, and the food of those who have been given the Book is made lawful, and your food made lawful for them; honorable wives among the faithful, and honorable wives from those given the Book before you, if you give them their wedding-portion, not lightly or as taking lovers. But he who rejects the faith renders his works useless, and in the world to come will be among the losers.

(*Sūra* 5:3–5)

He Rewards and Punishes

The commands and prohibitions of God are most serious and have very far-reaching consequences. Humankind will be rewarded or punished for commitment accordingly.

In the Name of God, the Merciful, the Compassionate

1. When the sun is darkened,
2. When the stars are scattered,
3. When the mountains are set moving,
4. When the ten-months-pregnant camels are neglected,
5. When the wild beasts are mustered together,
6. When the seas are set boiling,
7. When souls are reunited,
8. When the girl-child buried alive is asked
9. For what sin she was slain,

10. When the pages are opened,
11. When the sky is stripped,
12. When Hell is set ablaze,
13. When Paradise is brought nigh,
14. Every soul will know what it has prepared.
15. Nay, I swear by the star slinkers,
16. By the running planet sinkers,
17. By the night swarming,
18. By the dawn sighing,
19. This is indeed the word of an honored messenger,
20. Possessed of power, with the Lord of the Throne secure,
21. Obeyed and trustworthy.
(*Sūra* 82:1–21)

13. When the Trumpet is blown with a single blast,
14. And the earth and mountains are lifted and crushed with a single blow,
15. On that Day shall befall what shall come to pass,
16. And the sky shall be split, for on that day it shall be frail.
17. The angels eight shall be that day upon its fringes, bearing the Throne of your Lord aloft.
18. On that day you shall be exposed, not one secret hidden.
19. Then he who is given his book in his right hand shall say, "Here, read my book;
20. Surely I believed I would encounter my reckoning."
21. So shall they be in pleasant life
22. In a sublime garden,
23. Its clustered fruits nigh.
24. "Now eat and drink with pleasure, for what you did in days gone by."
25. But he who is given his book in the left hand shall say, "Would I was not given my book,
26. And never knew my account!
27. Would death had been the end;
28. My wealth avails me not,
29. My power is perished."
30. Take him and fetter him,
31. Then roast him in Hell!
32. Then in chain of seventy cubits' length insert him!
33. He had no faith in God the All-Mighty,
34. He never urged the feeding of the needy;

35. So he has here today not one loyal friend,
36. Nor any food save foulness
37. That none but sinners eat.
(*Sūra* 69:13–37)

In the Name of God, the Merciful, the Compassionate

1. When the Event befalls—
2. No denying its befalling—
3. Abasing, exalting,
4. When the earth reels in trembling,
5. And the mountains are crumbled,
6. And become dust scattered,
7. And you are three bands:
8. Companions of the Right—(who are they, of the Right Hand?),
9. Companions of the Left—(who are they, the Sinister?),
10. And the Winners of the race, the Far-runners;
11. Those brought near,
12. In the Garden of Delights;
13. A throng of the ancients,
14. And how few of later folk.
15. On couches finely wrought
16. Reclining face to face,
17. Immortal youths passing round about them,
18. With goblets and ewers, and a cup from a Source—
19. No head-throbbing from it, no intoxication;
20. And fruits such as they shall choose,
21. And flesh of fowls such as they shall desire,
22. And wide-eyed houris,
23. Like pearls in the shell,
24. A recompense for what they did.
25. There shall they hear no idle talk, nor cause of sin,
26. Only the saying, "Peace, Peace!"
27. The Companions of the Right Hand, O Companions of the Right!
28. Among thornless lote-trees
29. And blossoming acacias,
30. And spreading shade
31. And outpoured waters,
32. And fruit abundant
33. Never failing or forbidden,
34. And peerless companions

35. We formed as a creation,
36. Making them virgins,
37. Loving, companionable,
38. For the Companions of the Right Hand,
39. A throng of the ancients
40. And a throng of later folk.
41. The Companions of the Left, O Companions sinister!
42. Among scorching winds and boiling waters,
43. And shadows of black smoke,
44. Not cool and not agreeable.
45. Yet before they lived in ease,
46. And persisted in the great sin,
47. Saying ever, "What, when we are dead and turned to dust and bones? We shall be resurrected?
48. What, even our first forefathers?"
49. Say, "The ancient and the later
50. Shall be gathered to the appointment of the known day,
51. Then you, O erring and denying,
52. Shall eat of the Tree of Zaqqūm.
53. You shall fill your bellies with it,
54. Drinking over it boiling water,
55. Lapping it up like thirst-crazed camels."
56. That is their welcome, on the Day of Doom.

(*Sūra* 56:1–56)

In the Name of God, the Merciful, the Compassionate

1. By those sent consecutively,
2. By the whirlwinds blasting,
3. By the revivers quickening,
4. By the winnowers winnowing,
5. By those hurling reminder,
6. Excusing and warning,
7. Surely what you are promised shall befall!
8. When the stars are obliterated,
9. When the sky is rent asunder,
10. When the mountains are blown away,
11. When the messengers' time is set,
12. For what day is time appointed?
13. For the Day of Decision.
14. What shall teach you what is the Day of Decision?
15. Woe to the deniers on that day!

16. Did We not destroy the ancients,
17. And make follow them the later folk?
18. Thus we serve the sinners;
19. Woe to the deniers on that day!
20. Did We not create you from a base fluid
21. That We lodged secure
22. For a term decreed?
23. So We arranged; excellent was Our arranging.
24. Woe to the deniers on that day!
25. Made We not the earth a lodging
26. For the living and the dead?
27. Did We set in it soaring mountains, and pour for you flowing water?
28. Woe to the deniers on that day!
29. Be off to what you denied!
30. Be off to a triple-falling shadow,
31. Unsheltering and unprotecting from the flame
32. Shooting sparks like logs,
33. Like unto brassy camels.
34. Woe to the deniers on that day!
35. This is the day whereon they shall not speak,
36. Nor be given leave for excuses.
37. Woe to the deniers on that day!
38. This is the Day of Decision; We have joined you with the ancients.
39. If you have any shift, try now to shift Me!
40. Woe to the deniers on that day!
41. Surely the Godfearing shall be among shade and fountains,
42. And fruits such as they desire:
43. Eat and drink in pleasure, for what you did.
44. Even so We reward good-doers.
45. Woe to the deniers on that day!
46. Eat and enjoy a little while; surely you are sinners!
47. Woe to the deniers on that day!
48. When it is said to them, "Prostrate yourselves!" they do not.
49. Woe to the deniers on that day!
50. In what Speech after this will they then believe?
(*Sūra* 77:1–50)

II
THE NEWS OF GOD'S MESSENGER: THE *ḤADĪTH*

Next to the Qur'ān *itself, the most important body of Islamic textual material is the* Ḥadīth, *the sayings and actions ascribed to the Prophet. It is a second body of writings, comparable in importance to the New Testament in Christianity: the good news of how the Word came to humanity and the acts, preaching, epistles, and words of the Apostle and his disciples, as well as accounts of his visions and revelations.*

It has never been canonized: there are individual ḥadīths *which are clearly apocryphal, many about which no one is quite certain, and a core of material which is surely Muḥammadan. From early times, Muslims of differing factions have accused each other of tampering with* ḥadīths, *and each faction has its own corpus of* Ḥadīth.

Certain transmitters are regarded as untrustworthy; Shī'īs do not accept the collections of the Sunnīs, and Sunnīs do not accept those of the Shī'īs, while the Khārijīs have had their own collections. Every ḥadīth *has to stand or fall on its own merits, and there are differences of opinion even among the Sunnī majority of Muslims. The eponym of the Ḥanbalī law-school, Aḥmad b. Ḥanbal, was a great collector of* ḥadīths, *but his standards of criticism are not considered sufficiently rigorous by other law-schools, and his collection never won full acceptance outside his own group. The hallmark of fundamentalism in Islam has always been its tendency to make the widest application of* Ḥadīth, *and that of rationalism has always been its tendency to restrict the number of* ḥadīths *regarded as trustworthy.*

A ḥadīth *consists of two parts, a* matn *or text and its backing,* isnād, *composed of a chain or* sanād *of transmitters who handed it down. Change the* isnād, *and one has a new* ḥadīth.

One of the chief religious sciences of Islam rose to investigate the credentials of those who transmitted ḥadīths; *known liars, drinkers, and people of bias or bad character were not trustworthy. Encyclopedias of biographies were compiled, and some transmitters were controversial. No certain way was ever found to keep a forger from manufacturing a chain of reliable transmitters along with the text of an individual* ḥadīth.

Some Ḥadīth *scholars will criticize only* isnāds, *never* matns; *others will criticize both. It is generally true that religious differences in Islam always have to do with differences in* ḥadīths.

The point here is that the Ḥadīth *contains very precious material: virtually all the early history of Islam, the biography of the Prophet, and all the religious teaching of that period not already contained in the Qur'ān. To call for ignoring the* Ḥadīth *is clearly not feasible: the best that can be done is to sift it.*

Even ḥadīths *which are in themselves not from Muḥammad may still reflect the early consensus of Muslims about religious matters and thus have value for later generations.*

The Beginnings of the Revelation

Ibn Isḥāq of Madīna, who died ca. 768 C.E. (A.H. 151), was the first scholar to gather together the accounts of the Prophet's life and campaigns and weave them into a biography. He usually gave the source for the account but often omitted the chain of transmitters, because standards were not so rigorous in his day. Even in his own lifetime, he was accused by leading Ḥadīth *scholars of lying about* ḥadīths *he transmitted. Still, his material is the earliest and presumably the most authentic biography of the Prophet, as well as remarkably free of miraculous elements and pious fabrications.*

Later authors mined his accounts for materials, but his book was lost. It has been possible for modern scholarship to reestablish much of the original text.

Muḥammad's Revelations

In the seventh century of the Common Era the stony valley of Mecca was a well-watered stage on the ancient Incense Road which led from South Arabia to the civilizations of the Mediterranean. The people of Mecca had succeeded the Arabs of Petra and Palmyra in controlling what was left of the trade route. Their city-state also had one of the major cult-centers of West Arabia, the Ka'ba, a temple where all gods were honored, but especially sacred to the highest god, Allāh (El), who was seen as the father and chief of other gods.

*It was a confused, anarchic time, remembered for its barbarism (*jahl*, the opposite of urbanity or* ḥilm*). The values of the uncouth Bedouin nomads prevailed in most of Arabia. The old civilization of South Arabia had broken down, and the Yaman had been invaded by its daughter culture from across the Red Sea, Abyssinia, now Christianized by missionaries from Egypt.*

To the north, the Christian East Roman Empire of Byzantium was locked in a centuries-old struggle with the Zoroastrian Persian Empire, dangerously weakening them both. Both tried to dominate the people of the Arabian Peninsula. There were Christians in Arabia, seen as clients of the Byzantines, and Jews, seen as clients of the Persians. There were also Manichaeans, but the majority of the Arab tribes worshiped the idols of their ancestors.

Tribalism was the order of the day, and tribal wars and economic decline troubled the townsmen-traders of Mecca, the tribe of Quraysh.

Muḥammad was born among the Quraysh sometime around 571 C.E. His clan, the Banū Ḥāshim, had a history of differences with the oligarchic families who led the tribe and concentrated most of its resources in their own control. Although his grandfather, and later his uncle Abū Ṭālib, was head of the clan, Muḥammad was a poor boy. He was also trustworthy, enterprising, attractive, and likable.

Employed at the age of twenty-five by the high-minded widow of a rich merchant, Khadīja, a lady said to have been fifteen years his senior, he later agreed to a proposal of marriage from her. It was a happy marriage, and she bore him four daughters and at least one son, al-Qāsim, who died in infancy. He managed her business affairs well and seems to have used part of his leisure to ponder religious matters and the disordered affairs of Arabia.

Ibn Isḥāq: When Muḥammad the Messenger of God, God bless him and give him peace, reached the age of forty, God sent him in mercy to all beings to bring good news to the people.

From Wahb b. Kaysān, from ʿUbayd b. ʿUmayr b. Qatāda al-Laythī: The Messenger of God would withdraw to Mt. Ḥirāʾ every year for a month. This was part of the custom of *taḥannuth* [devotion] practised by Quraysh in pagan times. He would withdraw and feed all poor persons who came to him during this time. When he was finished the first thing he would do was go to the Kaʿba and circumambulate it seven times or as God willed, and then return to his house. In the year in which

God sent him as a prophet, in the month of Ramaḍān, he set forth to Mt. Ḥirā' according to his custom, with his family. When it was the night on which God honored him with his mission, Gabriel brought him God's command. The Messenger said later, "He came to me when I was asleep, with a saddle-cloth of brocade on which was writing, and said 'Recite!' I said, 'Recite what?' He wrapped me in it so that I thought this was death, then he let me go, and said, 'Recite!' 'Recite what?' I said. At that, he wrapped me so I thought it was death, then let me go, and said, 'Recite!' Then I said, 'What is it I should recite?' I only said this to deliver myself from him, lest he return to doing to me as he had done before. Then he said,

> Recite: In the Name of your Lord who created,
> Created Man of a blood-clot.
> Recite: And your Lord is the Most Generous
> Who taught by the Pen. [*Sūra* 96:1–4]

"So I recited it, and he left me. Then I woke from my sleep, and it was as though the words were written on my heart. I left, and when I was halfway down the mountain, I heard a voice from the sky saying, 'Muḥammad! You are the Messenger of God, and I am Gabriel!' I raised my head to heaven to look, and lo, there was Gabriel in the form of a man, his feet astride the horizon, saying, 'Muḥammad, you are the Messenger of God, and I am Gabriel.' I stood staring at him, neither advancing nor withdrawing, then I began to turn my face away from him, but wherever I looked in the heavens I saw him like that. I did not stop standing like that, moving neither forward nor backward, until Khadīja had sent her messengers looking for me. Finally he left me, and I set out to go back to my family, until I came to Khadīja, and sat down by her thigh and drew her close. She said, 'Why, Abū al-Qāsim [Father of al-Qāsim]! Where have you been? By God, I have sent messengers looking for you until they reached the upper part of Mecca and came back to me.' I said, 'I am surely an accursed poet or a man possessed.' She told me, 'I take refuge in God from that, Abū al-Qāsim! God would not do that to you; He knows your truthful speech, your great trustworthiness, your good character, and your abundant kindness. It cannot be, husband. Perhaps you saw something that upset you?' 'Yes, I did,' I told her, and related what I had seen. She said, 'Rejoice, husband, and be steadfast; by Him in whose hand is my soul, I have hope that you will be the prophet of this people!' "

She stood up, gathered her garments about her, and set off for Waraqa b. [ibn] Nawfal b. Asad, her paternal cousin. Waraqa had become a Christian. He recited the scriptures and had learned from the followers of the Torah and the Gospel. When she told him what the Messenger of God had seen and heard, Waraqa cried, "Holy, Holy! By Him in whose hand is my soul, Khadīja, if you are telling the truth, this is the great Nāmūs who has come to him, the Angel Gabriel, peace be upon him, who used to come to Moses, and he will be the prophet of this people! Tell him to take heart." Khadīja went back to the Messenger of God and told him what Waraqa had said, and that soothed his anxiety somewhat.

When he was finished with his seclusion and returned to Mecca, he circumambulated the Ka'ba first of all, according to his custom, and Waraqa met him as he was going around it. He told him, "Cousin, tell me what you saw and heard," so the Messenger of God told him. Then Waraqa said, "By Him in whose hand is my soul, you are the prophet of this community! The great Nāmūs has come to you, who came to Moses. You will surely be called a liar, and treated badly, and they will drive you out and seek to kill you. If I live to see it, I will help God's cause in ways known to Him." Then he brought his head near and kissed his forehead, and the Messenger of God went home to his house.[1]

The First Converts

Khadīja was the first to have faith in God and His messenger and the truth of what came from Him. By this, God lightened the burden on His prophet. He never met with hateful contradiction and accusations of falsehood which grieved him, that God did not comfort him through her when he went home to her. She strengthened him, lightened his burden, affirmed his words, and belittled people's opposition. May God Most High have mercy on her!

'Alī b. Abī Ṭālib [Muḥammad's young cousin] was the first male to have faith in the Messenger of God, pray with him, and affirm his message. At the time he was a boy of ten. Among the favors God granted 'Alī was that he was being reared in the care of the Messenger of God before Islam.

Ibn Isḥāq, from a learned man of Mecca: When the time of prayer would come, the Messenger of God would go out on one of the mountain paths around Mecca. 'Alī would go with him, unknown to his father, his uncles, or other people, and they would pray the ritual prayers. Abū Ṭālib came upon them once when they were praying thus and said to the Messenger of God, "Nephew, what religion is this I see you practicing?" He replied, "Uncle, this is the religion of God, His angels, and His messengers; the religion of our father Abraham. God has sent me as a messenger to His servants, and you are the most worthy of those I should advise and call to guidance, and most worthy to respond to me and assist me." His uncle replied, "I cannot leave the religion of my forefathers and their practices, but, by God, nothing you hate will reach you so long as I live." They mention that he said to 'Alī, "My son, what is this religion you practice?" He replied, "Father, I have put my faith in God and in the Messenger of God. I affirm that what he has brought is true, and I worship God with him and follow him." They allege that his father said, "Well, he wouldn't call you to anything but good, so stay with him."

Zayd b. Ḥāritha al-Kalbī [who had been bought by Khadīja as a child of eight and presented to Muḥammad, who set him free and adopted him as a son before the revelation came] was the first male to adopt Islam after 'Alī.

Then Abū Bakr, whose name was 'Atīq, son of Abū Quḥāfa, became a Muslim. He professed his faith openly and called others to God and His messenger. He was a man sought-after by his people, well liked and of easy manners, a merchant of excellent character and kindliness. He began to call to God and Islam all those whom he trusted among the people who sought his company.

Among those who accepted his invitation to Islam were 'Uthmān b. 'Affān the Umawī, al-Zubayr b. 'Awwām, 'Abd al-Raḥmān b. 'Awf, Sa'd b. Abī Waqqāṣ, and Ṭalḥa b. 'Ubaydallāh [all were later among the leading Companions of the Prophet].[2]

Around Muḥammad grew up a party of able men, critical of the tribal leadership, on whom the leaders looked with alarm and disfavor. They were not so much jealous for their gods as distrustful of signs of social and political innovation. There was little they could do to Muḥammad so long as his clan protected him, but his followers in their own and some other clans were more accessible.

The Prophet therefore sent a number of his followers to Abyssinia, where they sought the protection of the Christian king, the Negus. It seems possible that he was contemplating a political alliance with Abyssinia in the event that his followers came to control Mecca. The following story is almost certainly not historical in all particulars, but it is an early apologia for Islam.

The Emigration to Abyssinia

Muḥammad b. Muslim al-Zuhrī, from Abū Bakr b. ʻAbd al-Raḥmān al-Makhzūmī, from Umm Salama, wife of Abū Salama [after whose death she married the Prophet]: When we reached Abyssinia, the Negus received us most kindly; we practiced our religion, worshipped God Most High, suffered no harm, and heard nothing to dislike. When that got to the Quraysh, they decided among themselves to send two forceful men, ʻAmr b. al-ʻĀṣ and ʻAbdallah b. Abī Rabīʻa, to the Negus about us, and present him gifts of the choicest goods of Mecca. But the Negus summoned the Prophet's Companions, and when they came into his presence they found that he had summoned his bishops and they had spread out their scrolls around him. He asked them, "What is this religion for which you have separated from your people without entering my religion or that of any other community?"

Jaʻfar b. Abī Ṭālib [the cousin of the Prophet] answered, "O King, we were a barbarous people, worshiping idols, eating carrion, committing enormities, breaking the ties of kinship, mistreating our neighbors, the strong among us devouring the weak. Thus we stayed, until God sent us a messenger of our own, whose descent, truthfulness, trustworthiness, and forbearance we knew. He called us to acknowledge the oneness of God and worship Him, and renounce the stones and idols we and our forefathers had served. He ordered us to speak the truth, keep our word, observe the ties of kinship, be good neighbors, and cease from crime and bloodshed. He forbade us to commit abominations or devour the property of orphans or slander chaste women. He commanded us to serve God alone and associate nothing with him, and gave us commands about ritual prayer, the alms-tax, and fasting [he enumerated the commands of Islam]. We recognized his truth and put our faith in him, and followed him in all he brought us from God. At this, our people turned against us, persecuted us, and tried to seduce us from our faith, to make us go back to worshiping idols after worshiping God Most High, and consider as lawful the evil practices we had followed. When they oppressed us and came between us and our religion, we left for your country, choosing you above any other. We have sought your protection, and we hope that we shall not be wronged while with you, O King."

The Negus asked if they had anything with them which the Prophet had brought them from God. "Yes," said Jaʻfar, and he recited a portion of the *Sūra* of Mary. By God, the Negus wept until his beard was wet, and his bishops wept until their scrolls were wet, when they heard what he recited. Then the Negus said, "Truly, this and what Jesus brought both came from the same niche. You two men can go, for I will never hand them over to you, and they will not be betrayed."

The next day 'Amr b. al-'Āṣ told the king that the Muslims said a terrible thing about Jesus: that he was only a created being. The king sent for them and asked them, "What is it that you have said about Jesus, Son of Mary?" Ja'far said, "We say of him what our Prophet has brought us: that he is the servant of God, and His messenger, His spirit, and His word, which He sent into Mary the blessed virgin." The Negus took a twig from the ground, and said, "By God, Jesus does not exceed what you have said about him by this twig."

Some of his patricians around him snorted, but he said, "Though they snort, by God, go freely, for you are safe in my land. Whoever curses you will be fined. Not for a mountain of gold would I let one of you be hurt. Let these two take back their gifts."[3]

*A much loved story connected with the Prophet is that of his night-journey (*isrā'*), his ascension (*mi'rāj*), and his vision of the world to come. Art, poetry, and pious imagination have all lavished attention on this theme. It is now generally considered that Dante borrowed not only the general plan but many details of the* Divine Comedy *from a later fancifully developed treatment of the story, which was translated from Arabic to Latin. Ibn Isḥāq presents the earliest form of the story as he pieced it together. Its main elements are the journey from Mecca to Jerusalem, the ascent to the heavens, and the vision of the afterlife.*

The Night Journey and the Mi'rāj [*Ascent*]

Ibn Isḥāq: Then the Messenger of God was carried by night from the Mosque of the Ka'ba to the Aqsa Mosque, which is the Holy House of Aelia [Jerusalem].

The following *ḥadīth*s are from 'Abdallāh b. Mas'ūd, Abū Sa'īd al-Khudrī, 'Ā'isha, wife of the Prophet, Mu'āwiya b. Abī Sufyān [a brother-in-law of the Prophet], al-Ḥasan al-Baṣrī, Ibn Shihāb al-Zuhrī, Qatāda, and other learned men as well as Umm Hāni', daughter of Abū Ṭālib. The account is pieced together, each contributing something of what he or she was told.

'Abdallāh b. Mas'ūd: the Messenger of God was brought al-Burāq, the steed which the prophets before him used to ride, whose every step carries it as far as the eye can see.

Ḥasan al-Baṣrī said, the Messenger of God said: "While I was sleeping in al-Hijr, Gabriel came and stirred me with his foot. He brought me out to the door of the mosque, and there stood a white animal, between a mule and a donkey, with wings on its sides by which it propelled its feet, and each step carried it as far as it could see. He placed me on it, and left with me, not quitting me nor I him." They went their way until they arrived at the temple of Jerusalem, and found there Abraham, Moses, Jesus, and a company of the prophets. The Messenger then acted as their leader in the ritual prayer. He then was brought two vessels, one containing wine and the other milk. He took the vessel of milk and drank from it. Gabriel told him, "You have been guided to the primeval religion, and your community will be so guided, Muḥammad. Wine is forbidden to you." Then the Messenger went back to Mecca, and in the morning told the Quraysh what had happened. Most of the people said, "By God, the matter's clear! A caravan takes a month to go from Mecca to Jerusalem and a month to return, so how could Muḥammad do the journey there and back in one night?" But Abū Bakr said, "If he says it, it is true." Then he asked the Messenger to describe Jerusalem to him. Ḥasan says he was lifted up so he could see the Prophet speaking.[4] He began to describe Jerusalem to Abū Bakr, and he would say, "You have spoken truly: I testify that you are the Messenger of God!" Then the Messenger said, "And you, O Abū Bakr, are al-Ṣiddīq, [the Testifier to the Truth]." From that day on, the Muslims called him "al-Ṣiddīq."

'Ā'isha, the Prophet's wife, used to say: The Messenger of God's body remained where it was, but God moved his spirit by night.

I have heard that he used to say, "My eyes sleep while my heart is fully awake." God knows best how what happened happened, and how he saw what he saw. But whether he was asleep or awake, it was a reality, and actually happened.

From one I do not doubt, from Abū Sa'īd al-Khudrī, from the Messenger of God: "When my business in Jerusalem was finished, I was brought a ladder finer than anything I've ever seen. It is what each of you will gaze toward at the hour of death. Gabriel mounted with me until I came to one of the gates of heaven, called the Gate of the Watchers. In charge of it was an angel named Ismā'īl, in command of twelve thousand angels who each commanded twelve thousand other angels."

A learned man, from one who heard the Messenger say: "All the angels who met me as I entered the lowest heaven smiled in welcome and wished me well, until one angel met me who spoke as they did, but did not smile or show the joyful expression of the others. When I asked

Gabriel the reason, he said, 'If he were to smile at anyone, either before you or after you, he would have smiled at you, but he does not smile. That is Mālik, the Keeper of Hell.' I said to Gabriel, who has the position yonder that God describes, 'Obeyed there and charged' [Qur'ān 74:34], 'Will you ask him to show me Hell?' He said, 'Certainly! Mālik, show Muḥammad Hell.' At this he removed its cover, and the Fire blazed so high that I thought it would catch all I saw and said to Gabriel, 'Tell him to send it back!' He told him, and Mālik commanded the Fire, 'Subside!' It went back to its place, so it seemed to me most like the falling of a shadow, and he replaced the cover."

Abū Sa'īd al-Khudrī: The Messenger of God said, "When I entered the lowest heaven, I saw a man sitting there, with human souls passing before him. To one he would speak well and rejoice, saying, 'A good soul, from a good body!' To another, he would say 'Uff!' and look grimly, saying, 'A vile spirit, from a vile body!' Gabriel said, 'That is your father Adam, reviewing the souls of his offspring. When a faithful soul passes before him, he is pleased, and when the soul of a rejecter passes, he is disgusted.'

"I saw men with lips like camels, with pieces of fire like stones in their hands. They thrust them in their mouths, and they come out of their posteriors. Gabriel told me these are those who sinfully devour the property of orphans.

"I saw men like those of the family of Pharaoh, 'in the worst of all punishments' [Qur'ān 40:49], with such bellies as I have never seen, with something like thirst-maddened camels passing over them, treading them down as they are cast into Hell, while they cannot move out of the way. These are the usurers.

"I saw men with delicious plump meat before them, side by side with lean and stinking meat. They eat the latter and leave the former. Gabriel told me these are those who leave the women God has made lawful to them and go after those He has forbidden.

"I saw women hanging by their breasts. These are those who have fathered bastards on their husbands.

"Then I was taken up to the second heaven, and there were the two maternal cousins, Jesus, the son of Mary, and John, the son of Zachariah. Then to the third heaven, where there was a man with a face beautiful as the full moon. Gabriel told me, 'It is your brother Joseph, son of Jacob.' In the fourth heaven was Enoch [Idrīs]; 'And We raised him to an exalted place' [Qur'ān 19:58]. In the fifth heaven was a man with white hair and a great beard; never have I seen a handsomer elder. This was the beloved of his people, Aaron. In the sixth heaven was his brother Moses, a tall bronzed man with a hooked nose. In the seventh heaven was an older man sitting on a throne at the gate of the Immortal Mansion. Every day seventy thousand angels enter it, not to return until the Resurrection Day. I have never seen a man who looked more like myself. Gabriel told me, 'This is your father Abraham.' Then he took me into Paradise, and I saw a maiden with dark red lips. I asked her, 'For whom are you destined?' because I admired her when I saw her. She told me, 'For Zayd b. Ḥāritha.'" Thus the Messenger of God gave Zayd the good news that his place in Paradise was sure.

From 'Abdallāh b. Mas'ūd: Finally the Messenger of God came to his Lord, and the duty of five ritual prayers a day was laid on his community.[5]

The Opposition of the Quraysh

Khadīja, the daughter of Khuwaylid, and Abū Ṭālib both died in one year, and troubles followed thick and fast on the Messenger of God with Khadīja's death. She had been a faithful adviser to him in Islam, and he could tell her his problems. With the death of his uncle Abū Ṭālib he lost a support and refuge in his life, a defense and help against his tribe. This was three years before his emigration to Madīna. The Quraysh began to treat him in an offensive way they would never have dared use in his uncle's life. One young ruffian even threw dust on his head.

Hishām b. 'Urwa, from his father, 'Urwa b. Zubayr: When this happened, he went into his house with the dust still on his head, and one of his daughters rose and began to wash the dust away, weeping as she did so. He told her, "Don't weep, little daughter, for God is your father's Defender." At the same time he said, "The Quraysh never did anything hateful to me until Abū Ṭālib died."[6]

The Founding of the Community

The new leader of Muḥammad's clan, his uncle Abū Lahab, allied by marriage with the Meccan leadership, soon withdrew the protection of the Banū Ḥāshim from the Prophet. Muḥammad's life and mission were now in danger. In order for his preaching to become effective, he would have to create a political base for it. He began to look for a home with another tribe and found it with the Aws and the Khazraj of Yathrib, a sizable oasis later known as Madīna, some 250 miles (402 km) to the north.

The Hijra (622 C.E.)

When God wished to manifest His religion, glorify His prophet, and fulfill His promise to him, while he was offering himself to the Arab tribes at fairs as his custom was, he met at al-'Aqaba a number of the tribe of Khazraj of Yathrib, whom God desired to benefit.

'Āṣim b.'Umar b. Qatāda, from elders of his tribe of Khazraj: When the Messenger met them, he asked "Who are you?" They replied that they were of Khazraj, and clients of the Jews of Yathrib. He invited them to sit with him, called them to God, and expounded Islam to them, reciting to them from the Qur'ān. Among the things that God had done with them for Islam was that they lived among Jews, who were people of the scriptures and religious knowledge, though the Khazraj were polytheists and idolators. They had raided the Jews, and when there was a quarrel between them the Jews would say, "A prophet is to be sent soon; his time is at hand! We will follow him, and with him we will kill you all, like the death of 'Ād and Iram." Now when the Messenger spoke to them and called them to God, they said among themselves, "By God, people, you know this is that very prophet the Jews threatened you with! Don't let them get to him before you!"

Thus they responded when he invited them, and approved and accepted all he told them of Islam. They told him, "We have left our people, for no tribe is so divided by enmity and evil as they are. Perhaps God will gather them together through you, so we shall go to them and call them to your religion. If God unites them through it, then no man is greater than you are." Hence they returned to their country having accepted the faith and affirmed it.[7]

The Messenger had not been given permission to fight or shed blood up to this point. He had only been commanded to call people to God, endure ill-treatment, and forgive the ignorant. The Quraysh had persecuted his followers, to the point of seducing them from their religion and driving them from their country. They had to choose between giving up his religion, being tormented at home, or fleeing, some to Abyssinia and some to Madīna.

When the Quraysh became insolent to God, rejecting the grace He purposed, called His prophet a liar, and mistreated and exiled His servants, He gave permission to His messenger for fighting and self-protection against those who oppressed them. The first verses to be revealed on this, according to 'Urwa b. Zubayr and other learned men, were *Sūra* 22:40–41: "Permission is granted to those who fight because they were oppressed: God is well able to assist them, who have been driven wrongfully from their homes, only because they said, 'God is our Lord.' Had God not repelled some people by means of others, monasteries, churches, oratories, and mosques wherein the name of God is much-remembered would be destroyed. God will assuredly help those who help Him: God is Powerful and Mighty. Those We establish in the land will institute ritual prayer, give the poor tax, order the good, and forbid the reproved. God's is the issue of affairs."

When God gave permission to fight, and this group of the Helpers (Anṣār) from Madīna had given their allegiance and pledged to assist him and his followers, the Messenger ordered his Companions in Mecca to emigrate to Madīna and join their brothers the Anṣār. They went out in groups, and he stayed in Mecca awaiting his Lord's permission to emigrate to Madīna.[8]

The Hijra of the Prophet

Finally no one was left there with him, other than those confined by their clans or seduced from their religion, except Abū Bakr and 'Alī. Abū Bakr asked frequently to be allowed to emigrate, but he would say, "Don't be in a hurry; perhaps God will give you a companion." Abū Bakr hoped it would be the Messenger.

When the Quraysh saw that the Messenger now had a faction and followers not of their tribe and from outside their territory, and that his Companions were emigrating to them, they knew they had found a new home and protection against them. They feared that the Messenger would leave to join them and knew that he had resolved to fight them. They gathered in their council chamber, the house of Qusayy b. Kilāb, where they transacted their important matters, to take counsel as to what to do about him, for now they were afraid of him.

Then Abū Jahl, head of the clan of Makhzūm, said, "I have a plan which no one has suggested. Let us choose a young warrior from every clan, strong, well-born, and prominent, and arm him with a sharp sword. Let all of them strike him together and kill him, so that we are relieved of him. His blood will then be on all the clans, and the clan of 'Abd al-Manaf which is protecting him will not be able to fight the whole tribe. They will have to accept the blood-money for him from us, and we shall all contribute."

It was then that God gave His prophet permission to leave. Abū Bakr was a man of means, and he had bought two riding camels and kept them at his house, providing them with fodder in preparation. The Messenger told 'Alī he was leaving and ordered him to stay in Mecca until he was gone, to restore to their owners goods which had been left in trust with him, because of his well-known honesty and trustworthiness.

When the Messenger was ready to leave, he came to Abū Bakr, and they left by a window at the back of his house and made for a cave on Mt. Thawr below Mecca, which they entered. Abū Bakr told his son 'Abdallāh to listen to what people said of them by day and come to them each night with the news. He ordered his freedman, 'Āmir b. Fuhayra, to pasture his sheep and goats by day and bring them there to the cave at evening. His daughter Asmā' would bring food at evening to sustain them.

When the Quraysh missed him, they offered a reward of a hundred she-camels to anyone who would bring him back to them. After three days had passed, people thought they were gone. Then the man they had hired came with their camels and one of his own. Asmā' came to them with a bag of provisions, but, finding she had forgotten to bring a rope, she undid the girdle she was belted with and used it to tie the sack to the saddle. Thus she received the name "She of the Girdle."

They rode off, and Abū Bakr carried his freedman 'Āmir behind them to serve them on the way. 'Abdallāh b. Arqaṭ their guide was the fourth. [In Madīna, the clans] came to him and asked him to be their guest, but he said, "Let the camel go her way, for she is under orders." At last she came to the dwelling of the Banū Mālik b. Najjār and knelt at what was later the door of his house and mosque, which was then used as a floor for drying dates, belonging to two orphan boys of that clan. When she knelt, the Messenger did not dismount, and she rose and went a little distance and then returned and knelt where she had before. The Messenger dismounted and asked to whom the date-drying floor belonged. Mu'ādh b. Afrā' told him it was the property of two orphan boys; he would pay them for it, and the Prophet could take it for his mosque.

Then the Messenger ordered that a mosque (and lodgings for his family) be built, and joined in the work to encourage both the Muhājirīn and the Anṣār [Emigrant and Madīnan Muslims].[9]

The Call to Prayer

When the Messenger was firmly established in Madīna, and his brethren the Muhājirīn had gathered around him, and the Anṣār were united after their former quarrels, Islam was firmly established. The ritual prayers were instituted, the alms-tax and the fast were prescribed, the

Qur'ānic punishments for crimes were observed, the lawful and the forbidden were laid down, and Islam dwelt among them. At first the people gathered to him for the ritual prayers without any summons. The Messenger thought of using a horn like that of the Jews who call to their prayers with it. Then he disliked the idea and ordered a wooden gong [like those of the Eastern Christians] to be beaten when the Muslims should pray.

Meanwhile, 'Abdallāh b. Zayd b. Tha'laba of Balḥārith Clan of Khazraj heard a voice in a dream, and came to the Messenger saying, "A phantom passed me in the night. A man passed me wearing two green garments with a wooden gong in his hand. I asked him to sell it to me to call people to prayer, and he offered to show me a better way; it was to say three times,

> *Allāhu akbar!* [God is greater!] *Allāhu akbar!*
> I testify there is no god but God!
> I testify that Muḥammad is the Messenger of God!
> Come to prayer! Come to prayer!
> Come to salvation! Come to salvation!
> *Allāhu akbar! Allāhu akbar!*
> No god there is, but God!"

When the Messenger heard this, he said, "Truly I trust in God that this was a real vision. Go to Bilāl and acquaint him with it so that he can call to prayer in this way, for he has a more penetrating voice than you do." When Bilāl called to prayer with this, 'Umar b. al-Khaṭṭāb heard it in his house and came to the Messenger, dragging his cloak on the ground and saying, "Prophet of God, by Him who sent you, I saw the same vision!" The Messenger said, "God be praised for that!"

Muḥammad b. Ja'far b. Zubayr, from 'Urwa b. Zubayr, from a woman of the Banū Najjār: My house was the highest house around the mosque, and Bilāl would give the prayer-call from it every morning. He would come before daybreak and sit on the roof waiting for dawn. When he saw it, he would stretch out his arms and say, "O God, I praise You and ask Your help for the Quraysh, that they may accept Your religion!" Then he would give the prayer-call. I never knew him to omit those words for a single night.[10]

The Meccans led three campaigns to attack the Muslims at Madīna, but were repulsed each time. Muḥammad had hoped that the Jews of Madīna would recognize his claim to prophethood. They did not, and some of them ridiculed it and even intrigued with the Meccans. In this they were joined by the "Hypocrites" (munāfiqīn)*, Madīnan Arabs who had not sincerely accepted Islam. During Muḥammad's wars with the Meccans, most of the Jews were banished from Madīna, and some were killed. The direction of prayer for Muslims was changed from Jerusalem to Mecca, Judaizing features were dropped, and the Arabian nature of Islam was emphasized in new revelations.*

In the end, Muḥammad brought his native city over to his side in 630 C.E. by a skillful combination of economic, military, and political pressure. The Ka'ba was cleansed of idols and became the center of the Islamic world, the temple originally built by Abraham and Ishmael. The Quraysh, the ablest entrepreneurs of Arabia, were now Muslims, proud to be on the winning side. The Community was expanding by leaps, as one tribe after another entered into treaties with Muḥammad and agreed to let any of their people who desired to become Muslims do so unopposed. Jews and Christians were allowed to keep their own religions and laws, in return for payments of tribute.

Muḥammad continued to live simply in Madīna as the beloved teacher, lawgiver, commander-in-chief, and judge of his people. His religion was firmly established and his authority was unchallenged. The quarrelling tribes of Arabia were uniting—an obvious miracle to the Arabs—and the pagan cults were dying everywhere. No other founder of a world religion has known such success in his lifetime. In January 632, he led a final Pilgrimage to Mecca. In retrospect, it seemed to his followers that he was saying farewell, though none suspected it at the time. On June 8 of that year, only ten years after he had left Mecca, he died.

The Death of the Prophet

'Ā'isha, the wife of the Prophet, said: The Messenger of God returned from [a visit to the cemetery by night to pray for the dead] to find me suffering from a severe headache. I was saying, "Oh, my head!" He said, "No, 'Ā'isha, it is I who must say 'Oh, my head!' " Then he said, "What harm would it do if you died before me, so I could take care of you and wrap you in your shroud and pray over you and bury you?" I said, "I can just see you after doing that, coming back into my house and spending a wedding-night in it with a new wife!" He smiled at that, and then his pain overcame him in Maymūna's house. He called his wives and asked their permission to be nursed in my house, and they agreed.

'Ā'isha: The Messenger used to often say in my hearing, "God never takes a prophet without giving him the choice." When he was at the point of death, the last word I heard him say was, "No, the Exalted Companion of Paradise!" I said, "Well, then, by God, he's not choosing us!" I knew it was as he used to say, that a prophet does not die without being given the choice.

'Ā'isha: The Messenger of God died in my bosom, during my turn; I didn't wrong anyone about that. It was due to my ignorance and my extreme youth that the Messenger died in my arms. I placed his head on the pillow, and then I got up beating my breast and slapping my face with the other women.

Al-Zuhrī—Sa'īd b. Musayyib—Abū Hurayra: When the Messenger of God died, 'Umar b. al-Khaṭṭāb got up and said, "Some hypocrites are saying that the Messenger has died, but he has not died: he has gone to his Lord as Moses did when he was absent from his people for forty days, and then returned to them after it was said he was dead. And, by God, the Messenger will come back as Moses came back and cut off the hands and the feet of those who allege he is dead!"

When Abū Bakr heard the news, he came to the door of the mosque while 'Umar was speaking to the people. He paid no attention, but went into 'Ā'isha's house where the Messenger was lying, covered with a striped mantle. He uncovered his face and kissed it, saying, "You were more to me than my father and my mother. You have tasted the death that God decreed for you; death will never come upon you again after this!" Then he drew the mantle again over the Messenger's face. He went out where 'Umar was still speaking and said, "Go gently, 'Umar; be quiet." But 'Umar went on talking. When he saw that 'Umar would not be silent, Abū Bakr went forward to the people. When they heard him, they came to him and left 'Umar. He gave praise and thanks to God and said, "O people, if anyone worshipped Muḥammad, then Muḥammad is dead. If anyone worshipped God, then God is living and dies not." Then he recited *Sūra* 3:144: "Muḥammad is only a messenger. Messengers have passed away before him. If he died or were killed, would you turn back on your heels? He who turns back on his heel never harms God in any way, but God will reward the thankful." 'Umar said later, "By God, when I heard Abū Bakr recite this, I was so dumbfounded that my legs would not carry me. I fell to the ground, knowing that the Messenger of God was really dead."[11]

Muḥammad's unexpected death was the first great crisis of his umma *or Community, a shock from which it has never fully recovered. What was to happen now? Had he made any arrangement for the succes-*

sion? Khadīja was the only wife who had borne him children; his little son Ibrāhīm by his Christian concubine Māriya the Copt had died.

His closest relative was his cousin 'Alī, raised in his home, husband of Muḥammad's daughter Fāṭima and father of his only surviving grandsons, Ḥasan and Ḥusayn. But even the claims of a son to succeed to a chief's authority were not recognized in Arabian society, still less the claims of a son-in-law. Moreover, 'Alī was still a young man in a society which revered seniority.

The head of Muḥammad's clan, his uncle 'Abbās, might have had a claim, but he was a late convert and therefore under some suspicion.

The tribe of Quraysh did not intend to be dominated by a man from another tribe, and the Anṣār, the people of Madīna, felt they had the right to rule themselves now that their friend was dead.

People in other Arab tribes would consider that they had paid allegiance to a leader: now he was dead, and they must make their own arrangements. Something must be done swiftly.

Years later, his friend, early convert, and father-in-law 'Umar made a public pronouncement about the events on the night of Muḥammad's death.

The Succession (Caliphate)

When the Messenger of God was taken, this tribe [the Khazraj] of the Anṣār gathered around Sa'd b. 'Ubāda in the Portico of the Banū Sā'ida Clan.

'Abdallāh b. 'Abbās [the Prophet's cousin]: On the last Pilgrimage that 'Umar led, I was waiting for 'Abd al-Raḥmān b. 'Awf, and when he came he said, "You should have seen a man who came to the Commander of the Faithful ['Umar] and said, 'What do you think of a man who says, "If 'Umar died, I would go swear allegiance to So-and-so [i.e., 'Alī]. The allegiance given to Abū Bakr was only a hasty mistake which was then fulfilled."'" 'Umar was angry, and said, "God willing, I shall get up among the people this night and warn them of those who want to usurp the authority!" I said, "Don't do it in Mecca, Commander of the Faithful. Wait until you are in Madīna, for that is where it will be best understood." He said, "Then by God, if God wills, I shall certainly do it at the first opportunity in Madīna!"

We returned to Madīna, and on the first Friday, after the sun had set, 'Umar came out and sat in the pulpit, and when the callers to prayer were finished, he praised God in fitting terms and said, "I am telling you this day something I am destined to tell you, even if it is the last thing I ever say. Let those who understand it and heed it take it with them wherever they go. I have heard that someone said, 'If 'Umar died, I would go swear allegiance to So-and-so.' Let no-one deceive himself by saying that the allegiance to Abū Bakr was a hasty mistake which was then fulfilled. In fact, things happened as they did, but God averted the evil of it, and there is not a man among you today whom people would respect as they did Abū Bakr. If anyone pledges his allegiance to someone without consulting the Muslims, that allegiance has no validity and they are both in danger of being put to death. What happened was that when God took His prophet the Anṣār opposed us and gathered with their chiefs in the Portico of the Banū Sā'ida. 'Alī and Zubayr b. 'Awwām and those who were with them hung back from us, and the Muhājirīn gathered around Abū Bakr [in the mosque]. I said to Abū Bakr, 'Let us go to our brothers the Anṣār,' and we had set out to go to them when two honest fellows met us and told us what they were plotting. They said, 'You Muhājirīn don't need to go near them; just make your own arrangements.' I said, 'By God, we will certainly go to them,' and we found them in the Portico of the Banū Sā'ida. In the middle of them was a man all wrapped up. They told me it was Sa'd b. 'Ubāda and that he was ill. When we were seated, their spokesman gave testimony of the unity of God and the mission of His prophet, and praised God as is His due. Then he said, 'We are God's Helpers and the squadron of Islam. You Muhājirīn are our kindred, and some of you have come to settle among us.' There they were, trying to cut us from our origin and wrest the authority from us! When he was quiet I wanted to speak, and I had something prepared in my mind to say that pleased me, but Abū Bakr said, 'Gently now, 'Umar.' I didn't want to annoy him, so he spoke. He was a man with more knowledge and dignity than I, and he said everything I would have said or more, but said it better.

"He said, 'As for all the good things you say about yourselves, you deserve them. However, the Arabs will never recognize this government except in the tribe of Quraysh, since they are best of the Arabs in pedigree and homeland. I propose either of these two men to you; pledge your allegiance to the one you want.' Then he took hold of my hand and that of Abū 'Ubayda b. al-Jarrāḥ, who was sitting between us. It was the only thing he'd said I disliked, because I would have rather have stepped forward and had my head cut off—may no sin attach to me for saying it—than rule over a people of whom Abū Bakr was one.

"Then one of the Anṣār said, 'I'm a man to whom people come for the solution of problems. Let us have a leader from us, and one from you, O Quraysh.' That increased the clamor and voices were raised, until a real split was likely, so I said, 'Stretch out your hand, Abū Bakr!' He did, and I clasped it in allegiance. Then the Muhājirīn present gave him their allegiance, and after that the Anṣār. In this, we leaped on Sa'd b. 'Ubāda, and someone said we had killed him. I said, 'May God kill him!' "[12]

[In the account of Ṭabarī:] Abū Bakr said, "You know, Sa'd, that the Messenger of God said, 'The Quraysh are the custodians of the command: pious people follow them in piety, and immoral people follow them in immorality.'" Sa'd replied, "That is so. Let us be the ministers, and you be the rulers."

Ṭabarī, from Ibn Ḥumayd, from Jarīr, from Mughīra, from Ziyād b. Kulayb: When 'Umar proposed Abū Bakr, some of the Anṣār said, "We will pledge allegiance to no one but 'Alī."

The same sources: 'Umar came to the house of 'Alī [near that of the Prophet]. In it there were Zubayr and Ṭalḥa b. 'Ubaydallāh along with leading Muhājirīn. 'Umar said, "By God, you'll come out and pledge allegiance, or I'll burn the house down over your heads!" Then Zubayr came out at him with sword unsheathed, but he stumbled and dropped his sword. They then overpowered him and took it away.[13]

Ibn Isḥāq, from Anas b. Mālik: The next day after Abū Bakr had received the oath of allegiance at the Portico, Abū Bakr sat in the pulpit, and 'Umar rose and spoke before him. He praised God as is His due, and then said, "O people, yesterday I thought that the Messenger of God would continue to rule us so long as we lived. But God has left His Book by which He guided him, and if you hold fast to that, God will guide you as He did him. God has entrusted authority over you to the best among you, the Companion of the Messenger when they were two in the Cave [of Mt. Thawr], so rise and pledge your allegiance to him." Then the people pledged allegiance to Abū Bakr as a body, after the pledge at the Portico.[14]

A decision of great significance had been made in a sudden crisis. The umma *would have one leader, as successor (*khalīfa: *caliph) of the Prophet. Some would continue to feel that the family of the Prophet had been slighted.*

It was now necessary to enforce the decision on the other tribes, most of whom were refusing to send the zakāt *to Madīna or to obey Abū Bakr. Some were even turning to new "prophets" who claimed to have inherited Muḥammad's authority. It took the better part of two years to establish the rule of Madīna in Arabia, and many bitter battles. A sulky obedience ensued.*

To reunite the spirit of the Community, Abū Bakr and then 'Umar, whom he appointed as his successor, sent the Arabs on raids into the weakened Byzantine and Persian empires. The results surpassed the caliphs' hopes: the Fertile Crescent, Egypt, and Iran were all conquered for Islam, and the delighted Arabs gave thanks to the God of Muḥammad for an empire.

Muḥammad as Legislator and Founder

From the first, Muḥammad was seen as bringing his people a Law from God. Insight into divine Law is found in Islam by consulting the Qur'ān and the Ḥadīth. *The Prophet is seen as infallible—he must be, if the Qur'ān itself were not to be in doubt—and thus his practice (*sunna*), embodied in the* Ḥadīth, *is itself a secondary revelation for the Community.*

A fully "sound" ḥadīth *has a chain of known and approved authorities going back to a Companion of Muḥammad, followed by a text that is supported in other* ḥadīths. *Its form is as follows.*

Bukhārī, from Aṣbagh b. al-Faraj from Ibn Wahb from Yūnus from Ibn Shihāb from Abū Salama b. 'Abd al-Raḥmān from Abū Hurayra: A Bedouin came to the Messenger of God, may the benediction of God be upon him, and peace. He said, "Messenger of God, my wife gave birth to a dark-colored male-child, and I deny that it is mine!" "Do you have camels?" the Prophet asked. "Yes." "What color are they?" "Reddish." "Are they ever ash-colored?" "Yes, that happens." "How do you suppose that happens?" asked the Prophet. "Messenger of God, something in the blood changes them." "Then perhaps something in the blood changed the boy," said the Prophet, and he did not allow him to deny him.[15]

The following ḥadīths *have been taken from the Sunnī "sound" collections of al-Bukhārī, (d. 870/A.H. 256), and Muslim (d. 875/A.H. 261). I have kept the* isnāds *intact in those of Bukhārī, to give the original flavor, and omitted all but the first and last links of those drawn from Muslim or Muslim and Bukhārī both. Every mention of the Prophet in the originals is followed by the invocation "God bless him and give him peace." It is omitted here because the effect for non-Muslims may seem repetitive and monotonous, but Muslims do not tire of repeating it.*

Muslim and Bukhārī, from 'Abdallāh b. 'Umar: I heard the Messenger of God say, "Islam is built on five things: testimony that there is no god but God and Muhammad is the Messenger of God, performance of the ritual prayer [*ṣalāt*], payment of the alms-tax [*zakāt*], Pilgrimage to the Ka'ba, and the Fast of Ramaḍān."[16]

Bukhārī, from Sufyān from Manṣūr from Abū Wā'il from 'Amr b. Shuraḥbil from 'Abdallāh: I said, "Messenger of God, what is the greatest sin?" He said, "It is to make an idol for God, who created you." "Then what?" "To kill your child, fearing lest it will eat with you." "And then what?" "To commit adultery with your neighbor's wife."[17]

Bukhārī, from 'Alī b. al-Ja'd from Shu'ba from Qatāda from the *mawlā* [freedman] of Anas from 'Abdallāh b. Abī 'Utba, called Abū 'Abdallāh, from Abū Sa'īd al-Khudrī: The Prophet was shyer than a virgin in her retreat. Whenever he saw something he disliked, we knew it from his face.[18]

Bukhārī, from Muḥammad b. 'Uthmān b. Karāma al-'Ijlī from Khālid b. Makhlad from Sulaymān from 'Abdallāh b. Dinār from Ibn 'Umar: They brought the Prophet a Jew and a Jewish woman who had committed adultery. He said to the Jews, "What do you find in your book?" They said, "Our rabbis blacken the faces of the guilty and expose them to public ridicule." 'Abdallāh b. Salām, who had been a Jew, said, "Messenger of God, tell the Jews to bring the Torah." They brought it, but a Jew put his hand over the verse which prescribes stoning and began to read what comes before and after it. Ibn Salām said to him, "Raise your hand." There was the verse about stoning under his hand. The Messenger of God gave the order, and they were stoned. Ibn 'Umar added, They were stoned at the Balāṭ, [the paved square of Madīna], and I saw the man leaning over the woman to shield her from the stones.[19]

Bukhārī, from Maḥmūd b. Ghaylān from 'Abd al-Razzāq from Ma'mar from al-Zuhrī from Abū Salāma, from Jābir: A man who had become a Muslim came to the Prophet and confessed to fornication. The Prophet turned away from him. This happened until the man had confessed four times. The Prophet asked him, "Are you insane?" "No," the man said. "Are you married?" He said that he was, and the Prophet ordered him to be stoned at the Muṣallā [an oratory outside Madīna]. When the stones struck him, he ran away, but he was caught and stoned until he was dead. Then the Prophet, God bless him and give him peace, spoke well of him and conducted his funeral.[20]

Bukhārī, from Muslim b. Ibrāhīm from Hishām from Yaḥyā b. 'Ikrima from Ibn 'Abbās: The Prophet cursed men who act like women and women who act like men, and said, "Drive them from your houses." He expelled So-and-so, and 'Umar expelled Such-and-such.[21]

Bukhārī, from 'Alī b. 'Abdallāh from Walīd b. Muslim from al-Awzā'ī from Yaḥyā b. Abī Kathīr from Abū Qilāba al-Jarmī from Anas b. Mālik, the servant of the Prophet: A group of men from the tribe of 'Ukl came to the Prophet and accepted Islam. Then they became ill in Madīna, and he ordered them to go to the camel-herd of the public purse and drink the urine and the milk [as medicine]. They did, and were cured. Then they renounced their religion, killed the herdsmen, and stole the camels. He sent trackers after them, and they were captured. He then cut off their hands and their feet, burned out their eyes, and did not cauterize their wounds, so that they died.[22]

Bukhārī, from Aḥmad b. Yūnus from Ibrāhīm b. Sa'd from Ibn Shihāb from Sa'īd b. al-Musayyib from Sa'd b. Abī Waqqās: The Messenger of God refused to let 'Uthmān b. Maz'ūn make a vow of chastity. Had he allowed him, we would all have been castrated.[23]

Muslim and Bukhārī, from 'Ā'isha, wife of the Prophet: The Messenger of God said, "Whoever begins something in this matter of ours [Islam] that was not there, it is rejected." The version of Muslim says, "Whoever does something that has no order from us, it is rejected."[24]

Muslim and Bukhārī, from Ibn Mas'ūd: The Messenger of God said, "The blood of a Muslim is not lawful to shed except for one of these three: the married one who commits adultery, the one giving a life for a life taken, and the abandoner of the religion, who has split the Community."[25]

Muslim, from Jābir b. 'Abdallāh al-Anṣārī: A man asked him, "Messenger of God, is it your opinion that if I pray the prescribed prayers, fast during Ramaḍān, treat as lawful what is lawful, and avoid what is forbidden, adding nothing to that, I will enter Paradise?" He answered, "Yes."[26]

Muslim, from Abū Ya'la Shaddād b. Aws: The Messenger of God said, "Surely God prescribes benevolence in all things. Even if you kill, make it a good killing, and if you slaughter an animal, make it a good slaughtering. Let one sharpen the knife and dispatch the victim quickly."[27]

Muslim, from Abū Sa'īd al-Khudrī: I heard the Messenger of God say, "When one of you notices something rejected by God, let him try to change it with his hand, and if one cannot, then by the tongue, and if one cannot, then in one's heart, though that is the weakest of faith."[28]

Bukhārī, from Qutayba b. Sa'īd from Ya'qūb b. 'Abd al-Raḥmān from Abū Hāzim from Sahl b. Sa'd: A woman came to the Prophet and said, "Messenger of God, I have come to offer you my person." The Messenger of God gazed upon her, and looked her up and down, and then he lowered his head. When the woman saw that he had made no decision about her, she sat down. One of the Prophet's Companions rose and said, "Messenger of God, if you have no need of her, marry her to me!" He asked, "Do you have anything to give her [as a marriage portion]?" "No, by God, Messenger of God." "Then go to your people and see if you can find something." The man went and returned and said, "By God, I found nothing, Messenger of God." He said, "Look, even for a ring made of iron." He went and came back, and said, "No, by God, Messenger of God, there is not even a ring made of iron, but here is my waist-wrapper." Sahl added, it was not large enough so that he could have given her half and worn half. The Messenger of God asked, "What would she do with your waist wrapper? If you wear it, she will get nothing out of it, and if she wears it, you will have nothing on." The man sat down for a long time, and then he rose to go. The Messenger of God saw him leaving and ordered him to be called back. When he came, he said, "How much of the Qur'ān do you know?" He replied, "I know *Sūra* so-and-so, such-a-one, and such-a-one." He asked, "Could you recite them by heart?" "Yes," said the man. "Go along, then," said the Prophet. "I give her to you for what you have of the Qur'ān."[29]

Muḥammad as Model and Guide

The Prophet is not only the founder and legislator of the Community, he is the model for all Muslims. Since all his acts were preserved from moral error, all have moral value; they are part of his sunna *(practice). The way he wore his hair and beard, the way he cleaned his teeth or broke his fast, and the way he treated children are all worthy of study and imitation.*

Bukhārī, from 'Umar b. Ḥafṣ from his father from al-A'mash from Muslim from Masrūq from 'Ā'isha: The Prophet did something and permitted it for others, but some people still abstained from it. That came to the Prophet, and he put it in a sermon. He praised God, then he said, "What ails those people who refrain from a thing that I have done? For, by God, I know God better than they do, and I am more fearful of offending Him!"[30]

Bukhārī, from Ismā'īl from Mālik from Sumayy the *Mawlā* of Abū Bakr from Abū Ṣāliḥ al-Sammān from Abū Hurayra: The Messenger of

God said, "A man was walking on the road, and his thirst grew strong. He found a well and descended into it, drank, and was leaving, when he saw a dog hanging out its tongue and licking the ground from thirst. The man said, 'This dog's thirst is like the thirst I had,' and he went into the well again, filled his shoe with water and held it in his teeth while he climbed out, and gave it to the dog to drink. God approved of his act and pardoned his sins." They said, "What, Messenger of God, shall we be rewarded for what we do to animals?" He said, "Yes, there is a reward on every living creature."[31]

Bukhārī, from Muḥammad b. Yūsuf from Sufyān from Hishām from 'Urwa from 'Ā'isha: A Bedouin came to the Prophet and said, "Do you kiss little boys? We don't." At this the Prophet said, "How can I replace the mercy that God has taken from your heart?"[32]

Bukhārī, from Musaddad from Abū 'Awāna from Abū Bishr from Sa'īd b. Jubayr from Ibn 'Abbās: A woman came to the Prophet and said, "My mother vowed to go on the Pilgrimage, but she died before she could do it. Should I make a Pilgrimage in her place?" He said, "Yes, do it. If your mother had owed a debt, would you have paid it?" She said, "Yes." The Prophet told her, "Then pay what she owes, for God is most worthy that we keep promises to Him."[33]

Bukhārī, from Ismā'īl from Malik from 'Abdallah b. Dinār from 'Abdallāh b.'Umar: The Messenger of God said, "When any Muslim says to his brother, 'You infidel!' one of the two surely deserves the name."[34]

Bukhārī, from Isma'il b.'Abdallāh from Ibrāhīm b. Sa'd from his father from 'Abdallāh b. Ja'far b. Abī Ṭālib: I saw the Messenger of God eating fresh dates with cucumbers.[35]

Bukhārī, from 'Abdallāh b. Muḥammad b. Asmā' from Juwayriya from Mālik b. Anas from al-Zuhrī from Ibn Muhayriz from Abū Sa'īd al-Khudrī: We captured some women, and in coition practiced withdrawal [*'azl*], so as not to have children from them. We asked the Prophet about this, and he said, "Is that what you did indeed?" Then he said three times, "There is not a soul who is to be born from now until Resurrection Day but will be born." [This *ḥadīth* is used today to support birth control.][36]

Bukhārī, from Muḥammad b. Bashshār from Ghundar from Shu'ba from Ḥakam from Ibn Abī Layla from 'Alī: Fāṭima complained of the hardship she faced in grinding grain. Some prisoners were brought to the Prophet, so she went to see him but did not find him, and told 'Ā'isha [that she wanted one of the prisoners, to help her]. When the Prophet came home, 'Ā'isha told him of Fāṭima's errand. He came to visit us when we had already lain down to sleep. When I started to rise, he said, "Stay both where you are," and sat down between us, so I could feel the cold from his legs by my chest. Then he said, "Shouldn't I tell you something better than what you've asked me for? When you lie down, say thirty-four times, *Allāhu akbar* [God is greater]! Then say *Subḥān Allāh* [Glory be to God]! thirty-three times, and *al-Ḥamdu lillāh* [Praise be to God]! thirty-three times. That will be better for you both than a servant." [This hundredfold invocation is the Islamic rosary, recited with prayer-beads.][37]

Bukhārī, from Ḥajjāj b. Minḥal from Shu'ba from 'Āṣim from Abū 'Uthmān from Usāma b. Zayd: One of the Prophet's daughters sent him this message while Sa'd and Ubayy and I were with him: "We reckon that my son has come to the point of death." We said, "There is no god but God, and Muḥammad is His messenger!" and he sent her as follows: "Peace be yours. What God takes is His, and what He gives is His. Everything has its identity from Him, so take this into account, and be patient." Then she sent begging him to come, so the Prophet went, and we went with him. The child was placed on his lap. He was trembling, while his eyes flowed with tears. Then Sa'd said to him, "What is this, Messenger of God?" He replied, "It is compassion, which God places as He wills in the hearts of His servants. God has no mercy on those who do not have mercy."[38]

Bukhārī, from 'Umar b. 'Īsā from Muḥammad b. Sawā' from Rawḥ b. al-Qasim from Muḥammad b. al-Munkadir from 'Urwa from 'Ā'isha: A man came and wanted to speak to the Prophet. When he saw the man, he said, "Unhappy is the brother of his clan! Unhappy the son of his clan! (What an awful fellow he is!)" Then when the man came in and sat, the Prophet looked cheerily upon him and spoke kindly to him. When he went away, I said, "Messenger of God, when you saw him, you said this and that, but when he came in, you were cheery and kindly with him!" He replied, "Why, 'Ā'isha, when have you ever seen me act rudely with people? Surely the worst place on resurrection day will be that of the ones people avoided in fear of their mischief."[39]

Bukhārī, from Sa'īd b. Abī Maryam from Muḥammad b. Ja'far from Ḥumayd b. Abī Ḥumayd al-Ṭawīl from Anas b. Mālik: Three men came to the houses of the Prophet's wives to ask about his religious practice, and when they told them it was as if they belittled it. They said, "In what do we differ from the Prophet? Yet God has pardoned all his past and future faults." One of them said, "As for me, I shall pray all night long." Another said, "I shall fast every day." The third said, "I shall draw apart from women and never marry." Then the Messenger of God went to them and said, "Are you the ones who said thus and so? Yet I dread God more than you and revere Him more, but I fast and I break the fast; I pray and I sleep too, and I marry women. Whoever turns away from my practice [*sunna*] is none of mine."[40]

Muslim, from Abū Dharr: Some of the Companions of the Prophet said to him, "Messenger of God, the rich carry off all the rewards. They pray the ritual prayers as we pray them, and fast as we fast, and then they give alms with the surplus of their wealth." He replied, "Has God not given you the wherewithal to give alms? Every 'Glory to God!' is an alms, every 'God is greater!' is an alms, every 'Praise be to God' is an alms, and every 'Hallelujah' is an alms; every bidding to do good is an alms, every deterrence from evil is an alms. Lawful intercourse is an alms." They said, "Messenger of God, shall we receive a reward for satisfying our sexual appetite?" He replied, "What do you think? If God had made it forbidden, then it would be a fault, so if He commends marriage, there is a reward for it."[41]

Muslim, from Abū Hurayra: The Messenger of God said, "Do not envy one another, do not vie with one another, do not hate each other, do not be adversaries to each other, do not undercut one another in trading, but be servants of God and brothers. A Muslim is the brother of another Muslim; he does not oppress him, does not forsake him, does not deny him, does not despise him. Piety is here (and he pointed thrice to his breast). It is a sufficient misfortune for one to look down on a fellow Muslim. The blood, property, and honor of every Muslim are inviolable to another Muslim."[42]

Muslim, from Anas b. Mālik: The Messenger of God said, "No one of you really has faith, until one wants for a fellow Muslim what one wants for oneself."[43]

The following is a ḥadīth qudsī, *a word from God given by a prophet but occurring outside the Qur'ān.*

Muslim, from Abū Dharr: One of the things the Prophet related as coming from his Lord was that He says, "O My servants, I have forbidden wrongdoing in Myself, and made it a thing forbidden among you: do not wrong each other. O My servants, all of you are erring except for those I have guided, so ask guidance from Me: I will guide you. O my servants, all of you are hungry except those I have fed, so ask food of Me; I will feed you. O my servants, all of you are naked, except for those I have clothed, so ask clothing of Me; I will clothe you. O My servants, truly you sin night and day. I am He who forgives all sin, so ask pardon of Me; I will forgive you. O My servants, you will never attain My harm, so as to harm Me, nor My benefit, so as to benefit Me. O My servants, if the first and the last among you, all humans and all jinn, were as pious as the best heart among you, it would add nothing to My kingdom. O my servants, if the first and the last, the humans and the jinns among you, were as wicked as the worst heart among you, it would detract nothing from My kingdom. O My servants, if the first and the last, all humans and all jinns among you, were to stand on one high place and ask of Me, and I gave each among you all requests, it would not diminish what I have with me any more than the sea is diminished if you plunge a needle into it. O My servants, it is only your own actions which are reckoned, and for which you will account to Me, so let those who find good at the reckoning praise God, and those who find other than good blame no-one but themselves."[44]

The Science of *Ḥadīth*

The preservation of the sunna *of the Messenger in the study of the* Ḥadīth *has been Islam's way of preserving its link with the Apostolic period. The following essay on the branches of this study is by the great Ibn Khaldūn, a man of the Islamic Renaissance (d. 1406/ A.H. 808). He was from a Spanish Arab family of Tunis, a professor of* Ḥadīth *and jurisprudence, as well as a historian, statesman, philosopher, and diplomat. As one would expect, it is a magisterial discussion of the discipline from an eminent practitioner.*

The sciences of *Ḥadīth* are many and diversified, such as looking into *ḥadīth*s that abrogate or are abrogated. The possibility of abrogation is well-established in our religious Law, and its occurrence is a kindness from God to His servants, to assist them in matters of their welfare. As He says, "When We abrogate one verse or efface it, We bring another than it, or as good in its place" [Qur'ān 2:106].

When two traditions [*akhbār*] contradict each other completely, and it is known that one came earlier than the other, then the latter abrogates the first. Knowing the abrogating from the abrogated is one of the most important and difficult sciences of *Ḥadīth*. Al-Zuhrī [d. ca. 750 C.E.] said, "It is baffling and impossible for jurists to know an abrogating *ḥadīth* of the Messenger of God—God bless him and give him peace—from one that is abrogated."

Another science of *Ḥadīth* is study of the chains of transmission, knowing which traditions one must act upon because they have trustworthy authorities for them. One must act only on *ḥadīth*s of the Messenger of God that are in all probability true. Similar to this is the ranking of the transmitters among the Companions of the Prophet and the second generation.

Those learned in this subject have devised technical terms for the varying grades of material, such as "sound" [*ṣaḥīḥ*], "fair" [*ḥasan*], and "weak" [*ḍaʿīf*], which includes "dropping the first link" [*mursal*], "omitting one link" [*munqaṭiʿ*], "omitting two links" [*muʿdal*], "peculiar" [*shadhdh*], "odd" [*gharīb*], etc.

There is also the study of how transmission from one link to another took place, whether by reading or writing, by permission to set down or permission to recite from the transmitter.

Then there is the discussion of the texts conveyed by the chains of authority. These texts may be "odd" [*gharīb*], "problematic" [*mushkil*], "wrongly set down" [*taṣḥīf*], and so on. These matters form the greatest part of what the *ḥadīth* scholars investigate.

In the first generations [*salaf*], the conditions of *ḥadīth* transmitters were well known to the people of their cities. Whether in the Ḥijāz, in Baṣra or Kūfa of Iraq, or in Syria or Egypt, they were all well known and famous in their own time. The traditionists of the Ḥijāz had the shortest chains of transmission and were the soundest.

After this first period, the strongest in the Ḥijāzī tradition was the Imām Mālik, the leading scholar of Madīna. After him came his colleagues, such as Imām Shāfiʿī and Imām Aḥmad b. Ḥanbal [all three have schools of the Law named after them]. Knowledge of the religious Law at the beginning of Islam was entirely based on oral transmission. Then Mālik wrote his book *al-Muwaṭṭā'*, laying down the basic laws from sound, generally agreed-upon traditions, arranged in juridical categories.

Then came Muḥammad b. Ismāʿīl al-Bukhārī [d. 870] the imam of *ḥadīth* scholars of his time. He published the *ḥadīth*s accepted by the Sunnīs according to subject matter in his *Musnad Ṣaḥīḥ*. He combined all the ways of the Ḥijāzīs, the Iraqīs, and the Syrians, using *ḥadīth*s they agreed were sound and excluding those about which there was difference of opinion. He repeated *ḥadīth*s, bringing them into every chapter where they had some bearing. Thus it is said that his work comprised 7,200 *ḥadīth*s, of which 3,000 are repeated.

Then there came the Imam Muslim b. Ḥajjāj al-Qushayrī. He wrote his own *Musnad Ṣaḥīḥ,* in which he followed Bukhārī in transmitting those *ḥadīth*s generally agreed to be "sound." And still their two books did not contain all the "sound" traditions, so later scholars corrected them both on this.

Abū Dāwud al-Sijistānī [d. 888], Abū 'Īsā al-Tirmidhī [d. 892], and Abū 'Abd al-Raḥmān al-Nasā'ī [d. 915] all wrote *Sunan* books, which went beyond the "sound" *ḥadīths* to serve as a guide to the *sunna* and its practice.

These are the famous works on *ḥadīths* in the Community, the chief books of *ḥadīths* on the *sunna* [Ibn Khaldūn does not mention the *Sunan* of Ibn Mājā (d. 896) usually considered the sixth book, since it was never fully accepted in North Africa]. The discipline has a noble aim: knowledge of what traditions related on the authority of the Keeper of the Law [the Prophet] must be preserved. In our time, *ḥadīths* are no longer published, nor are the books of the earlier scholars corrected, since custom attests that these numerous religious leaders, close to each other in their own times, fully capable and exercising independent judgment, would not have neglected or omitted any tradition to be discovered by a later scholar far removed from their time. At this point, care is restricted to correcting the written sources and fixing the accuracy of transmission.

Bukhārī's *Ṣaḥīḥ* occupies the chief place among them. However, the religious scholars of the Maghrib [the Muslim West], unite in preferring the *Ṣaḥīḥ* of Muslim to that of Bukhārī.

Be also aware that the leaders in interpretation of the religious Law differ in the use they make of this branch of learning. Abū Ḥanīfa is said to have restricted his transmission of *ḥadīths* to about seventeen, while Mālik only approved as sound those in his book *al-Muwaṭṭā'*, at most some three hundred or so. Yet Aḥmad b. Ḥanbal has in his own *Musnad* some thirty thousand *ḥadīths*. Hence some odious and unfair persons have asserted that some of these great men transmitted few *ḥadīths* because they had small stock of them.

There are no grounds at all for such a conclusion about these great religious leaders. Abū Ḥanīfa only transmitted a few *ḥadīths* because he was very strict in the conditions he accepted for transmitting and retaining *ḥadīths*. He declared them weak in certainty if they were contradicted by the actions of individuals. Thus he was far from what is charged, and his position indicates that he was one of the greatest of those exerting themselves in this science.

His followers later permitted latitude in their conditions and increased their transmissions of *ḥadīths*.[45]

III
THE LAW OF GOD: *SHARĪ'A* AND *FIQH*

The most characteristic activity of Christian scholarship has been theology; that of Islamic scholarship has been the Law. The idea that Law comes from a divine source is very ancient in the Semitic Orient and in Islam it is reinforced by the Qur'ān, where God is seen as commanding and forbidding, and by the Ḥadīth *with the practice of the Prophet and the early Community seen as a model for Muslims. A system of divine Law may be deduced from these sources, and a system was needed. Early Arab Muslim society did not have a coherent legal system available to it, as early Christianity did in the laws of the Roman Empire. One may also put it this way: Christianity is a theological religion, deeply concerned with the right articles of faith to hold. Islam is primarily an ethical religion, deeply concerned with the right things to* do. *It sees civilization itself as depending on the right way to live.*

The name for the divine Law is shar', *the "prescribed" (by God and His messenger). Another name used is* sharī'a, *with its connotation of "the right way to the water." "The Religion is one, but the* sharī'a *is various," says Qatāda b. Di'āma, an early Muslim authority.*[1] *If an action is* shar'ī, *it is prescribed by the Law. However, humankind does not know every particle of* shar'; *God is most knowing of that. People may validly have* fiqh, *insight, into divine Law. There are different systems of* fiqh.

While classically Muslims recognized that there is more than one way to the water, in modern times there has been a tendency (fundamentalist in origin) to reify the sharī'a *and see it as a monolithic system. It has never been that, but each system of* sharī'a *Law has aimed to be all-embracing and govern every aspect of life, ritual, ethical, private, and public. For reasons of public welfare, the jurists grant the ruler the right to suspend the application of portions of the public law and substitute nonreligious laws; this has especially been true for penal law. Still, the* sharī'a *is not thereby revoked—one cannot revoke divine Law—it is simply not enforced, because for temporal reasons it may not be feasible at that time and place to do it, and it was given by God for human benefit. The collecting and sifting of the* Ḥadīth *was the chief activity of Muslim scholarship in the classical first four centuries. It went hand in hand with the development of systems of* fiqh; *after the chief* Ḥadīth *collections were set down, legal studies could truly become the major concern of the scholars.*

Virtually all religions have priesthoods. That of Islam is a priesthood of all. Any Muslim male may validly perform a sacrifice or lead prayers or officiate at a wedding or funeral. But there is a clerical class, similar to the rabbinate in Judaism, which has acquired social prestige and influence exactly similar to the clergy of other religions. These are the 'ulamā' *(learned: in the Law) and* fuqahā' *(the men of insight, or jurists).*

The legal texts which follow are all the work of medieval 'ulamā' *who were revered for their insight into divine Law. Their work is still studied by the* 'ulamā' *today. How much of it should be incorporated in the legislation of modern Muslim states is a matter of earnest discussion.*

The Acts of Servanthood

The first sections of the books of fiqh *always concern the laws governing human dealings with God (e.g., worship and ritual purity). The following sections are from the Ḥanbalī* madhhab *or school. Every Sunnī belongs to one of four schools which have supplanted all earlier schools: Ḥanafī, Mālikī, Shāfi'ī, or Ḥanbalī. Each has its own way of achieving* fiqh. *The Ḥanbalī school came after the others and attempted to redress what it saw as wrong turnings in interpretation. It is the fundamentalist school. The man for whom it is named (he did not found it), Aḥmad b. Ḥanbal of Baghdad (d. 855/*A.H. *241), insisted that the texts of Qur'ān and* Ḥadīth *must be applied without interpretation or question. Reasoning or traditional understanding is thus ruled out as a method of insight, though there is an appreciation of the school's own tradition. Ḥanbalism lies behind the Wahhābī insight into Law which predominates in Saudi Arabia, known for its strict application of such rules as amputation of the hands of thieves. Historically the Ḥanbalīs were the smallest of the Sunnī schools, and still are, but they have always had some following for their unwilling-*

ness to compromise and for the crystalline simplicity of their position. In Islam as in other religions, fundamentalism has especially recommended itself as a vehicle of renewal in the modern period. Thus the influence of Ḥanbalī Law goes far beyond its own adherents. The author Muwaffaq al-Dīn Ibn Qudāma of Jerusalem moved to Damascus in 1156 as a refugee from the Crusaders, fought against them with Saladin, and died in 1223 (A.H. 620).

Ritual Purity

Water

Water was created pure; it purifies a breach of ritual purity [*ḥadāth*], as well as impure matter [*najāsa*]. Purification does not take place with any other liquid.

Water to the quantity of two large jars [*qulla*] or running water is not made impure except by an alteration of color, taste, or odor. Apart from that, water mixed with impure matter becomes impure. Two large jars represent about 108 Damascus *raṭl*s of water [about 266 liters].

If one has doubts about the purity of water or some other liquid, one must use it only after certainty.

When one is not certain which place on a garment or other object has been rendered impure, one must wash it in such a manner as to be certain one has dispelled the impurity.

A person of faith who cannot tell whether the water in question is pure or impure and who has access to no other water must perform the ablution with dust or sand in *tayammum* [i.e., one may not use doubtful water].

Vessels

It is not lawful to use vessels of gold or silver for purification or any other thing, following the word of the Prophet, God bless him and give him peace: "Drink not from vessels of gold and silver, nor eat from platters of them: they are for others in this world, and for you in the world to come." The same is true of plated articles, unless it is silver plating of low value.

It is permissible to use all other vessels if they are ritually clean and utensils of the People of the Book and their garments, if they are not known to be impure [other schools do not all agree about this].

The wool or hair of an animal not ritually slaughtered is pure, but its skin is impure whether it has been tanned or not, and the same is true for its bones.

Any animal which has died without ritual slaughter is impure, except:

(1) Humans.

(2) Animals which live only in water, following the word of the Prophet, God bless him and give him peace, about the sea: "Its waters are pure, and what dies in them is permissible food."

(3) Animals without blood, provided they are not generated in filth.[2]

The Lesser Ablutions [Wuḍū']

Like all ritual acts, this is only made valid by intent. The Messenger of God, God bless him and give him peace, said, "Works are only judged according to their intention. To each is given according to one's intentions."

One should first say "In the name of God!" then wash the hands three times, and three times rinse out the mouth and snuff water into the nostrils, using water from the cupped hand for both acts at the same time.

One then washes the face three times from the hairline to the neck, the chin, and the openings of the nostrils. A man combs out his beard with wet fingers if it is thick and washes it if it is sparse. One then washes the hands up to the elbows, three times. One then proceeds to rubbing the head, including the ears, with both hands [wet], going from the forehead to the nape of the neck and back.

One then washes the feet three times, with the ankles, passing the fingers between the toes.

At the end, one raises the face to heaven and says, "I testify that there is no god but God alone, without partner. I testify that Muḥammad is His servant and His messenger."

It is *sunna* [recommended] to repeat each washing three times, but it is disliked to wash more than three times and waste water.

It is *sunna* to clean the teeth with a *siwāk,* or chewed stick, when the taste in the mouth alters, when one rises from sleep, or when one prepares for prayer, according to the Messenger of God, "Were it not that I fear my Community could not perform it, I would order them to use the *siwāk* before every prayer." It is recommended to clean the teeth at any time except when the sun is setting and when one is fasting during Ramaḍān.[3]

Things Which Annul Ablution

These are seven:

1. Whatever comes from the two natural orifices (urethra, anus).

2. Whatever comes from elsewhere in the body, if it is foul.

3. Loss of consciousness, except from a light sleep, whether seated or standing.

4. Touching the penis with the hand.

5. Touching a woman, if it is accompanied by desire.

6. Apostasy from Islam.

7. Eating camel's meat [most lawyers do not include this]. The Prophet was asked if one should make ablutions after eating camel's meat, and said, "Yes, go ahead." When asked if one should make ablution after eating sheep's flesh, he said, "If you wish, do; if not, don't."

The Great Ablution: [Ghusl]

Those things which obligate the greater ablution are:

1. Any seminal emission.

2. A meeting of the penis with the place of the clitoris.

Greater ablution obligates formulation of the ritual intention and washing the entire body, including rinsing the mouth and nostrils.

It is *sunna* to say "In the name of God!" and to rub the body with both hands.

It is not necessary to undo the hair, if one pours water over it.

If one has formulated the intention, one may accomplish the lesser ablution with the greater, and similarly with *tayammum* one may remove lesser and greater ritual impurities if one formulates the intention at the time, but if one formulates only one intention at a purification, one accomplishes only what one intended.

Ablution with Sand or Dust [Tayammum]

This consists of placing the hands once on clean dry earth, rubbing one's face with the hands, and rubbing the hands together. It is necessary to touch the soil only once, but not invalid if one does it more. There are four conditions for valid performance of *tayammum*.

1. The nonavailability of water for ablution.

2. The time: it can only be performed before one obligatory prayer [i.e., it must be repeated for the next prayer].

3. The intention.

4. The soil. It must be only pure soil containing dust.[4]

Menstruation and Ritual Purity

Menstruation prevents ten things: (1) performance of ritual prayer, (2) the obligation to perform it, (3) fasting, (4) circumambulation of holy places [*ṭawāf*], (5) reciting the Qur'ān, (6) touching a copy of it, (7) being in a mosque, (8) sexual intercourse, (9) formal repudiation of a wife, and (10) being counted in a period of voluntary continence.

Women issuing blood after childbirth are bound by the same law.[5]

Ritual Prayers [Ṣalāt]

Ubāda b. al-Ṣāmit stated, I heard the Messenger of God say, "Five prayers are prescribed by God for His servants in the space of a day and a night. Those who observe these have God's promise that He will let them enter Paradise. One who does not perform them has no promise from God. If God wills, He will punish the person, and if He wills, pardon."

The five prayers are obligatory for every Muslim who has reached the age of puberty and has the use of reason, except for women who are menstruating or recovering from childbirth.

If Muslims deny the necessity of prayer through ignorance, one must instruct them; if they deny it willfully, they have apostatized.

It is not permitted to delay a prayer, unless one has formulated the intention of combining it with another prayer, or was prevented from fulfilling the conditions for it [e.g., great ablution].

If Muslims abstain from saying the prayers from negligence, one should ask them three times to repent: if they repent, it is well, and if they refuse it is lawful to put them to death.[6]

Conditions for Ritual Prayers

These are six:

1. Ritual purity, according to the statement of the Messenger of God, God bless him and give him peace: "God will not accept the ritual prayer of one not in ritual purity."

2. The time: For the noon-prayer [*ẓuhr*] this falls from the time the sun begins to decline until the shadow of an object is equal to the length of that object.

The time of the afternoon-prayer [*'aṣr*], which is the central prayer, falls from the end of the time for noon-prayer until the sun turns yellow; after that it is not lawful to pray until the next time of prayer.

The time of the evening-prayer [*maghrib*] falls from the setting of the sun until the red has disappeared from the sky.

The time of night-prayer [*'ishā*] falls from that time until midnight. Then the delay of necessity begins, lasting until dawn.

The time for the dawn-prayer [*fajr*] begins at the true dawn and lasts until the sun is risen. [It is characteristic of differences in *fiqh* that exact times of prayer vary from school to school.]

3. Covering ritual nakedness. The nakedness of a man or a slave-woman is all that is between the navel and the knee, and every part of a free woman except her face and her hands.

4. Purity of body and clothing. If one prays in ignorance in a garment with an impurity on it, the prayer is accepted.

5. Facing toward Mecca.

6. Formulation of the intention.[7]

*The ritual prayers are a service to God, a liturgy which must be exactly performed. The instructions following are taken from a classic Mālikī manual, the Treatise of Ibn Abī Zayd al-Qayrawānī (born in Nafza, Spain, in 922 [A.H. 310], d. 996 [A.H. 386] in Qayrawān, Tunisia). The Mālikī school of Madīna spread to Spain and North Africa and prevails in Upper Egypt, the Sudan, and West and North Africa today. What distinguishes its method of attaining insight is its rigid dependence on traditionalism (*taqlīd*), seeking to maintain the practice of Madīna, the Prophet's capital. It is thus the most conservative of all Sunnī law-schools.*

Another distinguishing characteristic of the Mālikī school is its doctrine of istiṣlāḥ, *"finding the beneficial": whatever is in the interest [*maṣlaḥa*] of the Muslim Community is legally approvable. It was a recognized principle particularly after the eleventh century.*

Performance of the Ṣalāt

The consecrating act in prayer is to say *Allāhu akbar* [God is greater]! No other expression is permissible. You should raise your hands as high as your shoulders or less, and then recite from the Qur'ān. If you are in the morning-prayer, recite the opening *sūra* of the Qur'ān. Do not start with the formula "In the name of God, the Merciful, the Compassionate," either in this *sūra* or in the one which you recite after it. When you have said "nor of those who go astray," say "Amen," whether you are alone or praying behind a leader [imam], in a low voice. The imam also should not say it as loudly as the rest of the prayer, but in a low voice, though there is a difference of opinion about this.

Then recite a *sūra* from the last part of the Qur'ān [where the shortest *sūra*s occur]. If it is longer than that, there is no harm in it, but it should not exceed the space of time allotted for that prayer. Recite it in an audible voice.

When this *sūra* is finished, repeat "God is greater!" while leaning forward to begin the inclination [*rukū'*]. Place your hands on your knees, and keep your back straight, without arching it, not lifting your head up or ducking it. Be sure to preserve sincere humility in both the inclination and the prostration which follows. Do not pray while making the inclination: if you wish, say "Praise to my Lord, the Great! Glorified be He!" There is no fixed time for that, nor for the length of the inclination.

After this raise your head, saying "God hears those who praise Him." Then say "My God, our Lord, to You be praise!" if you are alone. An imam does not repeat these formulas. Those who pray behind an imam also do not say "God hears those who praise Him," but they do say "My God, our Lord, to You be praise!"

You should then stand erect serenely and quietly. Then begin the prostration, not sitting back on the heels but going directly into a prostration. Say "God is greater!" while leaning forward in the prostration and touch your forehead and nose to the ground, placing your palms spread flat on the ground and pointing toward Mecca, placing them near the ears, or somewhat to the rear of them. All of this is prescribed in a general manner, not strictly. Do not spread the forearms on the ground or clasp the upper arms to your sides, but hold them slightly away. Your feet should be perpendicular to the ground in the prostration, with the ends of the big toes touching it.

You may say in your prostration "Glory be to You, my Lord! I have wronged myself and done wrong. Forgive me!" or something similar. You may utter a private prayer in the prostration if you wish, and there is no set time for this, but at the least your members should remain still in a fixed position.

Then you should raise your head, saying "God is greater!" and sit back, folding the left foot in the time between the two prostrations and putting the right foot vertical to the ground with the bottoms of your toes touching the ground. Lift your hands from the earth and place them on your knees, and then make a second prostration as you did the first. Then rise from the ground as you are, supporting yourself on both hands, not returning to the sitting position before rising, but directly, as mentioned. While rising, say "God is greater!"

Then recite a part of the Qur'ān as you did at first, or a little less, doing it just as you did before, but add the invocation [*qunūt*] after the inclination, or if you prefer before performing it, after the end of your recitation. The invocation is as follows: "O God, I ask Your aid and pardon. We truly put our faith in You, we put our trust in You, we submit humbly to You, we confide in You, and we forsake all who repudiate You. O God, You only do we serve, to You we pray and prostrate ourselves, for You we strive. We put our hope in Your mercy, and fear Your grave chastisements. Surely Your chastisements shall attain those who repudiate You!"

Then make the prostration and sit back as has been described before. If you sit back after the two prostrations, place the right foot vertical to the ground with the bottoms of your toes touching it and place the left foot flat, letting your posterior come in contact with the ground. Do not sit on your left foot, and if you wish let the right foot incline from a vertical position until the side of the big toe touches the ground: this permits some latitude.

After this, you recite the *tashahhud,* as follows: "Unto God be all salutations, all things good, all things pleasing, all benedictions. Peace be upon you, O Prophet, and the mercy of God and His blessings! Peace be upon us all, and all righteous servants of God. I witness that there is no god but God, the Unique, without partner. I witness that Muḥammad is His servant and messenger." If after this you utter the final salutation, it is fitting and permissible, or you may add other formulas.

Then say "Peace be upon you" one time only, looking straight ahead in the direction of Mecca and turning the head slightly to the right. It is thus that an imam or one alone does; one praying behind an imam utters the salutation once, turning slightly to the right, and utters it again in response to the salutation of the man on the left. If there is no one there, he does not say anything to the left.

While reciting the *tashahhud* one puts one's hand in the lap and closes the fingers of the right hand, pointing with the index finger, the side of which is toward one's face. Opinions differ on whether it should move. Some hold that the believer with this gesture indicates his faith that God is one God; those who move it explain it as rebuking Satan. I myself believe one must explain it as a way of warning oneself of the things which in prayer might importune and distract the attention. The left hand should be left open on the right thigh, and one should not move it or point with it.

It is recommended to make two inclinations at dawn, before the regular dawn-prayer which follows the dawn. At each of these inclinations, one should recite the *Fātiḥa,* the opening *sūra* of the Qur'ān, in a low voice.

Recitation at the noon-prayer should be as long as that at the dawn-prayer or a little shorter, and nothing should be recited loudly. One should recite the *Fātiḥa* in both the first and the second inclinations as well as another *sūra,* in a low voice. In the last two inclinations of the noon-prayer, one should recite the *Fātiḥa* alone, in a low voice.

After this, one should perform supererogatory prayers. It is recommended to add four inclinations, saying the final salutation after each group of two. The same supererogatory prayers are recommended before the afternoon-prayer.

At the afternoon-prayer, one does as we have prescribed for the noon-prayer.

For the evening-prayer, one should recite audibly in the first two inclinations and recite the *Fātiḥa* with each inclination as well as one of the shorter *sūra*s. In the third, one should recite the *Fātiḥa* only, and the *tashahhud* and the salutation. It is reprovable to sleep before the night-prayer, or to converse after it, except for good reason.

"Reciting softly" in the ritual prayer means moving the tongue to form the words in the recitation. "Reciting audibly" is for one to hear oneself and be heard by a person standing next to one, if one is not acting as an imam. A woman should speak more softly than a man.[8]

[Friday is the Muslim day of congregational prayer. Friday does not have to be observed as a day of rest, though it often is. Noon-prayers are recited in congregation, led by an imam, and a public address or *khuṭba* is given.]

Funeral Rites

After the five daily offerings of liturgical prayer, the fiqh *books consider such matters as the the prayer of fear, night-prayers, those for rain, those in an eclipse, purification before touching the Qur'ān, and inappropriate things to do while facing toward Mecca, then pass on to rites at interment of the dead. This section is taken from the* Muwaṭṭā' *(the Beaten Path) of Mālik b. Anas (d. 795/A.H. 179), the jurist from whom the law-school of Madīna is named (he did not found it). His book was so admired in its time that no less a person than al-Shāfiʿī stated that it ranked in importance second only to the Qur'ān, and it forms the basis of Mālikī* fiqh. *It is a collection of traditions on the way that things were done in Madīna, in the Prophet's time and under his immediate successors. It is the example of Madīna, not only the example of the Prophet, that is held up as the model for Muslim practice, because Mālik assumes that the people of Madīna, the early capital, would have better insights than the people of other areas where Companions of the Prophet had settled. Madīnan tradition could thus supplement the Prophet's practice and was the true continuation of it.*

As collector of the traditions, Mālik is cited as the source. He did not write the Muwaṭṭā'; *he taught it, as traditions on various aspects of the Law. Some fifteen early recensions, from lecture notes of his students, survived.*

Washing the Dead

Yaḥyā from Mālik from Ja'far b. Muḥammad, from his father: The Messenger of God, God bless him and give him peace, was in his shirt when he was washed.

Mālik from Ayyūb b. Tamīma al-Sakhtiyānī from Muḥammad b. Sīrīn from Umm 'Aṭīya of the Anṣār: The Messenger of God came in where we women were when his daughter passed away and said, "Be sure to wash her three times, five times, or even more than that if you see fit, with water and lote-tree leaves. At the end, apply camphor, or something camphor-scented. When you have finished, call me." When we were finished, we called him, and he gave us a wrapper of his, saying, "Wrap her in this," meaning his waist-wrapper.

Mālik from 'Abdallāh b. Abī Bakr: Asmā' bint 'Umīs [Abū Bakr's wife] washed Abū Bakr al-Ṣiddīq when he died. Then she went and asked those of the Muhājirīn who were there, "I am fasting today and it is very cold. Do I have to make major ablution [*ghusl,* normally necessary after intimate contact]?" They answered, "No."

Mālik heard people of knowledge say: If a woman dies, and there is no woman there to wash her, no near kinsman, nor her spouse who could do this for her, *tayammum* should be performed for her. Her face and hands should be lightly rubbed with dust [to avoid uncovering her body].

Mālik said: If a man dies and no one is there but [stranger] women, *tayammum* should be performed for him as well.

Mālik said: Washing the dead is not so prescribed for us as to consist of an exact procedure, but they should be washed and purified.

Shrouding the Dead

Mālik from Yaḥyā b. Saʿīd: It has reached me that Abū Bakr asked ʿĀ'isha when he fell ill, "In how many shrouds was the Messenger of God buried?" She told him, "In three white garments of Yemeni stuff." He then said, "Take this garment"—pointing to a robe he had stained with musk or saffron—"and wash it. Then shroud me in it with two other garments." ʿĀ'isha said, "What about this one instead?" but he told her, "No, the living have more need of new clothes than the dead, and this is only for corpse-ichor."

Walking before the Bier

Yaḥyā from Mālik from Ibn Shihāb: The Messenger of God, may God bless him and give him peace, Abū Bakr and ʿUmar all used to walk before the bier at a funeral. So did the early caliphs, and ʿAbdallāh b. ʿUmar.

From Mālik: Ibn Shihāb said, "Walking behind the bier is a fault against the tradition [*sunna*]."

Saying "God Is Greater" over the Dead

Yaḥyā from Mālik from Ibn Shihāb from Saʿīd b. Musayyib from Abū Hurayra: The Messenger of God announced the death of the Negus of Abyssinia to the people of Madīna on the day he died. He went out of the town to the Oratory of the Muṣallā, formed them in ranks, and then cried "God is greater!" four times.

Mālik from Ibn Shihāb from Abū Umama b. Sahl b. Ḥunayf: A poor woman fell ill, and the Messenger of God was informed of her illness, for he—God's blessing and peace be upon him!—used to visit the poor and ask about them. He said, "If she should die, then call me." However, they took her out to be buried by night [washing and burial usually take place promptly after death], and they disliked to wake the Messenger of God. The next morning he was told what had happened and asked, "Did I not order you to call me for her?" They replied, "Messenger of God! We hated to get you out at night and wake you."

Then the Messenger of God went out with the people and put them in ranks at her grave, and cried four times, "God is greater!"

Funeral Prayers

Yaḥyā from Mālik from Saʿīd b. Abī Saʿīd al-Maqbūrī from his father, who asked Abū Hurayra [Companion of the Prophet], "How do you pray at a funeral?" Abū Hurayra replied, "As God lives, I shall tell you. First there is the procession, with the people following the bier, and when it is placed on the ground, I give the cry, 'God is greater!' and praise God and bless His prophet. Then I pray, 'O God, this is Your servant, the child of Your servant and child of Your handmaid. He used to testify that there is no god but You, that Muhammad is Your servant and Your messenger, and You know him best of all. O God, if he did well, then increase him in good deeds, and if he did wrong, then forgive his offense. O God! Deprive us not of his reward, and try us not after this his death.' "

Funeral Prayers in the Mosque

Yaḥyā from Mālik from Abū Nadr, the freedman of 'Umar b. 'Ubaydallāh, from 'Ā'isha, the wife of the Prophet, God bless him and give him peace. She ordered that the people pass by her at the mosque [her house was inside its walls] with the bier of Sa'd b. Abī Waqqāṣ after he died, so that she might pray for him. Some people found fault with her for this, and 'Ā'isha said, "How hasty people are! It was in this very mosque that the Messenger of God prayed for Suhayl b. Bayḍā'."

Mālik from Nāfi' from 'Abdallāh b. 'Umar: 'Umar b. al-Khaṭṭāb was prayed over in the mosque.

Burial of the Dead

Yaḥyā said that Mālik informed him that the Messenger of God died on Monday and was buried on Tuesday, and the people prayed over him one by one: no-one prayed behind a leader [as no-one yet had authority to lead the prayers in his place]. Some said, "He should be buried under his pulpit." Others said, "Bury him at the cemetery of al-Baqī'." Then Abū Bakr came forward and said, "I heard the Messenger of God say, 'No prophet is ever buried except at the place he died in.' " Thus they dug his grave in ['Ā'isha's] room. While they were washing the body, they wanted to remove his nightshirt, but they heard a voice say, "Do not remove the shirt!" Hence they did not, but washed him while it was on him.

Mālik from Hishām b. 'Urwa from his father: There were two men who dug graves in Madīna; one of them used to dig a niche for the body in the grave, and the other did not. They said, "Whichever of them comes first will do his job." The one who dug niches came first, so he dug one for the Messenger of God, may God bless him and give him peace [Muslim graves now usually have this recess at the side].

Mālik from Yaḥyā b. Saʿīd from ʿĀʾisha, wife of the Prophet: I dreamed that three moons fell into my chamber and told my dream to [my father] Abū Bakr al-Ṣiddīq. When the Messenger of God was buried there, Abū Bakr told her, "This is the first of the moons, and it is the best" [Abū Bakr and ʿUmar were both later buried there].[9]

Zakāt

The Shāfiʿī law-school was founded by Muḥammad b. Idrīs al-Shāfiʿī, a Meccan of the tribe of Quraysh, who studied the Law first in Madīna and then in Iraq. He set out to found a method of fiqh *that would combine the best features of both: the traditionalism of the Ḥijāz and the emphasis on reason and use of judgement of Iraq. For this, Shāfiʿīs like Ḥanafīs were sometimes accused by fundamentalists and traditionalists of being "People of Opinion," while their opponents were "People of* Ḥadīth.*"*

However, al-Shāfiʿī emphasized the critical study of Ḥadīth, *in order to know which were genuine so that they could be used in Law. He insisted that the Prophet's own example must be given precedence over any other (e.g., that of Madīna). He also emphasized the importance of* ijmāʿ *or consensus: when the infallible Community of the Muslims (or leading scholars) agreed on a practice, even though it was not mentioned in the Qurʾān or* Ḥadīth, *it had binding force. He moved to Egypt, taught at its capital, Fusṭāṭ, and was buried there in 820 (A.H. 204), where his tomb is a venerated shrine for his followers.*

The school spread from Lower Egypt to the Red Sea, South Arabia, and across the Indian Ocean to Malaysia, Indonesia, and the Philippines, areas where it is the only law-school of any importance. It played an important role in the return to Sunnism of the eleventh century (fifth century A.H.), partly because it appeared to be a broad middle way to fiqh *and thus had the support of the governing authorities.*

The following regulations for payment of the obligatory religious tax of the zakāt *are taken from the Shāfiʿī manual of Abū Isḥāq al-Shīrāzī, a Persian doctor of the school who died in 1083 (A.H. 476) Some of what it says (e.g., its emphasis on counting camels and goats) is clearly of antiquarian interest in modern times. Most people today figure a tax of 2.5 percent of their yearly income for this religious obligation. It is not simply alms to the poor, but must be spent for clearly stipulated Community purposes. In the early period, it was the only tax levied on Muslims. Later,* kharāj, *a tax on agricultural produce, was added.*

Who Is Affected by Zakāt

The obligation pertains only to a free Muslim who has complete ownership of the property on which it is due. Thus a contractual freedman [whose slavery has not yet been officially and legally terminated] does not owe *zakāt,* nor does one who has always been a non-Muslim. As to whether one owes it if one was a Muslim and then apostatized, there are three opinions:

1. One must pay it.
2. One need not.
3. One must pay it only if one returns to Islam.

Zakāt is due only on animals, agricultural products, precious metals, objects intended for sale, the product of mines, and treasure troves.

Zakāt *on Animals*

This is due only for camels, cattle, sheep, and goats, if one has the minimum number on which it is due and has been the owner for a full year. According to the soundest opinion it is then a religious obligation; according to another opinion it is not, if one is unable.

The increase of the flock born during the year is considered with the rest of the flock, even though the increase may not have been possessed for the full year.

The taxable minimum on camels is five. For each group of five, a goat is due. For a herd of twenty-five camels, a she-camel between one and two years of age is due. For thirty-six camels, a two-year-old female is due.

The taxable minimum on cattle is thirty head: on these, a one-year-old calf is due. For forty, a two-year-old heifer is due.

The taxable minimum on sheep and goats is forty head: on these, one goat is due. On 121, two goats are due; on 201, three goats are due; and after that a goat for each additional fifty.

Agricultural Products

This is only obligatory on cereals eaten for food and cultivated by people, such as wheat, barley, millet, sorghum, rice, and the like. It also applies to pulses, such as lentils, chickpeas, vetches, beans, and peas. Fruits are not subject, except for dates and grapes, to which al-Shāfi'ī used to add olives, turmeric, and saffron. The payment only becomes due when the grain or fruit has begun to show the marks of maturity.

The taxable minimum of each sort, when the grain has been threshed and the fruit dried, is five camel-packs, or 1,600 Baghdad *raṭl*s, but for rice and *'alas,* a grain which is left in the husk, the minimum is ten camel-packs.

Precious Metals

Whoever has the taxable minimum of gold or silver for a full year and is otherwise subject to the *zakāt* must pay the *zakāt* on precious metals. The minimum for gold is 20 *mithqal*s [1 *mithqal* = 1.5 drachms]: the *zakāt* is half a *mithqal* for each twenty [i.e., 2.5 percent]. For silver, the minimums is 100 drachms: one pays 5 drachms on each 100. Any adornment one may have for lawful use [e.g., women's jewelery] is exempted, according to one of two opinions, but if it is for an unlawful or reprovable use or in order to evade the tax, one must pay *zakāt* on it.

Zakāt *of Ramaḍān*

This is obligatory for every free Muslim who has something to spare from the provisions for himself and his dependents, which will allow him to pay it. Whoever owes it and can afford it owes it for all dependents who are Muslims.

This alms is due by the end of Ramaḍān, before the prayers on the Feast of Fast-breaking. It is lawful to make it at any time in Ramaḍān, but not to delay until the day after the Feast. If one does that, one has committed a fault which must be expiated.

One must give one measure of the quantity of the Prophet, God bless him and give him peace: 5 Baghdad *raṭl*s made up of those foods subject to *zakāt* [i.e., dates, raisins, wheat, barley, etc.].

Payment

Whoever has the obligation to pay *zakāt* and is able must pay it; if not, they commit a fault for which they must answer. If anyone refuses to pay it and denies its obligatory character they have committed apostasy and may be put to death. If they refuse it from motives of avarice, they shall have the amount taken from them and be given a sentence at the judge's discretion. The same is true for one who acts fraudulently.

It is reprehensible to transport the *zakāt* out of the district in which it was paid. If it is done, there are two opinions:

1. It may be considered permissible.
2. It may not.

If the *zakāt* is being paid on wealth found in a desert, the money shall be distributed among the designated classes in the nearest inhabited areas.

Distribution

The *zakāt* is to be distributed among the following eight classes of people:

1. The collectors, who should be free, versed in the Law, and trustworthy. They may not be Ḥāshimīs [i.e., of the Clan of the Prophet, since these are already entitled to Community funds].
2. The poor: those who cannot pay for their needs. These are given what is necessary to help them gain a living, such as tools or capital for a business.
3. The needy: those who are not able to support themselves fully; these are given a supplement.
4. Those whose hearts are to be conciliated: these are two categories:
   a. Infidels, of two sorts: those whose conversion is hoped for, and those from whom evil is feared. The latter are given part of the fifth of the fifth of the spoils of war (set aside for this purpose).
   b. Muslims, also of two sorts: important people who, it is hoped, will convert their (non-Muslim) followers, and tribes whose faith, it is hoped, will improve. The Prophet gave such tribes a share of the *zakāt;* in later times, there are three opinions:
   1. One should give them nothing.
   2. One should give them part of the *zakāt.*
   3. One should give them part of the twenty-fifth of the spoils of war (set aside for such purposes).
5. Slaves who are under legal contract to pay a certain sum for their freedom. They may be given what they are bound to pay, if they have no means to obtain it, but not more than that.

[Historically this assistance available to Muslim slaves was a powerful incentive for non-Muslim slaves in Muslim society to convert.]

6. Debtors.
7. Those who fight in "The Way of God;" that is, those who are not

entitled to an allotment, because they are volunteers not carried in the regular army registers. These are given a sum to outfit them for the *jihād*.

8. Travelers, whose travel is for lawful ends [e.g., to seek religious learning or go on the Pilgrimage].

The *zakāt* may not be given to an infidel, nor to a member of the Prophet's clan (who is entitled to another allotment).[10]

The Fast of Ramaḍān

These regulations are taken from a leading Shāfi'ī work, the Minhāj al-Ṭālibīn *of the Syrian Muḥyī al-Dīn al-Nawawī, who died in 1277 (A.H. 676). Ramaḍān in common has been a prominent Community-building experience for Muslims in history.*

The Obligation

The Fast of Ramaḍān becomes obligatory when thirty days of the preceding month of Sha'bān have passed, or when the new moon of Ramaḍān has been seen. This seeing is established with the testimony of one trustworthy witness, or some say two. If it is one witness, he must have the quality of full veracity and hence be neither a slave or a woman. If we should commence fasting on the basis of such testimony, and after thirty days did not see the new moon, we might still end the fast, even if the sky was cloudy.

Hence if fast is not yet obligatory in one area and a traveler from it came to a locality where the moon had been seen, the traveler should conform with the inhabitants and fast. Intention is a condition of the fast; it should be formulated each night. The full formulation in Ramaḍān is "I will fast tomorrow to acquit my duty to God of fasting during Ramaḍān this year."

The Conditions

To fast, one must rigorously avoid coition, vomiting, or introducing any substance to the interior of the body. It does not matter if the interior is in the head, the belly, the intestines, or the bladder; all can break the fast with the introduction of a substance by snuffing, eating, or through an incision or the like [e.g., injection].

According to the soundest opinion, putting drops in the nose or the urethra breaks the fast.

However, introduction must be through an open passage. Hence there is no harm if oil enters the pores by absorption, or eye cosmetic is used, and its taste is afterward perceived in the throat.

Introduction must be intentional, so that if a fly or gnat or dust of the road or flour-dust entered by accident, the fast would not be broken. It is also not broken by swallowing saliva.

It is broken, however, if saliva leaves the mouth and one brings it back into the mouth, even if one moistens a thread in one's mouth and then puts it back in the mouth still moist or swallows saliva in which a foreign substance is mixed.

If one swallows the saliva in the mouth it does not break the fast, but if one swallows water from the mouth and nose after the ablutions it does break the fast if it is in any quantity. If food remaining between the teeth is dislodged by saliva, it does not break the fast.

If one swallows something truly forgetting that one is fasting, it does not break the fast unless one repeats it, according to the soundest opinion.

Coition is like eating, according to our school (that is, if committed while truly forgetting, it would not break the fast), but any seminal emission otherwise does break the fast. [The time of fasting is from the time of night when a white thread can be distinguished from a black one—e.g., false dawn—until the sun has fully set below the horizon in evening.]

A traveler or sick person who is legally dispensed from fasting must fast the number of days missed when again able to do so. This is also true for menstruating women, for those who broke the fast without valid reason, for one who was unconscious for the entire day, for an apostate who reverts to Islam, but not for the period before one was converted to Islam.

A pregnant or nursing woman must fast for lost days when able. If she did not fast because she feared for her own health she need not pay expiation [*fidya*], but if she broke the fast fearing for the child, she does pay the expiation as well.

The expiation is a day's food given to the poor and needy.

One owes atonement [*kaffāra*] for breaking the Fast of Ramaḍan by coition. This consists of freeing a slave. If one cannot do that, one must fast for sixty days or, if one cannot do that, give sixty days' provisions to the poor. If one is unable to do all of this, the obligation remains, and one must do it if ever one is able. It is not possible for a poor person to pay the atonement to his own family.[11]

Pilgrimage [Ḥajj]

No rite of Islam has done more to unite its people than the Pilgrimage, where every year at the same time thousands of people meet and act together in complete equality. It is a transcendent demonstration of the fraternalism of Islam and a great opportunity for them to meet and exchange information. In medieval times, it also assisted the rapid dissemination of books from one end of the Muslim world to the other.

The following regulations are from the Mālikī Risāla *of Ibn Abī Zayd al-Qayrawānī. Qayrawān in North Africa was the real headquarters of the Mālikī legal scholars in the ninth century (third century* A.H.*). Mālikism became the law-school of all North and West Africa.*

The Obligation

Pilgrimage to the inviolate House of God in Bakka [i.e., Mecca] is a religious duty to every free adult Muslim who is able to make the way there, once in life. "Able" signifies having means of access and sufficient economic means, as well as the physical ability to arrive, whether riding or walking, in health of body.

Consecration

It is ordained that one take the ritual state of *iḥrām* [consecration for the Pilgrimage] at the proper post, or *miqāt*, on the routes. The post for the people of Syria, Egypt, and North Africa is Juḥfa. If they have passed by Madīna, it is better for them to use the post of its people: Dhū al-Ḥulaya. The post of the people of Iraq is Dhāt 'Irq, that of the Yemen's people is Yalamlam, and that of the people of Najd or Central Arabia is Qarn.

A pilgrim, or one who is only making the Visitation of the holy places [*'umra,* which can be undertaken at any time of year], should take the *iḥrām* either after one of the ritual prayers or after a supererogatory prayer. One then says, "I am here, Lord, I am here. I am here. You have no partner. I am here. Yours is the praise, Yours is the grace, Yours is the kingdom." One then formulates the intention to make the Pilgrimage or the Visitation in one's own words.

It is ordered that one perform the Great Ablution before taking the *iḥṛam* and that one remove all sewn garments. [Male pilgrim's garb is two seamless white garments, a waist-wrapper from navel to knee and a shawl covering the left shoulder, tied under the right. Women wear white garments covering all but the face and hands. Sandals may be worn, but not shoes.] It is recommended to make the Great Ablution on entering Mecca, and to continue using the formula "I am here [*labbayka*]" after one's prayers, on each elevation along the road, and when encountering fellow pilgrims. Great insistency in this is not mandatory.

Rites

When one has entered Mecca, one abstains from the formula until one has performed the Circumambulation and the Course. Then one continues to use it until sunset on the Day of 'Arafāt and the hasting to the Oratory at Muzdalifa.

It is recommended to enter Mecca by Kadā', the way above Mecca, and to leave it by Kudā, though if one does neither it is no sin.

Mālik says that on entering Mecca one should enter the Inviolate Mosque and that it is best to enter from the Gate of the Banū Shayba. Then one touches the Black Stone at the corner of the Ka'ba with one's lips, if one is able; if not, one puts one's hand on it and touches it to his lips, without kissing it. One then circumambulates the Holy House keeping it on one's left, seven times. Three times are quick, and four are walking. One touches the corner of the Ka'ba each time one passes it, in the way we have described, and says "God is greater!"

One should not touch the south corner with the lips, but with the hand, and place it on the lips without kissing. After the Circumambulation, one says a prayer of two prostrations at the "Station of Abraham," between the Ka'ba and the Gate of the Banū Shayba, and then touches the Black Stone, if one can reach it. Then one goes out to Mt. Ṣafā and stands on it while making an invocation. One then moves to Mt. Marwa, taking a brisk pace in the bottom of the valley. At Marwa, one stands on it, makes an invocation, and hastens to Ṣafā. One does this seven times, making in all four stops on Ṣafā and four on Marwa.

On the eighth of the Month of Pilgrimage, one goes out to Minā, and there prays the midday, afternoon, sunset, night, and dawn prayers. Then one goes to Mt. 'Arafāt, not ceasing to cry "I am here, O Lord!' until the sun sets and until one has arrived at the oratory of Mt. 'Arafāt. Before going there one must put oneself in the state of ritual purity and pray the noon-prayer and the afternoon prayer at one time under the direction of the imam of the pilgrims.

One then goes with the imam to 'Arafāt, and halts there until sunset. One then rushes with the throng and the imam to al-Muzdalifa and prays there the sunset, night, and dawn prayers. The pilgrims then make the "station" of the place called Mash'ar al-Ḥaram. When the sun is near rising, one hastens to Minā, driving one's mount on (if one is mounted) in the Valley of Muhassir. When arrived at Minā, one throws seven small stones at the first *jamra* [stone heap], called al-'Aqaba, and with each stone cries "God is greater!" [an ancient Semitic cursing ritual, regarded as recalling the stoning of Satan by Abraham.] Then a man shaves his head and goes to the Ka'ba to perform the seven prostrations and the inclination. One stays at Minā for seven days, and when the sun sets each day one throws seven stones at the three *jamras*, calling "God is greater" with each stone. When one has thrown for the third day, the fourth after the Feast of Sacrifice, one may leave for Mecca: the Pilgrimage is completed. If it is desired, one may compress the rites of Minā into two days and leave. On leaving Mecca, the Circumambulation of Farewell is made, and one performs invocations.

The *'umra* or Visitation is made as we have described, up to the hasting between Ṣafā and Marwa. Then one may cut the hair, and the Visitation is finished. Shaving the head is best, in Pilgrimage or Visitation, but merely cropping it is permitted. The *sunna* for a woman is cropping.[12]

Family Law

After dealing with 'ibādāt, *laws governing relations with God, the* fiqh *books pass to* mu'āmalāt, *the laws governing relations with one's fellow humans. The most universally observed of these are family laws: marriage, divorce, fosterage, inheritance, etc. According to a* ḥadīth, *"marriage is one half of Islam." Family law is only sketched here, in these sections from the* Hidāya, *by the Central Asiatic Burhān al-Dīn al-Marghinānī, of Farghāna, who died in 1196 (A.H. 593), a scholar of the Ḥanafī school.*

The Ḥanafīs developed from the law-schools of Iraq and took their name from Abū Ḥanīfa of Kūfa, who did not found the school, but did much to systematize its fiqh, *so that his followers were proud to call him their imam in* fiqh. *The Ḥanafīs are the school of reason and interpretation and tended at first to be wary of using many* ḥadīths, *which presented difficulties of reliability. Abū Ḥanīfa's disciples included Abū Yūsuf (d. 798/*A.H. *182), the chief justice of the 'Abbāsī caliph Hārūn al-Rashīd, al-Shaybānī (d. 805/*A.H. *189), as well as Zufar b. Hudhayl d. 775/*A.H. *158) and Ḥasan b. Ziyād. All are doctors of the school, though the first three rank highest, and in accord with their emphasis on the importance of reason and interpretation they have left many* ikhtilāfāt, *or permissible varying legal opinions, all of which could be used by later Ḥanafī scholars.*

This led traditionalists and fundamentalists to call the Ḥanafīs the school of mere "opinion," but they were always concerned with practical as well as theoretical questions in developing an Islamic society and government. They are perhaps the most developed of all schools, and their logical consistency and breath of vision recommended them to Muslim rulers. Ḥanafism was the school of the early 'Abbāsī Empire as well as of the later Mughal and Ottoman empires, and Ḥanafīs are found today chiefly in India, Pakistan, Afghanistan, China, Central Asia, Turkey, and the Fertile Crescent.

Nikāḥ *or Marriage*

[Nikāḥ, literally meaning sexual intercourse, is the term for the means by which intercourse becomes lawful.] It is contracted by means of declaration and consent. When both parties are Muslims, it must be contracted in the presence of two male or one male and two female Muslim witnesses who are free, sane, and adult. Their testimony is a condition of marriage, contrary to Mālik, who held that general knowledge was sufficient without testimony. Muslim witnesses are indispensable in the marriage of Muslims, since the testimony of infidels against Muslims is not valid. However, if a Muslim marries a woman who is a *dhimmī,* one of the People of the Book under Muslim protection, in the presence of two male *dhimmī*s it is valid, according to Abū Ḥanīfa and Abū Yūsuf. Zufar b. Hudhayl and Muḥammad al-Shaybānī differ, objecting that this amounts to accepting the testimony of infidels about a Muslim. The argument of the two earlier authorities in reply to this objection is that evidence is necessary merely in order to establish the husband's right to possess her, which is the object of the contract.

It is unlawful to marry one's mother, sister, grandmother, aunt, daughter, granddaughter, or direct descendant, or one's niece by his sister or brother. It is unlawful for a man to marry his wife's mother, his wife's daughter, any wife of his father or grandfather, or his son or grandson's former wife.

It is not lawful for a man to marry his foster-mother or foster-sister, God having commanded, "Marry not your mothers who have suckled you nor your sisters by fosterage," and the Prophet having stated, "Everything is forbidden in fosterage that is forbidden in kinship ties."

It is not lawful for a man to marry two women who are sisters or to cohabit with two sisters who are his slaves. However, if he marries the sister of a slavegirl with whom he has cohabited, the marriage is valid, providing he no longer cohabits with the sister who is his slave and renders her unlawful to himself by freeing her or marrying her to another man.

It is not lawful for a man to marry two women who are so closely related that marriage would be forbidden to them if one of them were a man. But he may marry a woman and her stepdaughter.

A man may not marry his slavegirl unless he sets her free first, and a woman may not marry her slave, since marriage has as its object that the children belong equally to both parents, and ownership and slavery are not equal states.

Marriage with a woman of the Book is lawful, but not marriage with a Zoroastrian woman, according to the statement of the Prophet, "Treat them as you would treat People of the Book, but do not marry their women or eat the animals they slaughter."

Similarly marriage with an idolatress is forbidden, until she accepts Islam or a religion of the Book.

But marriage with a Ṣābi'an is lawful, if they are of those with a prophet and a scripture [the Mandaeans], but if they are of those who worship the stars and have no scripture, it is forbidden. It is lawful for a free Muslim to marry a female slave, whether a Muslim or of the People of the Book [if she is not his own]; his children are then born in slavery.

It is not lawful for a man already married to a free woman to marry a slave, according to the statement of the Prophet, "Do not marry a slave after a free woman." This is an absolute prohibition according to us, in opposition to Shāfiʿī, who says such marriage is permitted if the man is a slave, and Mālik, who says it may occur with the free woman's consent. However, a man may lawfully marry a free woman after a slave.

A free man may marry four women, free or slave, but no more. It is unlawful for a slave to marry more than two women. Mālik holds that he may marry as many as a free man, even without his owner's consent. We, however, hold that slavery reduces both privileges and penalties by one half, so that the slave may marry two women and the free man four, to manifest the superiority of the free state. The "marriage of enjoyment" [permitted by the Shī'īs] is invalid. This is when the contract states "I will enjoy you until such a date, for such a consideration." Similarly, temporary marriage, as when a contract states "I will marry you for ten days," is invalid, whether the period be long or short, since a marriage should not contain a specification of time.

Guardianship

The marriage of a free adult sane woman may take place by her own consent without a guardian [*walī*], whether or not she is a virgin, according to Abū Ḥanīfa and Abū Yūsuf. According to Shaybānī, it may take place dependent on her guardian's consent. Mālik and Shāfi'ī hold that a woman can under no circumstances contract for herself, with or without her guardian's consent, and that she is not competent to contract for another [e.g., her daughter or her slave], because women are easily flattered and deceived. However such a marriage is illegal if there is inequality of the partners [e.g., in family, possessions, or status], according to our doctors.

It is not lawful for a guardian to force an adult virgin into marriage without her consent, contrary to Shāfi'ī. If when she is consulted by her guardian she smiles or is silent, this means consent, but not when she is asked by anyone who is not her guardian. A nonvirgin must in all cases verbally express her consent.

The contracting of a marriage for a boy or a girl who is under age by the guardian is valid, the Prophet having stated, "Marriage is committed [i.e., arrangements are entrusted] to the paternal kindred." If the marriage is contracted for children by the fathers or grandfathers, no option remains to them after they reach puberty, but if it is contracted by any other, the party may confirm or annul the contract upon reaching puberty.

Mahr

A marriage is legal even if there is no mention of the *mahr* paid to the bride by the husband, though Mālik holds the contrary. If he marries without specifying a *mahr*, she shall receive ten dirhams [pieces of silver], the Prophet having stated, "There is no *mahr* less than ten dirhams." If he should then divorce her before having been in *khalwa* [completely alone together for the time in which intercourse could be possible] with her, he must pay her one half of the agreed on *mahr,* or five dirhams, whichever is greater.

The *mahr* is payable to the bride before the consummation of the marriage, unless she has agreed to take the payment of all or part at a later time. She may lawfully refuse to go into *khalwa* with him if the *mahr* has not been paid.

Qism [*partition*]

If a man has two or more wives, all free women, he must make equal partition (of his attention, time, and gifts) to them, as the Prophet said, "A man who has two wives and is partial in partition to one of them will incline to one side on the Day of Resurrection." It is stated by ʿĀ'isha that he was scrupulous in partition with his wives and would pray, "O God, I make equal partition of what is in my control; do not hold against me that which I do not control," that is, degree of love. It is understood that equality of cohabitation is residence, not coition, since that depends on a matter which is not always in the man's control.

Divorce

Divorce is of three sorts: most laudable, acceptable, and irregular [*bidʿī*]. The most laudable is when the husband repudiates his wife by a single formula [e.g., "I divorce you"] during a period of ritual purity [between menstrual periods] during which he has not had marital relations with her and leaves her untouched for the period of her *ʿidda* or period of waiting to ascertain that she is not pregnant. This is most laudable, because

(1) The Companions of the Prophet considered it the best, and

(2) The husband still has it in his power to reverse his divorce during the *ʿidda,* if he desires, and the woman remains a lawful object of remarriage to the husband even after the *ʿidda* (whereas by another method she would have to first be married to another man before he could remarry her).

Acceptable divorce is when a man repudiates his wife by three formulas of divorce, each in a successive period of ritual purity.

Irregular divorce is when a man repudiates his wife by three formulas at one time or three formulas within one period of ritual purity. If the husband divorces her in this way it holds good, but he commits an offense. Shāfiʿī holds that all three forms are equally permissible, because divorce is by its nature a lawful act, even if the divorce was pronounced during her menstrual period.

If the woman is not subject to regular periods or is pregnant, then one period is assumed to be one lunar month.[13]

Wills

Wills bequeathing a part of one's property after death are not obligatory [since the property will be divided among the legal heirs by the provisions of the Law], but they are recommended. However, one may not bequeath more than one third of one's total property, unless it is by consent of all the legal heirs. One may not favor one or several of the heirs with a third of the property at the expense of the others, unless it is with their consent. A bequest to one who then kills the person making the will becomes invalid.

A bequest to an infidel or a bequest from an infidel is valid for a Muslim, firstly since God says, "God does not forbid you from kindness and fair dealing to those who have not fought with you about religion or expelled you from your homes" [Qur'ān 60:8], and secondly because by making the contract of *dhimma* they are equal with the Muslims in their transactions. However, a bequest to a hostile infidel is invalid, since God says, "He only forbids you from those who fight with you about religion and expel you from your homes or aid in your exile" [Qur'ān 60:9].

An insolvent person may not make a bequest, since his/her debts take precedence over what he/she would bequeath.

If a person bequeaths one-third of his/her property to one person and another third to another person, and the heirs refuse their consent, one-third of the property is divided between the two, and similarly for any bequests exceeding one-third of the total.[14] [Note: Islamic inheritance law is a complex matter. Certain categories of relatives are permitted to inherit in varying shares, with females in each category receiving half of what males in that category receive.]

Government of the Community

Islam is also a polity; a community which seeks governance. The first century and a third after the Prophet's death were racked by religious-political disturbances over the vital question of who had the right to be his khalīfa *(successor or caliph), the Imam or leader of his* umma*. The sects of Islam developed out of these events, and the question has* *never been fully settled, even among the Sunnī majority, who constitute about 86 percent of the total number of Muslims.*

The classical views of the jurists are well expressed in "The Governing Statutes" (al-Aḥkām al-Sulṭānīya) *of the Shāfiʿī jurist al-Māwardī of Baghdad, who seems to have written sometime before 1033 (A.H. 424). The successor of the Prophet is the sole legitimate authority, and all Muslim authority must be derived through delegation from him.*

Al-Māwardī was moved more by theoretical than by practical considerations. In his time, the ʿAbbāsī caliph had gone from being the ruler of a world empire to the status of a prisoner of a family of Shīʿī Persian dictators, the Būyīs. There were rival caliphs in Cairo, the Ismāʿīlī Shīʿī Fāṭimīs, and in Spain the Umawī caliphs of Córdoba. Still, al-Māwardī sees his Imam-caliph as the fountainhead of all legally exercised Muslim power.

The Imamate is placed on earth to succeed the Prophet in safeguarding the Religion and governing the world. It is a religious obligation to contract it with that person in the *umma* who will perform these duties, according to the consensus [of Sunnī *ʿulamā*], even though al-Aṣamm [who held that a model community should not require a leader] stands against them on this.

Opinions differ on whether this duty is necessitated by reason or by the Law. One party holds that reason necessitates it, since it pertains to intelligent beings to submit themselves to a leader who will keep them from wronging one another and will judge between them in their contentions and disputes, so that, if there were no supremacy, there would be anarchy and the human race would be a confused rabble. As al-Afwā al-Awdī the pre-Islamic poet says,

> Ill for Mankind is chaos, with no chiefs their own,
> and no chiefs there are, when the ignorant lord it.

According to another party, it is necessitated by the Law, which goes beyond reason, since the Imam has to carry out prescriptions of the Law which reason might not perceive that God's service demands.

Reason therefore (they say) does not necessitate it: reason only demands that intelligent people forbid themselves to commit wrongs against each other or cut relations with one another, and act in accord with justice in equality and friendly conduct, and thus follow their own reason, not that of another. As it is, the Law has come down to give jurisdiction to its delegate in the Religion, for God the Mighty and Glorious has said, "O you who have faith, obey God and obey the Messenger, and those set in authority among you" [Qur'ān 4:58], so that He has made it obligatory for us to obey the ones set in authority, the Imams reigning over us.

The obligatory nature of the Imamate is thus established, but it is only an obligation for those necessary to perform it, like *jihād* or the seeking of religious knowledge. If no one takes it on, two groups of people emerge:

(1) The people suited to choose, until they select an Imam for the *umma,* and

(2) The people suited to be Imam, until one of them is invested with the office.

Those who do not belong to these categories commit no crime or sin if they delay in choosing an Imam. The qualifications of those suited to choose are three:

(1) **Rectitude**, with all its qualifications.

(2) **Religious knowledge** sufficient to arrive at knowledge of who deserves to be the Imam.

(3) **Judgment and wisdom** to select the best man suited for it.

As for those fitted for the Imamate, there are seven qualifications:

(1) **Rectitude,** with all its qualifications.

(2) **Religious knowledge** necessary to interpret the Law in revealed and religious matters.

(3) **Soundness of the senses** of hearing, sight and speech so that these function normally.

(4) **Soundness of limb** from any defect which would prevent freedom of movement and agility.

(5) **Judgment** for governing and administration.

(6) **Courage and bravery** to protect his flock and wage *jihād.*

(7) ***Nasab*** [correct genealogy]. He must be of the Quraysh. The Prophet, may God bless him and give him peace, said, "Give precedence to the Quraysh and do not go before them." There is no pretext for any disagreement about this, and no word one may raise against it.

There are ten things the Caliph must do in public affairs:

(1) **Maintain religion** according to its established principles.

(2) **Apply legal judgments** for litigants so that equity reigns, without aiding the oppressor or weakening the oppressed.

(3) **Protect the flock** and keep the wolf from the fold, so that people may gain their living and move from place to place securely.

(4) **Apply the *ḥudūd*** or punishments of the Law, so as to secure God's prohibitions from violation.

(5) **Fortify the marches** so that the enemy will not appear due to neglect, shedding the blood of any Muslim or protected person.

(6) **Wage *jihād*** against those who reject Islam so that they become either Muslims or protected people.

(7) **Collect the *zakāt* and the taxes** on conquered territory in conformity with the Law, without fear or oppression.

(8) **Administer treasury expenditures.**

(9) **Delegate loyal and trustworthy people.**

(10) **Directly oversee** matters and not delegate his authority seeking to occupy himself either with pleasure or devotion.[15]

With time, the 'Abbāsī caliphate at Baghdad was destroyed by the pagan Mongols, in 1258. Until 1517, their descendants were given the caliphal title and an allowance by the Mamlūk sultans of Cairo; symbols of Islamic unity and legality. The prominent Mālikī scholar and judge Ibn Khaldūn wrote in this context an opinion in his Introduction to History (Muqaddima) *which was widely accepted in later times: any ruler who rules Islamically is the successor of the Prophet.*

The Meaning of Caliphate

The truth about royal authority is that it was a necessary institution for the human species, and it required domination and force, which both rise from wrath and animality. The rulings of one who had royal authority usually deviated from justice and were injurious to those under his authority.

Thus it was difficult to obey him, and this led to disturbance and killing. In this situation it was necessary to have recourse to ordained political rules accepted by the people, to which they would submit, such as the Persians and other peoples had. A dynasty which had no such policies would not endure for long.

If these rules were ordained by the intelligent, great, and far-seeing men of state, the result was a rational polity. If they were ordained by God through a lawgiver who decreed and prescribed them, it was a religious polity, useful to life both in this world and in the world to come.

This is because the purpose of humankind is not only for this world, for it is all trifling and vain, since its final end is only death and annihilation. And God says, "Did you reckon that We created you for trifling?" [Qur'ān 23:115]. The purpose of humankind is service to God, which leads them to happiness in the world to come. Political laws only consider the interests of this world, but the purpose of the Lawgiver for humankind is their welfare in the world to come. It is necessary therefore to cause the masses to act in accord with divine laws in all their affairs, both in this world and in the world to come. The authority to do this was possessed by the prophets, and after them by their successors.

Thus it becomes clear what caliphate means. The king in the natural state causes the masses to act in accord with his purpose and desire. The king in the political state causes them to act according to rational insight so as to obtain their worldly interests and avoid harm. The caliphate, however, causes the masses to act in accord with religious insight for their welfare in the world to come as well as in this world. Thus it is really a successorship to the giver of the religious Law, serving to protect religion and lead this world for him, so understand this and keep it in mind.

It is called "caliphate" and "Imamate," and the incumbent is called "caliph" and "Imam." [In later times he has been called the sultan.] It is a necessary position. Some, like the Mu'tazilī al-Aṣamm and some of the Khārijīs, seeking to escape from kingship and its overbearing, dominating, and worldly ways, have said that it is not necessitated by either reason or the Law. However, the Law does not censure kingship as such, or the exercise of it, but its abuse. When no Imam is set up, a king will be set up, since kingship is a natural institution. That is the very thing they wanted to avoid. [It is not permissible to appoint two men as Imam in the same region, or where they would be near each other, but where there are great distances, and one Imam is unable to control the farther region, some (Mālikī) scholars hold it is permissible to set up another Imam to take care of public welfare.][16]

Ritual Slaughter and Animal Sacrifice

There are correct legal procedures in Islam for slaughtering animals, whether for food or for animal sacrifice, which is still enjoined. The following discussion is from the Hidāya *of al-Marghinānī the Ḥanafī.*

Dhabḥ [ritual slaughter]

Slaughter is a necessary condition to make lawful the flesh of the warm-blooded animal slaughtered, according to God's Word: "Forbidden . . .

unless duly slaughtered" [Qur'ān 5:3], because in this way the unclean blood is separated from the clean flesh. Thus *dhabḥ* renders clean all animals lawful for food, and those not normally eaten [e.g., cats, dogs, rats, which might be used for medicine or eaten in case of necessity].

It is of two sorts: (1) the method of choice, by cutting the throat, and (2) contingent, by cutting the veins in another part of the body. The latter may only be substituted for the first when the first cannot be accomplished, because the first is more effective in removing the blood. But the second is acceptable when the first is impossible (for example, a spearthrust in hunting), since obligation under the Law is only according to ability.

It is a condition that the slaughterer be a member of a community believing in the one God, either a Muslim or a Person of the Book, according to God's Word, "The food of those who have been given the scripture is lawful for you" [Qur'ān 5:5], and it is lawful if they mention God in performing the slaughter and do it correctly even if they are a child, insane, or a woman. If it is not performed correctly (by cutting the animal's veins) and the name of God is not mentioned, the animal is not lawful food.

An animal slaughtered by a Zoroastrian is not lawful, because the Prophet said, "Treat them like People of the Book, but do not marry their women or eat what they slaughter," and because they do not profess monotheism. Meat slaughtered by an apostate from Islam or an idolator is also not lawful, but a Person of the Book who has changed his or her religion is reckoned by the community to which they have changed.

Game slain by a person in consecration for the Pilgrimage is unlawful, even if it was not killed in the sacred territory.

If the slaughterer willfully omitted mentioning the name of God, the meat is carrion and may not be eaten, but if he omitted it through forgetfulness it is lawful. Shāfiʿī opines that it may be eaten in either case, and Mālik holds that it is unlawful in either case. Shāfiʿī's opinion about willful omission is contrary to the consensus of scholars before his time.[17]

Sacrifice

It is obligatory on every free mature male Muslim possessed of means to offer a sacrifice on the tenth of the Month of Pilgrimage, for himself and for his minor male children. This is the opinion of Abū Ḥanīfa, Shaybānī, Zufar b. Hudhayl, and Ḥasan b. Ziyād of our school, but according to one opinion of Abū Yūsuf and according to Shāfi'ī, it is only *sunna* [recommended].

It is not an obligation if one is on a journey.

The sacrifice for one person is a goat or sheep, and for any number up to seven it may be a cow or a camel. Only goats, sheep, cows (including buffaloes), and camels are lawful as sacrifices. They may not be blind, lame, sick, emaciated, or missing more than a third of an ear or the tail. A missing or broken horn, however, does not render an animal unsuitable. A kid may be sacrificed, but a cow must be at least two years old, and a camel five.

It is lawful for the one making the sacrifice to eat the meat or to give it to others, whether rich or poor, but it is preferable to give at least one-third in charity.

It is best for the sacrificer to slay the animal himself, if he knows how, or at least to be present when it is slain, and it is disliked for him to choose a Person of the Book to slay it, though it is lawful.[18]

Things Disliked and Things Forbidden

The jurists classify all human actions in five categories: obligatory, recommended, permissible, disliked, and forbidden. Different law-schools may classify an action differently (e.g., what is disliked in one school may be forbidden in another). It is important to notice that a disliked action is still ḥalāl *or permitted. This discussion of the disliked and non-permissible is from the* Hidāya *of al-Marghinānī.*

Things Disliked in the Law

It is related of Shaybānī that he regarded everything disliked [*makrūh*] in the Law as forbidden [*ḥarām*], but since he could find no conclusive text establishing this, he did not use that word. Abū Ḥanīfa and Abū Yūsuf opine that the disliked comes close to the forbidden (but is still permitted).

Abū Ḥanīfa has said it is disliked to consume the meat or milk of an ass and the urine of camels. Abū Yūsuf says there is no harm in using the urine of camels, if used medicinally. Since milk is produced from the meat of an animal, the milk is exactly similar to its meat.

It is not permitted to men or women to eat or drink or keep unguents or perfumes in vessels of gold and silver, because the Prophet said of those who drink from a vessel of gold and silver, "The fire of Hell will gurgle in their bellies." This being true of drinking, it will also be true of unguents and the like, and of eating with spoons of gold and silver, or using applicators of these materials for *kuḥl* to the eyes. Abū Ḥanīfa permitted utensils and furniture ornamented with silver.

If one is invited to a wedding-feast and finds there [frivolous] diversion or singing, there is no harm in one's sitting and eating, because responding to such an invitation is *sunna,* and the Prophet said, "If one refuses such an invitation, he has not obeyed me." One may not leave the wedding-feast because of the innovations of others, just as one may not leave a funeral because there are hired mourners present. If one can prevent them, one may; but if not one must endure it.

This is if one is not regarded as an exemplar by others; such a person must withdraw if he or she cannot prevent this behavior, because remaining there would be a deformation of religion and open the door for disobedience by the Muslims. All this applies if it occurs after one's arrival, for if one knows in advance that there will be inappropriate behavior, one should avoid the occasion whether one is an exemplar or not.

It is not permitted for a man to wear silk, but it is permitted for a woman. A number of the Companions including ʿAlī related that the Prophet once came out with a piece of silk in one hand and a piece of gold in the other, and said, "These are both forbidden to the men of my Community and permitted to its women."

There is no harm in wearing material with a woof of silk and a warp of any other material, in battle.

It is not permitted for a man to wear gold or silver, except for silver on a ring, on a belt, or on a weapon. It was the opinion of Abū Ḥanīfa that gold should not be used to mend teeth, if silver would serve as well, while the opinion of Shaybānī is that there is no harm in using gold for this purpose.

Seeing and Touching between the Sexes

It is not permissible for a man to look at a strange woman [i.e., from outside his immediate family], according to God's Word: "They shall not display their adornment except for what shows" [Qur'ān 24:31]. [The Prophet's cousins] ʿAlī and Ibn ʿAbbās explained that this means eyeshadow and rings and the place they appear, the face and hands. Moreover, a woman frequently needs to bare her hands and face in transactions with men. Abū Ḥanīfa said it was also permitted to look at her feet, and Abū Yūsuf said it was permitted to look at her forearms as well, since they are frequently bared in giving, taking, etc. However, if a man is not secure from feeling lust, he should not look needlessly even at the face or hands, to avoid sin. He is not allowed to touch her face or hands with his hands even if he is secure from lust, whether he be young or old.

A man may look at or touch a female child who does not yet have sexual appetites, since there is no fear he will seduce her. A judge or a notary in taking evidence from a woman may look at her face even if he fears he will be aroused. A man who wants to marry a woman may look at her even though he knows he will be aroused. A physician may look at whatever place she is ailing, but should take care to keep other areas covered and have a woman apply the treatment, if this is feasible.

A man may look at any part of a man except the area between his navel and his knees. A woman may look at what a man may look at as well, if she is secure from feelings of lust, and she may look at the same parts of a woman that a man may see of a man.

A man may look at his wife or slavegirl in any part and may see the head, face, arms, breasts, or legs of a female relative in the forbidden degrees for marriage in kinship and may touch those parts he is permitted to see, if he is free from lust. He may be alone with her or travel with her.

A man may see those parts of the slavegirl of another person that he is permitted to see of his relatives. He may look at and touch those same parts of a slavegirl whom he thinks of buying, even if there is fear that it will arouse him.

A slavegirl must be properly clothed when she reaches adulthood, a eunuch must observe the same rules in looking at and touching women as a male who is whole, and a male slave may see only the face and hands of his female owner.[19]

It is disliked for a man to kiss another on the mouth or hand or any other part, or to embrace him, in the opinion of Abū Ḥanīfa and Shaybānī, but Abū Yūsuf held that there is no harm in embracing and kissing, since the Prophet, may God bless him and give him peace, embraced Ja'far when he arrived from Abyssinia and kissed him between the eyes. Our learned men hold that the contradiction has to do with embracing when wearing only a waist-cloth, but that there is no harm in it if both are fully clothed, and this is the soundest view.

There is no harm in joining hands in greeting, since the Prophet said, "Whoever joins his hand with his brother Muslim's and shakes it will be forgiven his sins."[20]

Sales

There is no harm in selling animal manure, but it is disliked to sell human excrement.

If a Muslim sells wine and takes its price to pay a debt, it is disliked for his debtor to accept it, but if the seller is a Christian there is no harm in it, for wine is not lawfully in the possession of a Muslim, but it is the right of a *dhimmi* [protected non-Muslim] to own it and sell it.

It is disliked to corner the market in food for humans or animals if it occurs in a town where this may prove harmful to the people. It is disliked to sell weapons in a time of turmoil.

There is no harm in selling fruit juice to someone who will make wine of it, since the transgression is not in the juice but in the wine after it has been changed.

Miscellaneous

It was disliked to put points and vowels in a copy of the Qur'ān according to the Companion Ibn Masʿūd, but in our time learned men hold there is no getting around it for non-Arabs, so that they may learn the text.

There is no harm in a *dhimmī*'s entering the Inviolate Mosque [at Mecca]. Shāfiʿī said it was disliked, and Mālik said it was improper for such a person to enter any mosque. The argument of Shāfiʿī is God's Word: "Those who associate others with God are impure; let them not approach the Inviolate Mosque after this year" [Qur'ān 9:28], and that an infidel is never free from impurity since they never perform the necessary ritual ablutions, and the impure should avoid the mosque. Mālik used the same argument and extended it to include all mosques. Our Ḥanafī doctrine is based on the example of the Prophet, who lodged members of the tribe of Thaqīf in his own mosque even though they were infidels, and because the impurity is in their beliefs and does not lead to pollution of the mosque. The verse from the Qur'ān refers to the pagan Arabs being present in a haughty and coercive manner or to their pre-Islamic custom of circumambulating the Kaʿba naked.

It is disliked to employ eunuchs, because the demand for them incites people to make eunuchs, and it is a forbidden mutilation. There is no harm in castrating animals, or in mating a donkey to a mare to produce an [infertile] mule, because the first brings benefits to both animals and people and because the Prophet himself used to ride a mule.

There is no harm in visiting a Jew or Christian in their illness, because it is a sort of kindness that is within their rights, and because the Prophet paid a sick-call on a Jew in his neighborhood who was ill.

It is disliked for one to say in a prayer, "I ask you, O God, by the right of (any person or prophet)," because no creature has any right from the Creator.

The games of chess, backgammon, "fourteen," and all such games are disliked, because if anything is wagered it is gambling, which is expressly forbidden, and if nothing is at stake, then it is a foolish pastime, and the Prophet said, "All pastimes are vain for a man of faith, except exercising his horse, bending his bow, and amusing himself with his family." Some have said that the game of chess is permitted because of its tendency to sharpen the thoughts and quicken the understanding, and the opinion is also ascribed to Shāfi'ī. Against this is a saying ascribed to the Prophet, "Whoever plays at chess and backgammon has just plunged a hand in pig's blood."[21]

Forbidden Beverages

Note that there is a Ḥanafī opinion that drinks made from grain or honey fall outside the prohibition on wine. This doctrine is not shared by the other law-schools, yet because of it many Muslims today drink beer in good conscience.

Forbidden drinks are four:

1. *Khamr,* the juice of the grape fermented until strong, gathering foam which settles,
2. That juice, boiled until less than a third of it is gone,
3. The infusion of dates, which is *sakar,* and
4. The fermented infusion of raisins.

The first of these is *khamr.* Some people say it is a name for every inebriating drink, according to the Prophet's *ḥadīth* "Every inebriator is *khamr.*" He also said, "*Khamr* is made from these two trees," and pointed to the grapevine and the palm.

The prohibition of *khamr* is absolute, but the prohibition of other drinks is suppositious. Yahyā b. Ma'īn disputed the authenticity of the first *ḥadīth.* The second is the demonstration of the ruling, establishing the name *khamr* for all strong fermented drinks made from these two sources.

Khamr is forbidden in its essence, independently of whether it produces drunkenness. Some have asserted that it is only forbidden when it is drunk in quantity sufficient to inebriate, but that is pure infidelity, since the Qur'an terms it *rijs* [filth], and filth is forbidden in its essential nature (not in its quantity). Moreover the Prophet forbade it in sound independently attested *ḥadīth*s, and there is consensus of the scholars about this. This is not true of other intoxicants which are not *khamr,* though Shāfiʿī was of that opinion, which is extreme and contrary to tradition.

Khamr is filth in an extreme degree, like urine.

A Muslim who says it is lawful becomes an infidel [exposed to the penalty for apostasy].

It cannot constitute property for a Muslim, so there can be no penalty for destroying or usurping it, and a Muslim cannot legally sell it or profit from it [unlike a Person of the Book].

It may not be put to use in any way [e.g., as medicine].

One who drinks it in any quantity receives the legal penalty, eighty lashes, unless it has been boiled. Then the drinker is only given the penalty after intoxication, because the punishment is for a small quantity of the raw wine, and this has been cooked.

It may be lawfully changed into vinegar however, contrary to Shāfiʿī.

As for the second liquor, grapejuice boiled until less than a third is gone (called *bādhiq*) or until half is gone (called *munaṣṣaf*), which is then fermented, it is forbidden, according to Abū Yūsuf and Shaybānī when it grows strong, and according to Abū Ḥanīfa when it ferments, grows strong, foams, and settles.

The third liquor, *sakar,* is made by steeping dates when fresh in water and is forbidden.

The fourth, *naqīʿ zabīb,* is made by steeping raw raisins in water and becomes forbidden when it is fermented and grows strong, contrary to Awzāʿī.

The degree of prohibition in relation to these three liquors is less than that of *khamr,* so that the one who declares them lawful does not become an infidel, because the prohibition is based not on revelation but on opinion. The legal punishment does not become obligatory for drinking a small quantity of them, providing they do not inebriate the drinker. Their degree of filth is less. They may be sold and may constitute property, according to Abū Ḥanīfa.

Drinks made from honey, figs, wheat, millet, barley, etc., are lawful even if they have not been boiled, according to Abū Ḥanīfa and Abū Yūsuf, providing they are not drunk in a wanton manner. There is a difference of opinion as to whether one who drinks a beverage made of grain until drunk may be given the legal punishment, but the soundest opinion is that one may.

Grape juice boiled until it is one-third of its original volume, *muthallath,* is lawful even if it has become strong, according to Abū Ḥanīfa and Abū Yūsuf, if the intention is to use it as a tonic, though Shaybānī, Mālik and Shāfi'ī hold it is forbidden. If it is taken as a wanton pastime, all hold that it is forbidden.[22]

Enjoining Good and Preventing Wrong (*Ḥisba*)

*The Muslim Community is to enjoin right behavior on its people and deter them from wrong. This aspect of Islamic ethics (*ḥisba*: reckoning) creates a degree of being one's brother's keeper that might be looked upon as highly officious in other societies. Here again the principle is that human society depends on people's living as they were intended to do. The* muḥtasib *in premodern societies was the custodian of public morality and the inspector of markets. The excerpts following are instructions for the* muḥtasib *taken from a* ḥisba *manual written by the Shāfi'ī jurist Ibn al-Ukhūwa of Cairo (d. 1329/A.H. 729). Even though there is no* muḥtasib *today, Muslims are expected to do his job.*

Market Regulations

The *muḥtasib* must order transporters of goods when they stay long in one place to unload the pack-animals, for if the animals stand long with loads it will hurt them, and that is cruelty. The Messenger of God has forbidden cruelty to animals.

The *muḥtasib* should order the market people to keep the market free of filth which collects there and will hurt the people. He should allow no one to spy on his neighbors from the roofs or through windows, or men to sit in the paths of women needlessly. He must correct anyone who does anything of this sort.[23]

Money-changers

Earning a living by changing money is a great danger to the religion of one who practices it. Indeed, there is no preserving the religion of such a one, except through knowledge of the Law so as to avoid forbidden practices. It is the duty of the *muḥtasib* to search out the money-changers' places of business and spy on them, and if he finds one of them practicing usury or doing something illegal in changing money he must punish that person.[24]

Barber-Surgeons

These people must carry with them tools for circumcision, that is, razor and scissors, for circumcision is a religious obligation for men and for women, according to most [Shāfi'ī] people of learning. Abū Ḥanīfa says it is confirmed *sunna* [hence recommended] for men, but not obligatory. Our guide is the *ḥadīth* of the Prophet, God's blessing and peace be upon him, when he told a man who had become a Muslim, "Get rid of the long hair of paganism and be circumcised." Also, cutting off a part of the body is a part of God's right upon us, like the amputation of the hand of a thief. This being established, circumcision for a man consists of cutting off the foreskin, and for a woman in cutting the clitoris [excision of the organ or only its prepuce: practiced mainly by Shāfi'īs, occasionally by Mālikīs, and virtually never by Ḥanafīs.]. Thus it is obligatory for men and women to do this for themselves and for their children, and if they neglect it, the Imam [i.e., the 'Abbāsī caliph in Cairo and his appointees] may force them to do it, for it is right and necessary.[25]

Shipmasters

Owners of ships and boats must be prevented from loading their vessels above the usual load, for fear of sinking. For this reason the *muḥtasib* must also prevent them from sailing during windstorms. If they carry women on the same boat with men, there must be a partition set between them.

Pottery-sellers

Sellers of earthenware jars, pots, and vessels are not to overlay any that are pierced or cracked with gypsum made into a paste with fat and egg white and then sell them as sound. If any vessels of such description are found among them, they must be disciplined so as to deter others like them.

Punishments

The first order of the *ḥisba* is prohibition, the second is admonition, and the third is deterrence and restraining. Deterring is for the future, punishment is for the past, and restraining is for the present. It is not for one of the common people to do anything more than restrain. What goes beyond stopping illegal acts is for the authorities.

Admonition is useless from one who does not admonish himself or herself, and one who knows that his words will not be accepted because people know of his delinquency should not undertake the *ḥisba* by admonishing, since there is no good in it. How shall one who is not honest make others honest?

The second stage is putting the fear of God in the culprit and threatening him with physical punishment until he is deterred from what he is doing.

The third is reviling him and upbraiding him with rough words, though not libelously, but with words that do not count as moral excess, such as "Libertine!" "Stupid!" "Ignorant! Will you not fear God?" "Reprobate!" and that sort of thing, for if one is a libertine, one *is* stupid—if one were not, why would one offend God?[26]

The Interpretations of the Jurisconsults

The general tendency of the 'ulamā' *was to expand the practical application of the Law to give religious value to every act of life.*

While a qāḍī *or judge hears cases and administers the Law, a* muftī *gives a legal opinion when it is requested, either because it is not fully covered in the* fiqh *books or because the questioner wishes to be legally covered in an action that is planned. Thus new situations could be met within the Law, even when it was held by many jurists that the "gates of interpretation* [ijtihād]*" were closed, following the destruction of Baghdad. The answer of the* muftī *is called a* fatwā, *and it helped form precedent and determine practical application of the Law. It is sometimes called "the lesser* ijtihād.*"*

The following fatwas *are based on the rulings of the Ḥanafī jurist Abū Su'ūd (d. 1574/A.H. 982), grand* muftī *of the Ottoman emperor Sulaymān the Regulator and his son. Through his rulings, he was able to bring the* qanūns, *or decrees of the emperors, into agreement with the Law of Islam. He insisted that the competence of the judges derived from their appointments by the emperor, who held in his time the power of the caliphate, and they must therefore follow imperial directives in applying the* Sharī'a. Fatwās *are always given as a response to a question.*

Question: When in several Muslim villages there is not one mosque, and the inhabitants do not perform the congregational prayers, must

the authorities force them to build a mosque and punish those who neglect to pray there?
Response: Yes. In A.H. 940 [1533] express edicts were issued for the attention of the local rulers of the empire, that they must compel the inhabitants of such villages to construct mosques and establish regular prayers. Abū Su'ūd wrote as follows: "The Call to Prayer is one of the distinguishing characteristics of Islam, so if the people of a city, town, or village refuse it, the Imam should force them. If they will not do it, he should take up arms against them. If they neglect the Call to Prayer, the performance of prayer, and the congregational prayers, he must fight them, for these are earmarks and outward signs of the Religion."[27]

Question: One of the conditions of marriage is the *walī* [guardian of the bride], who is a necessary condition for the valid performance of marriage for minors, the mentally ill, and slave women. There is disagreement in the case of a mature free woman of sound mind as to whether she may legally contract marriage for herself. Abū Sulaymān [disciple of the Ḥanafī doctor al-Shaybānī] reports Shaybānī as holding her marriage as null and void. Abu Ḥafṣ [also his disciple] reports him as saying it is permissible if she has no representative, but if she does it depends on his consent; if he refuses the marriage is void, regardless of whether the husband is her equal or not. What effective decision may a judge make on this conflicting ruling?
Response: In the year 951 [1544] the judges were enjoined to accept no marriage contract without the assent of the bride's *walī*. Abū Su'ūd wrote this.

Question: In the *Muḥīṭ* law-book, it states: "A Ḥanafī may reckon by Shāfi'ī law as regards eating hyena flesh and meat slain by one neglecting to say 'In the name of God!' [lawful for Shāfi'īs, but not ordinarily for Ḥanafīs], and a Shāfi'ī may reckon by Ḥanafī law as regards drinking wine boiled to a third of its volume [not ordinarily lawful for Shāfi'īs] and marriage without a *walī*." Now if the *qāḍī* says, "In this matter the opinions and precedents differ, so I shall follow the other doctrine here and regard her marriage as legal," is his verdict legally valid?
Response: Since it is illegal, it is certainly not valid. The authority of the *qāḍī* derives from the permission and authority of the holder of the caliphal power. Moreover, the *qāḍī*s have been enjoined to make use of the soundest opinion, so the option of basing themselves on this legal

disagreement is taken from them, particularly since the general corruption of our era is obvious [and few can correctly interpret the Law].

The original of the Imperial Decree forbidding such practices is preserved in the law courts of Istanbul, Pera, and Üsküdar. The corruptness of such practices is clearer than daylight; if they are followed, the families of certain people will come to ruin![28]

Question: If the Jew Bakr says to the Christian Bishr, "Your Prophet Jesus (God's blessing be upon him) was (God forbid!) an illegitimate child," what must be done to the accursed one according to the Law? *Response:* Those unbelievers who publicly abuse the prophets, may God's blessing be upon them all, shall be put to death. Abū Su'ūd has written this.[29]

IV
INTERIOR RELIGION: ṢŪFISM

Important though the Law is, there is another aspect of Islam that has been almost equally important for Muslims. This is Ṣūfism or mysticism: the search for the experience of God as ultimate reality. There is no necessary contradiction of course between the Law and mysticism: many Ṣūfīs have been fundamentalists or legalists of the most uncompromising sort. Still, emphasis on direct personal experience has at times led Ṣūfīs into conflict with scholars of the Law and brought discredit on their followers. This has occasionally led to persecution of the Ṣūfīs and in modern times to hostility toward them. Yet as long as there is Islam, there will be Ṣūfism; it is an essential aspect of the faith, even though not for all *Muslims.*

The Ṣūfīs were the great missionaries of Islam, and those parts of the Islamic world like India and Anatolia converted by them have been drenched in Ṣūfī faith. Their interpretation of the message of Muḥammad, by focusing on universals and on experience, is often still the most attractive aspect of Islam for people of other traditions.

Ascetics

In the century after the death of the Prophet, the Arab Muslims conquered a great empire, stretching from Spain to Pakistan and Central Asia. In new garrison cities they dwelt apart, supported by the taxes of their subjects and by booty from continuing campaigns of expansion. They surrounded themselves with captive concubines and slave retainers and lived on a scale of luxury the first Muslims had scarcely dreamed of. They regarded themselves as a chosen people, and those of their subjects who adopted Islam were rarely treated fraternally by the Arab masters. This produced social discontent and unrest.

*Pious Muslims saw this situation with sorrow and dismay. They recalled the simplicity of early Islam and felt that the faith was now in danger. In their malaise, they found some of the ascetic practices of the Christian monks congenial. They clothed themselves in rough wool (*ṣūf*), and tried to stay aloof from the* dunyā, *the "lower" material world. They studied the sayings of Muḥammad and the earlier prophets and laid the foundations of Islamic Law and the religious sciences.*

al-Ḥasan al-Baṣrī

This religious ferment was particularly strong in the port and camp-city of Baṣra in lower Iraq, and no one was more typical of it than al-Ḥasan al-Baṣrī *(d. 728/A.H. 110), a revered religious scholar. "He is our leader in this doctrine [Ṣūfism]; we walk in his footsteps and have our light from his lamp," a tenth-century work on mysticism says.*[1] *In fact however, Ḥasan was more an ascetic than a mystic, and asceticism was found among some of the Companions of Muḥammad, such as 'Imrān b. Ḥuṣayn, who had settled at Baṣra and taught Ḥasan* ḥadīths. *Mortification of the flesh and constant meditation on the Qur'ān purified the heart and led to a deeper relationship with God. It was the beginning of mysticism, and thus mystics after this were called Ṣūfīs: wool-wearers.*

Ḥasan said: The good things have departed; only the reprehensible remains, and whoever is left among the Muslims is afflicted.

Ḥasan said: The believer wakens grieving and goes to bed grieving, and this is all that encompasses him, because he is between two fearful things: sin which has occurred so he knows not what God will do with him and the allotted term which remains so he knows not what deadly things will strike him in it.

Ḥasan said: The believer wakes grieving and goes to bed grieving, overturned by the certainty of grief, and there suffices for one what suffices a little gazelle: a handful of dates and a drink of water.[2]

Ḥasan said: Repolish your hearts, for they are quick to rust, and check your selves, for they are profligate: if you give them what they desire, they will bring you down to the depth of evil.[3]

Ḥasan preached to his companions, saying: The lower world is a house of labor. One who companions it to its loss while abstaining from it will be happy and profit from its companionship. One who companions it in desire and love for it will be rendered wretched by it, and one's portion of it will be laid waste by God. It will deliver one to punishments from God for which there is no patience and no enduring. Its worth is small and its goods are little, and its passing written upon it. God is the administrator of its legacy, and its people will exchange it for dwellings which will not wear out, nor long stay change so they may leave them. So beware this dwelling-place, and remember much where you must go. Child of Adam, cut away your anxiety about the lower world![4]

In 717 a pious member of the ruling Umawī dynasty came to the caliphal throne in the new capital of Damascus. This was 'Umar b. 'Abd al-'Azīz (d. 720/A.H. 101), hailed by many of his contemporaries as the man to restore the true faith. He chose the righteous first two caliphs, Abū Bakr and 'Umar, as models, fought corruption, preached conversion to the conquered people, and offered them equality within Islam so that they embraced it in great numbers. Ḥasan's correspondence with him has been in part preserved.

Ḥasan wrote to 'Umar b. 'Abd al-'Azīz, saying: Reflection calls us to good, and to labor for it, and regret for evil calls us to take leave of it. Beware this world with all wariness. It is like a serpent, smooth to touch, but its venom kills. Turn away from what delights you in it, for the little companioning you will have of it. The more it please you, the more be wary of it, for whenever one who has it feels secure in any pleasure from it the world drives him over into something hateful. Whenever he attains a part of it and mounts it, it turns him upside down. The pleasing in it proves a pit, and what is useful in it proves harmful; ease of life is followed by misfortune. Beware it, for its securities are lies, its hopes are false, its life is harshness, and its clarity muddied. You are in peril from it; in transient bliss, in imminent trial, in painful calamity, or in decisive doom. It has diminished one's life, if one but knew it: from comforts one is in danger, from trials in wariness, from the ultimate fate in certainty. Even if the Creator had not informed us about it, nor struck any similitude for it, nor charged us to abstain from it, the house itself would have waked the sleeper and roused the unheeding. How much more now, seeing that God has sent us a warning against it and admonition about it! For it has no worth or weight with God; it weighs not a pebble nor a clod with Him. It was offered to our Prophet with all its keys and treasures, and it would not have diminished him with God by a gnat's wing, but he refused to accept it. Nothing prevented him, but he knew that God despised the thing, and he despised it. Muḥammad bound a stone upon his belly when he was hungry; as for Moses, the skin of his belly was seen green as grass; he asked of God only food to eat in hunger. Should you wish for a third, there is he of the Spirit and the Word [Jesus]. In his matter there is a marvel: he used to say, 'My daily bread is hunger, my ensign is fear, my raiment is wool, my steed is my foot, my lantern by night is the moon, my brazier in winter is the sun, my fruits and fragrant herbs are what the earth brings forth for the animals. I sleep having nothing, yet there is none richer than I!' For a fourth, there is Solomon, son of David: he was no less wonderful than these. He ate barley bread with his elite and fed his family on bran meal, but fed his people on fine wheat. At night he clothed himself in sackcloth, chained his hand to his neck, and stayed weeping until dawn, eating rough food and wearing hairshirts. All these hated what God hates, and despised what He despises, abstaining and ascetic. Thus righteous people have followed their path and walked in their footsteps.[5]

Ibrāhīm b. Adham

Ṣūfism seems to have traveled with the Arab army from Baṣra who settled in Khurāsān, the eastern marches of the old Persian Empire. Here many Iranians were Buddhists, and there were Nestorian Christians as well as Zoroastrians among them. One of the early Khurāsānī ascetics was Ibrāhīm b. Adham, an Arab whom legend makes the descendant of native princes of Khurāsān. The legend of his conversion has reminded some of that of Gautama Buddha, and the objects adopted by some Khurāsānī Ṣūfīs, such as the begging bowl, rosary, needle, and staff, are like those of Buddhist monks. While techniques or articles from other traditions were sometimes useful to Ṣūfīs, one must remember that Ṣūfism was a native Islamic growth, born of early meditation on the Qur'ān and the search for full commitment to God.

My father was one of the princes of Khurāsān, said Ibrāhīm, and I was a youth and rode to the chase. I went out one day on a horse I had with my dog along and raised a hare or a fox. While I was chasing it, I heard the voice of a speaker I did not see, saying, 'O Ibrāhīm, was it for this you were created? Was it this you were commanded to do?' I felt dread, and stopped. Then I began again and urged my horse on. Three times it happened, just like that. Then I heard the voice—from the horn of my saddle, by God!—saying, "It was not for this that you were created! It was not this that you were ordered to perform!" I got off my horse then.

I came across one of my father's shepherds and took his woolen tunic and put it on. I gave him my mare and all I had with me in exchange and turned my steps toward Mecca.[6]

Behind the legend, there is a real Khurāsānī Arab who left home for Syria around the middle of the eighth century and worked at odd jobs for sustenance, disdaining to beg. He wandered in the Syrian desert and is reported to have said that he learned gnosis from a Syrian monk. Several encounters with Christian anchorites occur in the stories handed down from him, such as this one with a stylite.

I passed by a monk whose hermitage was built on columns on the top of a mountain. Whenever the wind blew, it swayed. I called to him, 'O monk!' and he did not answer. I called to him again and he did not reply, so I called him a third time, saying, 'By Him who has confined you in your hermitage, please answer me!' Then he put his head out of his hermitage and said, 'Why are you shouting? You call me by a name of which I am not worthy: 'monk,' and I am no monk [*rāhib*]; a monk is one who fears [*rahab*] his Lord.' 'What are you, then?' I said, and he replied, 'A prison-keeper. I have a fearful beast confined here.' I said, 'What is that?' He said, 'My tongue is a harmful beast; if I let it go, it would injure people. O Ḥanīfī, God has servants who are deaf yet hearing; mute yet speaking, blind yet seeing; they pass among the houses of oppressors and feel lonely in the company of the ignorant; they rear the fruit of knowledge in the light of sincerity and sail on the wind of certainty until they harbor on the shore of the light of devotion. As God lives, they are servants whose eyes are anointed by night vigils! You should see them in the night, when people's eyes are closed, standing in their circles, crying on Him whom neither slumber nor sleep overtakes. O Ḥanīfī, you should follow in their path!' I said, 'Do you practice Islam, then?' He said, 'I know no religion except Islam [commitment]. But Christ covenanted with us and described for us the end of your time, and the world has been cleared for you. Your religion is a new one, though God created it.' The man who heard this from Ibrāhīm added, 'Scarcely a month after that, Ibrāhīm fled away from people.'[7]

One day he saw a beggar complaining of his poverty. He observed, "Perhaps you paid little for your poverty." "And is poverty for sale, then?" asked the man. "Certainly," Ibrāhīm replied. "I bought mine with the kingdom of Balkh. I have never regretted it."[8]

Ibrāhīm prayed, 'O God, You know that Paradise does not weigh with me more than the wing of a gnat. If You will befriend me with remembrance of You, and sustain me in Your love, and make it easy for me to obey You, then give Paradise to whomever You will!'[9]

Ḥātim al-Aṣamm

Khurāsān remained a notable center of Ṣūfism. One of Ibrāhīm's pupils was Shaqīq of Balkh, who with pupils such as Ḥātim al-Aṣamm (d. 852/A.H. 237), began the development of a school of self-discipline.

Ḥātim al-Aṣamm was asked, "On what do you base your trust of God?" He replied, "On four principles. I learned that no-one can eat my daily bread except me, and I calmed my Self with this knowledge. I learned that no-one performs my acts but me, and so I busy myself with them. I learned that Death will come suddenly, and so I run to meet him; and I learned that I am never hidden from God's sight wherever I am, so I behave modestly before Him."[10]

Rābi'a al-'Adawīya

A very great ascetic of Baṣra was the saintly Rābi'a al-'Adawīya (d. 801/A.H. 185), a former slavewoman who had been trained as a flute-player before she turned to the contemplative life. In her passionate sayings and poetry we find full mystical doctrine: God discloses Himself to the heart which loves Him with sincere devotion; the surest and sweetest relationship with Him is love.

Rābi'a prayed, "O my God, will you burn in Hellfire the heart that loves you?" Then an unseen speaker told her, "We do not do such things. Do not think on Us with evil thought!"[11]

At night she would go up to her roof and pray thus: "O my Lord, the stars are shining and the eyes of men are closed and kings have shut their doors, and every lover is alone with his beloved, and here am I alone with Thee."[12]

Rābi'a prayed, "O my God, whatever portion You have for me of worldly things, give to Your enemies; and whatever You have for me in the world to come, give to Your friends; for You are enough for me!"[13]

The Ṣūfīs of Baṣra urged Rābi'a to obey the Law and choose a husband from among them. She replied, "Willingly. Who is the most learned among you, that I may marry him?" They replied that it was Ḥasan. She said to him that if he could give her the answer to four questions, she would become his wife.

Then she asked, "What will the Judge of the world say when I die?" Ḥasan answered, 'That is among the hidden things known only to God Most High.' Then she said, "When I am put in the grave and Munkar and Nakīr, the angels who question the dead, query me, will I be able to give a good answer or not?" He replied, 'This also is known only to God.' Then she asked, "When people are assembled on the Day of Resurrection, and the books are distributed, in which hand will I be given mine: in the right, or in the left?" He replied, 'This is also hidden.' Finally she asked, "When humankind are summoned, some to Paradise and some to Hell, to which shall I be summoned?" He replied, "This too is hidden, and none knows what is hidden except God, His be the glory and the majesty!"

Then she said to him, "Since this is so, and I have these four questions with which to occupy myself, how shall I need a husband with whom to be occupied?" [And she remained unmarried.][14]

Someone asked her, 'Do you love the Lord of Glory?' She replied, "I do." Then they asked, 'And do you hate Satan?' "No," she said. Asked 'Why not?' she replied, "My love for the All-merciful leaves me no room for hating Satan. I saw the Prophet in a dream, and he asked me, 'Rābi'a, do you love me?' I said, "Messenger of God, who is there that does not love you? But passion for the Reality [God] has so filled my heart that there is no place there for 'loving' and 'hating.' "[15]

Rābi'a said, "It is a bad servant who serves her Lord from fear and terror, or from desire for a reward, though many there are!" They asked her, 'Why do you worship God, then? Have you no desire for Paradise?' She answered, "First the Neighbor, then the House. Is it not enough for me that I am given permission to worship Him? If Paradise and Hell were not, would it not behoove us to obey Him? Is He not worthy of worship without intermediary motives?"[16]

Ḥārith b. Asad al-Muḥāsibī

In 750, the Umawī dynasty was swept away by a revolution engineered by the descendants of the Prophet's uncle 'Abbās. In 762, the 'Abbāsīs founded Baghdad in Iraq, as a new capital for the caliphate. As chief city of Islam, it quickly drew to itself eminent exponents of religious life, including mystics. A Ṣūfī who moved there from Baṣra was Ḥārith b. Asad al-Muḥāsibī (d. 857/A.H. 243). By his time, self-denial was being seen chiefly as preparation for a selfless love of God.

God has appointed self-mortification for the seekers, for the training of the soul. People are ignorant of the high station of the one who is preoccupied with his Lord, who is seen to be thinking little of this world, who is humble, fearful, sorrowful, weeping, showing a meek spirit, keeping far from the children of this world, suffering oppression and not seeking revenge, despoiled, yet not seeking requital. He is disheveled, dusty, shabby, thinking little of what he wears, wounded, alone, a stranger—but if the ignorant were to look on the heart of that seeker, and see how God has fulfilled in him what He promised of His favor, and what He gives him in exchange for what he renounced of the vain glory of this world and its pleasure, they would desire to be in that one's place and would realize that it is he, the seeker after God, who is truly rich, who is fair to look upon, who tastes delight, who is joyous and happy, for he has attained his desire and has secured that which he sought from his Lord. Let one who wishes to be near to God abandon all that alienates one from God.[17]

The love of God in itself is the illumination of the heart by joy due to its nearness to the Beloved. When the heart is illumined with such joy, it finds delight in being alone with recollection of its Beloved . . . and when solitude is combined with secret intimacy with the Beloved, the sweetness of that intimacy overwhelms the mind, so that it can mind no longer this world and what is in it.[18]

Ecstatics

Abū Yazīd al-Bisṭāmī

*Mystics illumined by the joy that al-Muḥāsibī mentions underwent emotional transports where they were flooded with the awareness of God, sometimes to the point that they took leave of the Self and were conscious only of the Divine Unity. The father of the "intoxicated" Ṣūfīs was Abū Yazīd al-Bisṭāmī or Bāyazīd (d. 875/*A.H. *261), who spent most of his life in his town of Bisṭām on the western border of Khurāsān. His ecstatic accounts of his unitive experiences of God created problems for more sober Ṣūfīs and scandalized many Muslims. Yet he was much revered and gave his name to two Ottoman emperors.*

Abū Yazīd al-Bisṭāmī said: When He brought me up to the Divine Unity, I divorced my Self and turned to my Lord, calling on Him for assistance. 'My Master,' I cried, 'I call on you with the cry of one who has nothing else!' When He recognized my sincerity in this cry and how I had despaired of myself, the first sign that came that He had answered this prayer was that He let me forget myself completely, and forget all creatures and all dominions. So He drew me near, appointing a way to Him nearer than soul to body. Then He said to me, "Abū Yazīd, all of them are my creatures, except you." I replied, "So I am You, and You are I, and I am You!"[19]

A man came to Abū Yazīd and said, "I have heard that you can fly through the air." "What sort of wonder is that?" asked Abū Yazīd. "A carrion-eating bird can fly through the air; is not a believer nobler than a bird?"[20]

Abū Yazīd said: Paradise holds no danger for those who love God; they are protected by their love.[21]

Abū Yazīd said: I gazed upon my Lord with the eye of certainty, after He had turned me away from any other than Him and illumined me with His light; and He showed me marvels of His Mystery. He also showed me His Selfhood, and I looked upon my I-ness with His Selfhood, and it passed away: my light was His Light, my glory was His Glory, my power was His Power.[22]

Junayd of Baghdad

Junayd of Baghdad (d. 910/A.H. 298) was al-Muḥāsibī's disciple and is the spiritual father of the "sober" mystics. He was familiar with Abū Yazīd and tried to find rational explanations for his dangerous sayings. He was also one of the first Ṣūfīs to develop a mystical system. Some Ṣūfīs seemed to be fascinated by the intoxication of an emotional state, which could be assisted by chanting the Qur'ān, music, dancing, and songs or poetry in which God is addressed as the Divine Beloved. Junayd proved to be a doctor of penetrating, original, and sober mystical doctrine which would be cited to render Ṣūfism acceptable to religious scholars alarmed by Ṣūfī excesses. Yet he attests to mystical experiences of a high order in his poems and sayings. Here he comments on the original covenant of humankind with God, mentioned in Qur'ān 7:172.

> When your Lord took from the Children of Adam, from their loins their seed, and made them bear witness as to themselves: "Am I not your Lord?" They said, "Yes, we bear witness!"—lest you should say on the Day of Resurrection, "Really, we were ignorant of this."

Junayd commented: In this verse, God tells you that He spoke to them at a time when they did not exist, except so far as they existed in Him.

This existence is not the same type of existence that is usually attributed to God's creatures; it is a type of existence which only God knows and only He is aware of. God knows their existence; embracing them He sees them in the beginning when they are non-existent and unaware of their future existence in this world. The existence of these is timeless.[23]

Love means that the attributes of the lover are changed into those of the Beloved. Now one lives in accordance with the saying of God related by the Prophet: "Whoever treats a friend of mine as an enemy, on that one I shall declare war. None of my servants approaches me with anything I like better than what I have laid on them as incumbent duty. My true servant will continue to draw near me with supererogatory acts of worship until I love him. When I love him, I shall be the hearing by which he hears, the vision by which he sees, the hand by which he takes, the foot by which he walks. If he asks of Me, I shall surely give him, and if he takes refuge with me, I shall surely give him refuge."[24]

Abū Muḥammad al-Jarīrī said: We once met at Abū Ja'far al-Ḥaffār's, near the Damascus Gate in Baghdad—Junayd and Abū Ṣāliḥ al-Malāmatī and Abū al-'Abbās ibn Masrūq were with us. There was a cantor [*qawwāl*] with us, and when the chant began, Abū Ṣāliḥ rose and went into an ecstacy until his knees buckled, whereupon he fell down. Ibn Masrūq rose and went into an ecstasy and then walked off barefoot, so Junayd and I remained. I said to him, "Sir, do you feel nothing similar to what has happened to them?" He replied, "You shall see the mountains that you suppose fixed passing by like clouds" [Qur'ān 27:88]. Then he said to me, "And you—do you feel nothing at the *samā'*?" I replied, 'Oh yes—sometimes I am present with someone whom I respect and honor, so I control myself, but when I am alone, I release the ecstasy upon my inmost heart, and become ecstatic.'[25]

Junayd said: al-Ḥārith al-Muḥāsibī used to come to our house and say, "Come out with me; we shall grind." I would tell him, "Will you take me from my solitude and peace with myself to the streets, the allurements, and the beholding of sensual things?" He would say, 'Come forth with me; there is nothing to fear,' and the street would be empty; we would see nothing to dislike. When I arrived with him at the place where he would sit, he would say, "Ask." I would say, "I have no question to ask you." Then he would say, "Ask whatever comes into your mind." Then the questions would rush upon me, and I would ask him, and he would answer me then and there. Then he would go back to his house and make them into books.[26]

Abū al-Ḥusayn al-Nūrī came to Junayd and said, 'It has reached me that you talk about everything, so talk about anything, and I shall discuss it with you.' Junayd said, "What shall I talk about?" Nūrī said, "About love." Then Junayd said, "I shall tell you an allegory. Once a group of my companions and I were in a walled orchard, and the one who was to come bringing some things we needed was detained, so we climbed up on the wall. Then we became aware of a blind man who had with him a beautiful youth, and the blind man was saying to him, 'You have ordered me to do such and such, and I have done it. And you have forbidden me such and such, and I have abandoned it, nor do I oppose you in anything you desire, so what more do you wish of me?'

"The youth said, 'I want for you to die.' The blind man replied, 'Why, then, here I die,' and he lay down, covered his face, and closed his eyes. I said to my companions, 'This blind man has tried everything—he even makes it appear that he is dead! But death in reality will hardly be possible for him.' Then we climbed down and went out to where he lay and moved him. Lo, he was dead." Then Nūrī rose and went his way.[27]

In these verses Junayd describes his experience of union and separation from God.

In my secret soul I have realized You;
My tongue has whispered with You.
We are united in profoundest way,
Though we are parted in a deep sense.

Your magnitude has absented You
To the perception of my eyes,
Yet ecstasy has shown You present
To the very depths of my being.[28]

Ṣūfism means that God makes you die to yourself and makes you alive in Him. It is to purify the heart from the recurrence of creaturely temptations, to say farewell to the natural inclinations, to subdue the qualities which belong to human nature, to keep far from the claims of the senses, to adhere to spiritual qualities, to ascend by means of divine knowledge, to be occupied with what is eternally the best, to give wise counsel to all people, faithfully to observe the truth, and to follow the Prophet in respect of the religious Law.[29]

Ḥusayn b. Manṣūr al-Ḥallāj

It was a younger contemporary of Junayd who brought down the crisis that had been threatening between the Ṣūfīs and the scholars of the

Law. This was Ḥusayn b. Manṣūr al-Ḥallāj, who seemed to have learned more from Abū Yazīd than from Junayd. Like many Ṣūfīs, he considered Jesus the model for an ascetic, but he wrote a hymn in extravagant praise of Muḥammad, whom he considered to have beheld the essence of God on his Night Journey. He held that God manifests Himself on earth in His friends and in mystical experience permits them a real if temporary union with Him. This was little more than Junayd had taught, but al-Ḥallāj refused all discretion. He was believed to work miracles and had a great following in Baghdad, where he kept a model of the Ka'ba in his house. It was said that he told poor people who could not afford the Pilgrimage that they could fulfill their obligation by a visit to it. Others he told to "circumambulate the Ka'ba in their own hearts." He drew the lightning by his notorious, apparently repeated, statement "I am Reality" (ana al-Ḥaqq)*. Since* al-Ḥaqq *is one of the divine names, he was accused of claiming to be God. He was condemned by leading scholars of Baghdad and in 922* [A.H. 309] *was given the most severe penalty in Islamic Law, reserved for "those who war against God and His messenger": scourging, amputation of the hands and feet, and crucifixion. His image among many later Ṣūfīs is that of a misunderstood martyr; among some he is seen as one who had to die because he had disclosed the great secret.*

Between you and me there lingers an "it is I" that torments me.
In grace to me, take this "I" from between us!

I am Whom I love, and Whom I love is I,
If you see me, you see us both.
We are two spirits in one body.
If you see Him, you may behold me.[30]

The lights of prophecy appeared from his light; his name preceded the Pen, he whose name is Aḥmad [Most Praised]. Muḥammad lifted the cloud, he pointed out the Holy House, he the complete, he the magnanimous, the one commanded to break idols, sent to mortals and to veneration. Above the clouds thundered, below him lightning flashed and enlightened; it rained and fructified. All sciences are a drop from his ocean, all wisdoms a dipping from his river, all times an hour of his age. The Reality is with him, and in him truth . . . he abjured his fancy and attained the desire; "his heart lied not in what it beheld," "at the Lote-tree of the Boundary" [Qur'ān 53:12, 14].[31]

Ibrāhīm b. Fātik, his servitor, said: When al-Ḥallāj was brought to be crucified and saw the cross and the nails, he prayed a prayer of two prostrations while I was standing near him. In the first he recited the Opening of the Qur'ān and the verse 'We shall try you with something of fear and of hunger' [Qur'ān 21:35]. In the second he recited the Opening and the verse 'Every soul shall taste of death; then unto Us you shall be returned' [Qur'ān 29:57]. When he was finished he said some words I do not remember, but in the part I remember he said, 'O my God, who are revealed in every place, and are not in any place, I beseech You by the truth of Your Divine Word which declares that I am, and by the truth of my weak human word which declares that You are, sustain me in gratitude for this Your grace, that You hid from others what You revealed to me of the glory of Your countenance, and forbade to them what You permitted to me: the sight of things hidden by Your mystery.

"And these Your servants, who are gathered together to kill me in zeal for Your religion, seeking Your favor; forgive them. For if You had revealed to them what You revealed to me, they would not have done what they have done; had You withheld from me what You have withheld from them, I would never have been tried with this trial. To You be praise in all You do; to You be praise in all that You will."

Then he was silent. The headsman stepped up and dealt him a smashing blow which broke his nose, and the blood ran onto his white robe. Al-Shiblī the mystic, who was in the crowd, cried aloud and tore his garment, and al-Ḥusayn al-Wāṣitī fell fainting. So did other famous Ṣūfīs who were there, so that a riot nearly broke out. Then the executioners did their work.[32]

Antinomians

A wave of persecution of the Ṣūfīs of Baghdad followed the execution of al-Ḥallāj, and many Ṣūfīs moved to Khurāsān and Transoxania, where the Samānī princes were more tolerant. There they performed a great service to Islamic Civilization as missionaries, converting the Turkish peoples of Central Asia to Islam. Antinomianism, a strong hostility to the scholars of the Law and their concerns, often characterized the Khurāsānī Ṣūfīs. They accused the 'ulamā' *of "the murder of God's lovers," separated faith from works, and were hospitable to theosophical ideas found among gnostic sects. The subjective "state" seemed to be given priority over the observable and verifiable act.*

Abū Sa'īd b. Abī 'l-Khayr

Abū Sa'īd b. Abī 'l-Khayr (d. 1049/A.H. 440), was a great Khurāsānī Ṣūfī. After a period of extraordinary austerities, followed by self-abasement in service to the poor, he became known as a spiritual guide and settled in an urban khānqāh *or Ṣūfī convent. At the end of his life, he lived "more like a sultan than a Ṣūfī," as his biographer remarked, accepting with complacency the veneration of his followers and the masses, organizing extravagant entertainments for his Ṣūfīs at which they were encouraged to feast, dance, and worship God with grateful hearts, and feeding the poor. He never failed to find generous donors for these activities, in part because of his gift of thought-reading and other "miracles."*

He is credited with many rubā'īyāt *or quatrains, some of them impertinent enough to be attributed to 'Umar Khayyām. While many of them are probably spurious, they form part of his image. He referred to the Ka'ba as "a house of stones" and the Law as bondage and was accused of infidelity by the fundamentalist Ibn Ḥazm of Córdoba, but he held that "the shortest way to God lies in giving comfort to the heart of a Muslim."*[33]

The Qalandars mentioned here were notorious people who dropped out of Muslim society and mocked all its rules, claiming—not always convincingly—to be doing so from spiritual insight.

Quatrains

Your sinful servant I—Your mercy, where now?
In my heart darkness lies—Your comfort, where now?
Obedience can buy Your paradise—why then,
A merchant are You—Your goodness, where now?

Till every madrasa and minaret beneath the sun
Lies desolate, the Qalandar's work will not be done.
Not one true Muslim will appear,
Till truest faith and infidelity are one.[34]

I said to Him, "For whom does Your beauty thus unfold?"
He answered me: "For Myself, as I am I was of old.
For Lover am I and Love and I alone the Beloved,
Mirror and Beauty am I: Me in Myself behold."

> Your Path, wherein we walk, in every step is fair.
> Meeting with You, whatever way we go, is fair.
> Whatever eye doth look upon Your face, finds beauty there.
> Your praise, whatever tongue doth give it You, is fair.[35]

If people wish to draw near to God, they must seek Him in the hearts of others. They should speak well of all people, whether present or absent, and if they themselves seek to be a light to guide others, then like the sun, they must show the same face to all. To bring joy to a single heart is better than to build many shrines for worship, and to enslave one soul by kindness is worth more than the setting free of a thousand slaves.

The true friend of God [or saint] sits in the midst of his fellow-beings, and rises up and eats and sleeps and buys and sells and gives and takes in the bazaars among other people, and marries and has social intercourse with other folk, and never for an instant forgets God.[36]

Muḥyī al-Dīn Ibn al-ʿArabī

Beside those who claimed that man may become God, there were those who claimed that God is everything: since there is no god but God, all that exists must share in His essence. Monism, or pantheism, has been a constant temptation for the Ṣūfīs, and its greatest theosopher is the Spanish mystic Muḥyī al-Dīn Ibn al-ʿArabī (d. 1240/ A.H. 638). He has had a profound influence on later Ṣūfism, and doubtless on Christian and Jewish mysticism as well. His very prolific writings, filled with striking images and strange expressions, brought Ṣūfism to a rather dangerous state of explicitness. They have remained controversial in Muslim circles until today, being regarded as sheer infidelity by some. The problem with monism for Islam is that if everything shares in one divine essence, then evil is finally an illusion, and the Law is a delusion. Such Ṣūfism is likely to become a speculative system of metaphysics, self-indulgent and devoid of moral earnestness. Yet Ibn al-ʿArabī also wrote about the mystical implications of Islamic Law; one cannot say that he is hostile to it, only that his vision transcends it. His stay in Mecca was a time of great spiritual exaltation. The Kaʿba represented for him the point of contact between the visible and invisible worlds, and a lady whom he met there represented for him all perfection. She inspired some beautiful poetry that—he wrote later—must be interpreted spiritually.

O doves that haunt the *arāk* and *bān* trees, have pity!
Do not double my woes by your lamentation!
Have pity! Do not reveal by wailing and weeping
my hidden desires and my secret sorrows!
I respond to her, at eve and morn, with the plaintive cry
of a longing man and the moan of an impassioned lover.
The spirits faced one another in the thicket of *ghaḍā* trees,
and bent their branches toward me, and it annihilated me.
And they brought me divers sorts of tormenting desire
and passion and untried affliction.
Who will give me sure promise of Jam' and al-Muḥaṣṣab of Minā?
Who of Dhāt al-Athl? Who of Na'mān?
They encompass my heart moment after moment, for the sake
of love and anguish, and kiss my pillars,
Even as the best of mankind [Muḥammad] encompassed the Ka'ba
which the evidence of reason proclaims to be imperfect,
And kissed stones therein, although he was a Prophet.
And what is the rank of the Temple compared with Man?
How often did they vow and swear that they would not change,
but one dyed with henna does not keep oaths.
And one of the most wonderful things is a veiled gazelle,
who points with red finger-tip and winks with eyelids,
A gazelle whose pasture is between the breast-bone and
the bowels. O marvel! A garden amidst fires!
My heart has become capable of every form: it is a pasture
of gazelles and a convent for Christian monks,
And a temple for idols and the pilgrim's Ka'ba
and the tables of the Torah and the book of the Qur'ān.
I follow the religion of Love: whatever way Love's
camels take, that is my religion and my faith.[37]

Ibn al-'Arabī's most remarkable book is Fuṣūṣ al-Ḥikam *(The Gems of Wisdom), written in 1232, in which he treats of the esoteric message of 28 major prophets as dictated to him by the Prophet in a vision in Damascus. This is the section on Adam, the father and archetype of Humanity.*

The Gem of Divine Wisdom in the Word of Adam

The Reality desired to see the essences of His most beautiful names, whose number is immeasurable—or, if you like, to see His own essence in one universal being who when endowed with existence would reveal all the Divine Command, so that He might behold His mystery in it. For the vision of oneself is not like beholding oneself in a polished metal mirror, for then one is manifest in a form resulting from the place one beholds, which is the mirror.

He created the entire world as a fully formed body without a spirit, so that it was like an unpolished mirror. It is a rule of the divine activity to prepare no locus which does not receive a divine spirit. This is no other than the actualizing of the potentiality of the locus to receive some of the everlasting revelatory outpouring, which ever was and ever shall be. It was Adam who became the polish of that mirror and the spirit of that body.

The angels were faculties of that form of the world which the people of gnosis call "The Great Man" [each man is a microcosm, and the macrocosm is a Man], so that they are to it like the spiritual and physical forms of the human organism. Each of these faculties is veiled from the others by its own nature and can conceive of nothing finer than itself, so that it is its property to hold that it is entitled in itself to the high place that it has with God.

This is a matter which reflective reason cannot grasp; understanding can come here only by the divine unveiling. Only by this unveiling can one know the origin of the cosmic forms which receive their spirits. This being God named Man [*insān*] and viceregent [*khalīfa*]. He is to the Reality as the pupil of the eye [*insān al-'ayn*]; through him Reality sees its creation and has mercy on it. Thus humanity is both created accident and eternal principle, being created and immortal, the Word which defines and which comprehends. Through him all things came to be; he is the bezel stone of the signet ring, on which is inscribed the sign with which the King seals His treasures. Thus he is the King's viceroy, who bears his seal and safeguards His treasure, and the world shall not cease to be safeguarded so long as the Perfect Man [*insān kāmil*] remains in it.[38]

In the section on the Wisdom of Seth, Ibn al-'Arabī discusses the spiritual reality of Muḥammad as Seal of the Prophets. This reality is the preexistent Logos, from which all prophets received. This reality finds its hypostasis in the Perfect Man, a great saint, for Muḥammad was also the Friend of God.

Some of us are ignorant of knowledge of God, and say, "To know that one cannot know Knowledge is knowledge." Others of us know and do not say such a word, which is the last word; to them knowing gives silence, rather than ignorance. Such a one is the highest knower of God, and such knowledge is given only to the Seal of the Messengers and the Seal of the Friends of God.

Every prophet from Adam to the last Prophet [Muḥammad] receives light from the niche of the Seal of the Prophets, even though his clay was formed after theirs, since in reality he was present always, according to his word, God bless him and give him peace: "I was a prophet when Adam was between water and clay." Other prophets only became prophets at the time when they were sent. Similarly, the Seal of the Saints was a Friend of God when Adam was between water and clay, and other saints only became such after they fulfilled the conditions of nearness to God by taking on divine qualities, for He says, "I am the Friend, the Much Praised."

Thus even the messengers of God, as friends of God, receive from the niche of the Seal of the Saints.

Apostlehood and prophecy (and I mean by this the bringing of sacred Law and the mission) cease, but Sainthood never ceases.

The Seal of the Prophets, by virtue of his friendship with God, participates in the Seal of the Saints just as the other prophets do in him. He is at once Messenger, Friend, and Prophet.

The Seal of the Saints is the friend and the heir, who partakes of the Source, and contemplates the hierarchies of being. He is one of the virtues of the Seal of the Prophets, Muḥammad, upon whom be peace and God's blessing; foremost of the Collectivity and lord of the sons of Adam by opening the gates of intercession.[39]

*Ibn al-ʿArabī held that there are three great journeys: the journey from God, which is being born in the material world, the journey to God, which one undertakes with a spiritual guide to arrive at junction with the Universal Intelligence, and the journey in God, which remains in God (*bāqī billāh*), and never ends. In the final section of* Fuṣūṣ al-Ḥikam, *on the Wisdom of Muḥammad, he discusses man's contemplation of the Divine Reality in woman.*

Muḥammad is the Seal of the Prophets, the first of the three singulars [Ibn al-ʿArabī held that the Divine Reality expressed Itself in the triplicity of Essence, Will, and Word], since all other singulars derive from it. Since his reality was given the primal singularity by being given triplicity in its makeup, he said concerning love, "Three things I have been given to love in your world: women, perfume, and prayer." He began with woman because woman in the manifestation of her essence is a part of Man.

Because of this, he loved women because of the perfect contemplation of the Reality in them. [Reality delights in union with Its created image.] Contemplation of the Reality devoid of any base is never possible, since God in His essence does not depend on creation. Since a base is necessary, contemplation of the Reality in women is the greatest and most perfect sort. The greatest union is that of man and woman, since it is like the divine turning to the one He created in His own image, to make him his viceregent and behold Himself in him.

One who loves women truly loves them with a divine love, while one who loves them in carnal lust approaches his wife or any other woman only for pleasure, without realizing Whose that pleasure is. If he only knew Whom he is enjoying and Who is the enjoyer, then he would be perfect.[40]

Poets

Ṣūfī poets made an immortal contribution to Islamic literature, especially after the development of Persian vernacular literature that began in the tenth century. Eastern Iran had been hospitable to the Ṣūfīs. Wherever Persian rather than Arabic became the literary language—in Persia, Turkey, India, and Central Asia—their poems have inspired Muslims. After the eastern Islamic world had been devastated by the Mongols in the thirteenth century, Ṣūfī poets writing in Persian were able to offer Muslims a vision of divine consolation and beauty.

'Abdallāh al-Anṣārī

'Abdallāh al-Anṣārī of Herat in Khurāsān, or Pīr-i Anṣār (d. 1088/ A.H. 481), was a Ḥanbalī Ṣūfī who composed early Persian devotional poetry. Some of the Ṣūfī poetic symbols he uses are the rose, the Beloved; the wine, ecstacy; the wine-bearer, God. This selection begins with a ḥadīth *the Ṣūfīs treasured.*

"Poverty's my pride!" Your lovers raise to heaven their battle cry,
Gladly meeting men's derision, letting all the world go by.
Such a fire of passion's potion Pīr-i Anṣār feels,
That distraught, like Laylā's lover, through a ruined world he
reels.

O God, accept my plea,
And to my faults indulgent be.
O God, all my days I have spent in vanity,
And against my own body have I wrought iniquity.

O God, do You bless,
For this is not given to any man;
And do You caress,
For this no other can.

O God, though succory is bitter,
Yet in the garden with the rose it blends;
And though ʿAbdallāh is a sinner,
Yet is he among Your friends.

O God, You said, "Do this,"
And did not let me,
You bade me, "Do this not,"
And did permit me.

Small profit was my coming yesterday:
Today life's market's not more thronged or gay.
Tomorrow I shall go unknowing hence.
Far better were it to have stayed away.

Know that God has built an outward Kaʿba out of mud and stone,
And fashioned an inward Kaʿba of heart and soul alone.
The outward Kaʿba Abraham did build,
The inward Kaʿba was as the Lord Almighty willed.

O God, all other men are drunk with wine
The Wine-bearer is my fever.
Their drunkenness lasts for but a night,
While mine abides forever.[41]

Farīd al-Dīn ʿAṭṭār

ʿAṭṭār was a Khurāsānī Ṣūfī believed to have perished in Genghis Khan's invasion of eastern Iran in 1220. He collected the sayings and anecdotes of Ṣūfī teachers and was an able poet, devoted to the memory of al-Ḥallāj, with a clear tendency to pantheism. His most grandiose composition was Manṭiq al-Ṭayr *(The Speech of Birds), a mystical epic. The birds, led by the hoopoe, set out to find their King, the Phoenix (*Sīmurgh*). At the end of the quest, only thirty birds (*sī murgh*) survive. They recognize that they are He whom they sought and lose individuality in union with Him. Here is the culmination, the Phoenix's speech.*

The sun of my Perfection is a Glass
Wherein from *Seeing* into *Being* pass
All who, reflecting as reflected see
Themselves in Me, and Me in them, not *Me,*
But all of Me that a contracted Eye
Is comprehensive of Infinity.
Not yet *Themselves;* no Selves, but of the All
Fractions, from which they split and whither fall.
As water lifted from the Deep, again
Falls back in individual Drops of Rain—
Then melts into the Universal Main.
All you have been, and seen, and done, and thought,
Not *You* but *I* have seen and been and wrought;
I was the Sin that from Myself rebelled,
I the Remorse that toward Myself compelled:
I was the Tajidar who led the Track:
I was the little Briar who pulled you back:
Sin and Contrition—Retribution owed
And cancelled—Pilgrim, Pilgrimage, and Road,
Was but Myself toward Myself: and your
Arrival but *Myself* at My own Door:
Who in your fraction of Myself behold
Myself within the mirror Myself hold
To see Myself in, and each part of Me
That sees himself, though drown'd, shall ever see . . .
Rays that have wandered into Darkness wide
Return, and back into your Sun subside![42]

In this poem from his Diwān, *'Aṭṭār gives Ṣūfī meaning to the doctrine of the fundamentalists that matters of faith must be accepted* bilā kayf, *without asking how.*

His beauty if it thrill thy heart,
If thou a man of passion art
Of time and of eternity,
Of being and non-entity,
   Ask not.

When you have passed the bases four,
Behold the sanctuary door:
And having satisfied your eyes,
What in the sanctuary lies
   Ask not.

The Heavenly Tablet and the Pen
Are certainly your tongue and brain:
Do you the pen and tablet know,
But of the Pen and Tablet, O
   Ask not.

Your breast is the Celestial Throne
And Heaven the heart that it does own.
Yet but a cipher are the twain
And what the cipher is, again
   Ask not.

When unto this sublime degree
You have attained, desist to be:
But lost to self in nothingness
And, being not, of more and less
   Ask not.

Be you a particle of shade
Whereon the sun's light is displayed
And when you shall no longer be,
Of happiness and misery
   Ask not.

'Aṭṭār, if you have truly come
Unto this place, that is your home,
In your enjoyment of the Truth

Do you of anguish and of ruth
Ask not.[43]

'Umar b. al-Fāriḍ

The greatest mystical poet of the Arabic language was 'Umar b. al-Fāriḍ, a friend and contemporary of Ibn al-'Arabī from Cairo (d. 1235/ A.H. 632). He spent some fifteen years in Mecca and Madīna, where he had a vision of the Prophet. His poems are mystical hymns to the Beloved, written to be sung at the samā', *the Ṣūfī concert. The Beloved with which he seeks union, however, is the "Muḥammadan Truth"; the Prophet as the preexistent Logos of God, the emanating principle between God and creation, which we found Ibn al-'Arabī discussing. For some Ṣūfīs, Muḥammad had come to occupy a place very similar to that of Jesus in orthodox Christianity. While love and praise for the Prophet is easily accepted, a cult of Muḥammad quite analogous to what they have found objectionable in the idea of the Christian cosmic Christ is very troubling to many Muslims (it is to attack the cult that the fundamentalist Wahhābīs later tried to destroy the tomb of Muḥammad in Madīna). There is no escape from mentioning it in a discussion of later Ṣūfism, however, so I do so with apology.*

If any messenger came to me with words of kindness from you
and my life were mine, I would cry to him "take it!"
Surely enough blood has flowed from my wounded eyelids
for you: is what has come to pass enough for you?
So guard from your hate one much afflicted because of you,
who desired only you, before he even knew what love is.
Grant that the slanderer in ignorance forbids your lover
to come to you, yet tell me—who forbids you to unite with him?
Beauty has summoned him to adore you; who then,
think you, called you to turn him away?[44]

Even in translation, the odes of Ibn al-Fāriḍ can be as lovely as poems by Shelley or Keats, and the imagery is not dissimilar.

Though he be gone, my every limb beholds him
In every charm and grace and loveliness:
In music of the lute and flowing reed

Mingled in consort with melodious airs,
And in green hollows where in cool of eve
Gazelles roam browsing, or at break of morn;
And where the gathered clouds let fall their rain
Upon a flowery carpet woven of blooms;
And where at dawn with softly-trailing skirts
The zephyr brings to me his balm most sweet;
And where in kisses from the flagon's mouth
I suck wine-dew beneath a pleasant shade.[45]

Even in his own lifetime, Ibn al-Fāriḍ seems to have been attacked for the scandals in his imagery, but it did not prevent the people of Cairo from venerating him as a saint then and today. The spiritual reality of Muḥammad, which he believes to have enlightened all the prophets and saints, he often pictures as the illuminating moon in the dark night. Badr *mentioned here was the Prophet's first great victory; it also means full moon.*

O happy, happy night in which your vision
I hunted after with my net of waking!
The full moon, being your copy, represented
To my unslumbering eye your face's image,
And in such alien form your apparition
Cooled my eye's fever: I saw you, none other.
Thus Abraham of old, the friend of [God],
Upturned his eye, what time he scanned the heavens.
Now is the pitchy gloom for us made dazzling,
Since you your splendor gave me for my guidance,
And when you from my eye in outward seeming
Are gone, I cast it inward, there to find you.
Of Badr are they with whom by night you fared—
No, not of Badr: they journeyed in your daylight.
That men do borrow radiance from my outward
Is not strange, when my inward is your dwelling.
Ever since you to kiss your mouth did call me,
Musk lingers wheresoe'er my name is spoken . . .
The beauty of all things seen tempted me, saying
"Enjoy me," but I said, "I aim beyond you.
Beguile not me, yourself by my Beloved
Distraught, in whom you seem but an idea . . .
For his sake I exchanged my truth for error,

My right for wrong, my modesty for ill-fame.
My heart confessed his love One: then my turning
To you were dualism, a creed I like not."[46]

Jalāl al-Dīn Rūmī

This great poet, the theologian of Persian poetry, was the son of a Khurāsānī scholar and Ṣūfī who emigrated with his family from Balkh to Anatolia (Rūm), and then to Konya, capital of the Rūm-Saljūq sultans, shortly before Genghis Khan devastated eastern Iran. The family is said to have called on Farīd al-Dīn 'Aṭṭār in Nishāpūr, who predicted the boy Jalāl al-Dīn's future status.

Jalāl al-Dīn succeeded his father as professor in a madrasa, or academy of religious sciences, after being initiated into Ṣūfism by a disciple of his father, and studied in Syria, where he probably met Ibn al-'Arabī and his chief disciple, Ṣadr al-Dīn of Konya.

However, the great change in Rūmī's life came in 1244, when as an academician in Konya he met the wandering antinomian dervish Shams al-Dīn of Tabrīz, who was probably connected with the Qalandars. Jalāl al-Dīn conceived a tremendous passion for this eccentric and captivating figure, the first of three important men who inspired him to pour forth his torrent of poetry, and in whom he felt that he was able to contemplate the eternal Beloved. Shams-i Tabrīz seems to have tried to keep Jalāl al-Dīn from books and from his disciples and occasioned so much scandal that some of the disciples murdered him in 1247 and threw his body in a well, concealing what they had done. Jalāl al-Dīn was distraught by his loss and went twice to Damascus to search for Shams, only at last to find him, he thought, in himself; thus for him it was Shams who wrote Rūmī's Diwān *of Shams-i Tabrīz. Mawlānā (Our Master) Rūmī died in 1273. Under his son Sulṭān Walad, who led them from 1283 to 1312, the disciples became the Mevlevī (Turkish for Mawlāwī) order of dervishes, whose sedately turning mystical dance in the* samā' *has given them their name of "whirling" dervishes.*

From the Diwān-i Shams-i Tabrīz

What to do, O Muslims? for I do not recognize myself;
  not a Christian I nor Jew, Zoroastrian nor Muslim.
Not of the East am I nor West, nor land nor sea;
  not of Nature's mine, nor of the wheeling spheres.

Not of earth am I nor water, not of air nor fire.
  Not of the Throne am I nor carpet, not being nor entity.
Not of India am I nor China, not Bulgar-land nor Turkistān;
  not the Kingdom of Both Irāqs nor the Land of Khurāsān.
Not of this world am I nor the next, not of heaven nor hell;
  not of Adam nor of Eve, not of Paradise nor Riḍwān.
My place is no place, my trace has no trace;
  not body nor soul, for I belong to the soul of Love.
Duality have I put aside, I have seen both worlds as one.
  One I seek, One I know, One I see, One I call.
He is the first, He the last; He the outward, He the inward.
  Except "Yā Hū" [O He!] and "Yā man Hū," none I know.
I am drunk with Love's cup; the two worlds past my ken.
  No business have I save in drink and in carouse.
If once in my life I spent one day without you,
  from that time and that hour I repent of my life.
If my hand is given one day with you, in this retreat
  both worlds I shall trample to dance in triumph.
O Shams-i Tabrīz, I am so drunk that in this world
  apart from drink and and revelry I have no tale.[47]

The Mathnawī *or Rhyming Couplets, Rūmī's long theological poem, has been called "the Qur'ān of the Persian language," that is, its inimitable and inspired revelation. It was inspired by the third of Mawlānā's mystical love-bearers, Ḥusām al-Dīn, who succeeded him as shaykh of the disciples after his death. When Ḥusām al-Dīn suggested that Rūmī should write a* mathnawī *like that of 'Aṭṭār, it is said that Rūmī immediately plucked eighteen verses of the introduction which follows from his turban, already written. They are still sung with flute music today in the* samā' *and tell of the longing of the soul for God, the ground of its existence.*

Hearken to the tale of the reed flute,
  complaining of the pangs of separation:
"Since they tore me from the reed-bed,
  my laments move men and women to tears.
O for bosom torn like mine with wound of severing,
  that I may tell it of the pain of longing!
One who is far from the place of origin
  longs for the day of the Return.
In every company I sing my complaint,

with sorrowful and joyful am united.
Yet each becomes my friend for his own sake;
none cares to know the secrets of my heart.
My secret is not far from my complaint,
yet eye and ear lack light to discern it.
Body from soul, soul from body are not veiled,
but to none is it given to see the soul."
Fire, not wind, is this song of the reed-flute!
May one who has no fire be naught.
The fire of Love has caught the reed;
the ferment of Love has changed the wine.
The reed is comrade to one who has lost the Friend;
but its tones rend our defenses from us.
Who has seen a poison and an antidote like the reed's?
Who has seen sympathy and longing like the reed's?
The reed-flute tells of a Path filled with blood,
it recounts the love of the madman for Laylā.
Only to the senseless is the sense given,
and the tongue has no customer but the ear.
In our care life's days are grown untimely;
all my days keep company with burning grief.
Though they pass away thus, let them go!
You remain to me, Incomparable Purity.
One not a fish is soon sated with the Sea;
one without bread is soon tired of the Day;
And one who is raw will not understand ripeness,
therefore let my words be brief, and peace.
Arise, O my son, burst your bonds and be free!
How long will you be fettered with silver and gold?[48]

The Mathnawī *is an astonishing fountain of anecdotes, sermons, and allegories dictated to Ḥusām al-Dīn over a long period, a six-volume work of unquestioned genius and deep feeling, yet without artistic unity as one usually understands it. A brief homily of Mawlānā on the love of Woman will serve as a sample here.*

Though outwardly you seem to rule your wife,
inwardly you are ruled by her whom you desire.
This trait is found in Humankind alone;
such love lacking in animals shows their inferiority.
The Prophet said Woman prevails over the intelligent,

and dominates wise men possessed of hearts,
While ignorant men seek to prevail over women.
Men like that are slaves to animality.
For tenderness, kindness, and affection are human,
but harshness, lust, are animal in nature.
For Woman is a ray of God, no worldly beloved.
She is creative; one may say she's uncreated.[49]

'Abd al-Raḥmān Jāmī

The Mongols were driven from Iran in the late fourteenth century by the terrible lord of Samarqānd, Lame Tīmūr (Tamerlane), a Muslim Turk who ravaged all the cultural centers of Islam in Asia, but whose descendants patronized a brilliant fifteenth-century renaissance of Persian culture from their court at Herat, in Khurāsān. One of the ornaments of that court, an accomplished scholar, poet, and mystic, was the last great Ṣūfī poet to write in Persian, Mawlānā 'Abd al-Raḥmān Jāmī (d. 1492/A.H. 898). By 1507, the wild Uzbek Mongols had destroyed the power of the Tīmūrīs, but a Tīmūrī prince founded the Mughāl Empire of India and continued Tīmūrī patronage of the arts. This is from Jāmī's long poem about the beautiful Joseph and Potiphar's wife Zulaykhā, who, given no choice but to love him, learned to perfect her love.

Each speck of matter did He constitute
A mirror, causing each one to reflect
The mirror of His visage. From the rose
Flashed forth His beauty, and the nightingale
Beholding it, loved madly. From that Light
The candle drew the luster which beguiles
The moth to immolation. On the sun
His Beauty shone, and straightway from the wave
The lotus reared its head. Each shining lock
Of Laylā's hair attracted Majnūn's heart
Because some ray divine reflected shone
In her fair face. 'Twas He to Shīrīn's lips
Who lent that sweetness which had power to steal
The heart from Parvīz, and from Ferhād life.
His Beauty everywhere doth show itself,
And through the forms of earthly beauties shines
Obscured as through a veil. He did reveal

His face through Joseph's coat, and so destroyed
Zulaykhā's peace. Where'er you see a veil,
Beneath that veil He hides. Whatever heart
Doth yield to love, He charms it. In His love
The heart hath life. Longing for Him, the soul
Hath victory. That heart which seems to love
The fair ones of this world, loves Him alone.[50]

Dervishes

Darvīsh *is the Persian rendering of the Arab word* faqīr, *one who is poor for God's sake, who cares nothing for worldly things. It can be used for any Ṣūfī, but has particularly been used for the followers of a Ṣūfī* pīr *or shaykh, who seek to come to the truth through him.*

All the early shaykhs had their circle of disciples, and the building and endowing of khānqāhs,[51] *quasimonastic establishments for Ṣūfīs, along with the academies of the scholars of the Law, the* 'ulamā', *was a favorite activity of patrons and rulers after the eleventh century. By the thirteenth century, shaykhs deputized disciples to lead* khānqāhs *in other cities, so that regular orders with daughter chapters grew up, keeping a rule and established order of* samā' *or* dhikr *(remembrance of God). Central to this was the Ṣūfī doctrine of* wilāya: *that* walīs, *or friends of God (usually translated saints) have divine gifts or charisms on which they may draw for their followers in life and after death and that following their path will bring one to an intimate relationship with God.*

For example, the dervishes who follow the way of 'Abd al-Qādir Jilānī, the great Ḥanbalī Ṣūfī of Baghdad (d. 1166/A.H. 561) are the Qādirī Ṭarīqa, or path, an international order. The followers of Mawlānā Rūmī are the Mevlevīs. Others are the Naqshbandīs, with a silent dhikr, *who began in Central Asia and are still active in the renewal of Islam, the Chishtī Ṭarīqa of India, and the Shādhilī Ṭarīqa of North Africa.*

When organized society in the East broke down or was transformed following the Mongol invasions, the ṭarīqas *offered flexible and useful social groupings which could undertake defense, relief, and security. In some areas they governed cities, led revolutions, and converted pagans. The Safavī empire of Iran was founded by a family of Ṣūfī shaykhs brought to power in the sixteenth century by their disciples among the Turkoman tribes there.*

Most notably, however, ṭarīqa *Ṣūfism brings Ṣūfī teachings down to the level of the common people. No world religion has been more successful than Islam in teaching mystical religion to the masses—that has been one of its remarkable characteristics. The legal scholar took care of the* sharīʿa; *the Ṣūfī shaykh or* pīr *took care of the interior life. They were two distinct classes of religious practitioners, though one man might have both occupations. The interplay between* sharīʿa *and* ṭarīqa *gives Islam a rich and complex weave.*

Central to the life of each ṭarīqa *is usually its* dhikr *or service of "mentioning God," which is communally undertaken in a* ḥaḍra, *sometimes a session like that of the* samāʿ *of the Mevlevīs, and sometimes less sedate. Al-Ghazālī has this to say of these.*

The general merit of *dhikr* is testified to by the Word of God: "Remember Me, and I will remember you" [Qur'ān 2:152]. Thābit al-Bunānī said, "Verily I know when my Lord remembers me." So the people became alarmed at him and asked, "How do you know that?" He said, "When I remember God, He remembers me."

From Muslim: The Messenger of God said, "Whenever people sit in a gathering mentioning God, the angels welcome them, and grace descends upon them, and God mentions their names to those who are beside Him."

Dhikr has both a beginning and an end. The beginning of it requires intimacy and love, and its aim is intimacy and love. In the beginning the novice sometimes exerts himself to turn from the insinuation of Satan by the mention of God. If he is successful in persevering, he obtains intimacy with *dhikr,* and love for the One is implanted in his heart.[52]

The following prayers are from manuals of still widely used prayers of the saints, once composed for the dervishes.

O saints of God, lo I am sick, and before you is
  medicine and healing.
Then of your favor, look on me for treatment, and
  grant me of your goodness what is needed.
How many a sick one sought you at your door,
  and left it, sickness gone from him in healing.
How many a chronic sufferer have you helped,
  bedridden, whom your bounty has sufficed.
You are the door, and God is generous.
  One then who comes to you finds grace and health.[53]

[Muḥammad ʿAlī, Muftī al-Jazā'ir]

Praise to You, glorified be Your Majesty, while I live, and when I die, and when I am brought forth to You astounded by the awful cry summoning to the Assembly, and when I stand dumbfounded in Your presence at the publishing of the pages of my past life. And when You question me, and my very members are witnesses for You against me.[54]

[Prayer for the first day of the Muslim year]

O Lord, call down a blessing on Muḥammad in the cooing of doves, in the hovering of birds, in the pasturing of cattle, in the girding on of swords and the brandishing of lances and in the health of bodies and spirits.[55]

[al-Ṣalāt li-al-Buṣīrī]

O God, You are my Lord. There is no God but You. In You we trust. You are the Lord of the Glorious Throne. There is no might and no power save in You, the Exalted, the Magnificent. What God wills is, and what He does not will does not exist. I know that God is powerful over all things, and comprehends everything in knowledge and counts everything in number. O God, verily I take refuge in You from the evil of my soul and from the evil of every beast, whose forelock You hold. Verily my Lord is on a straight path.[56]

[Prayer of Abū al-Dardā']

My God and my Lord, eyes are at rest, stars are setting, hushed are the movements of birds in their nests, of monsters in the deep. And You are the Just who knows no change, the Equity that swerves not, the Everlasting that passes not away. The doors of kings are locked, watched by their bodyguards; but Your door is open to him who calls on You. My Lord, each lover is now alone with his beloved, and You are for me the Beloved.[57]

[Ṭahārat al-Qulūb]

V
THE STATEMENTS OF THEOLOGIANS: *KALĀM*

Muslims have often preferred to do without theology altogether; there is no orthodoxy in Islam—there is not even a word for it in Arabic. Hence theology has always come after the Law and mysticism in importance. All that one is obliged to believe is that there is no god but God and that Muḥammad is the Messenger of God. What one believes has never been so important as what one does: orthopraxy has been what Muslims were concerned with, and that of course has a Arabic term: sharʿī.

From the time of Aḥmad b. Ḥanbal, who reproved any discussion of matters of faith, fundamentalists have tended to hold that faith needs no rational interpretation or discussion. Ibn Ḥanbal was reacting to the lively discussion of faith among the first generations of Muslims, particularly in the circle of Ḥasan al-Baṣrī (important in theology as well as early fiqh *and Ṣūfism) at Baṣra. Both the Law and theology were included in the term* fiqh, *or insight, with* fiqh fī-'l-ʿilm *(insight in correct knowledge) used for the Law and* fiqh fī-'l-dīn *(insight in religion) used for theological doctrine.*

The word for religious discussion, kalām, *is the Muslim name for theology. Some of the earliest exponents of it seem to have been among the Ibāḍī Khārijīs (see chapter 6), and there were also those who began by trying to withdraw* (iʿtazila*) from political quarrels. These Muʿtazila also engaged in the rational defense of Islam against non-Muslim (often Christian) criticisms. They are usually credited with being the first theological school of Islam, yet there were other theological positions.*

Abū Ḥanīfa

The following doctrinal statement, derived from the statements of Abū Ḥanīfa and used by the early Hanafīs, states that insight in matters of religion is superior to insight in matters of knowledge—that faith must take precedence over works.

Such a creedal statement in Islam is not like a Christian creed, intended to be binding on the whole Community of Faith; it simply states what a group holds for itself. Still, this "creed" eschews positions held by other Muslims which are felt to be wrong.

The Fiqh Akbar I

1. We do not hold anyone to be an infidel on account of sin, and we do not deny their faith. [This is against the position of the Khārijīs, that those who commit grave sin cease to be Muslims.]

2. We enjoin what is good and forbid what is wrong. [This rejects quietism: keeping still in the face of wrong.]

3. What reaches you could not have missed you, and what misses you could not have reached you. [This seems to affirm predestination, but is not saying that one has no control over one's own actions, only that one has no control over the things that befall one.]

4. We do not disavow any of the Companions of the Messenger of God, and we do not adhere to one rather than another. [This is against the Shī'īs, who exalted 'Alī, as well as the Khārijīs, who held both 'Uthman and 'Alī to have committed infidelity (see chapter 6).]

5. We leave the question of 'Uthmān and 'Alī to God, who knows things secret and hidden. [This is very close to the position of the early Mu'tazila: one must withdraw from the political quarrels of the adherents of 'Uthmān and 'Alī and leave the matter to God. The followers of Abū Ḥanīfa included many Mu'tazilīs.]

6. Insight in matters of religion is better than insight in matters of knowledge and law.

7. Difference of opinion in the Community is a sign of God's mercy. [Muslims have been generally very tolerant of difference of opinion, so long as it does not lead to wrong acts.]

8. Whoever believes all that they are supposed to believe, except that they say, "I do not know whether Moses or Jesus (peace be upon them) were messengers of God or not," is an infidel. [Such a position would contradict revelation and clearly put one outside the Abrahamic tradition.]

9. Whoever believes all that they are supposed to believe, except that they say, "I do not know whether God is in Heaven or on the earth," is an infidel. [The position of the Mu'tazila later was that God is not to be localized. The Ka'ba is His "house," and He is "established on the Throne above the heavens," but He is not contained.]

10. If anyone says, "I do not know about the punishment in the tomb," they belong to the sect of the Jahmīya, which will go to hell. [*Ḥadīth*s state that, although the dead will sleep in their graves until the Day of Judgment, sinners will be tormented there by burning, pressure, and evil dreams. This is an unusually strong anathema, and clearly the Jahmīya are not acceptable Muslims in the eyes of these Ḥanafīs.][1]

Since faith takes precedence over works, and only God knows what is in one's secret heart, Abū Ḥanīfa held that one must refrain from saying on the basis of their actions that other Muslims have apostatized. Extreme proponents of this doctrine of postponing judgment (murji'-ism) *held that all who professed Islam would be saved. Abū Ḥanīfa's epistle to 'Uthmān al-Battī makes the point that nothing was more terrible than the wars of the Prophet's Companions, but who shall judge them except God? We shall never know all the truth about the matter. In the same way, it is not just works of the Law that make one a Muslim; it is faith.*

The Epistle of Abū Ḥanīfa to 'Uthmān al-Battī

From Abū Ḥanīfa to 'Uthmān al-Battī. Peace be upon you. I extol to you God: there is no god but He. As for what follows, I counsel fear of God and obedience to Him: He is sufficient as Reckoner and as Compensator. Your letter has reached me, and I have understood your advice in it. You say that you were moved to write it by my earlier letter to preserve you in good and give you counsel. You mention that it has reached you that I am of the Murji'a, and hold that one of true faith may err, that this distresses you, and that there is no excuse among friends of God for a thing that keeps one apart from God; that there is nothing for our guidance in what mere humans create and innovate; that the imperative is to be found in what the Qur'ān brought and in what Muḥammad preached and his Companions agreed on until the people fell into divisions and anything beyond this is human creation and innovation.

Now understand what I am writing to you. Be prudent in your opinions, and take care lest Satan enter. May God preserve us both in obedience to Him; we ask the help of His mercy for us both. I would inform you that the [Arab] people were idolators before God sent them Muḥammad, on whom be blessing and peace. Then He sent them Muḥammad to call them to Islam, so he called them to testify that there is no god but God, the Unique, without associate, and to profess what he brought them from God.

One who entered Islam became a believer, free of idolatry, with blood and possessions inviolate, and was entitled to the rights of a Muslim and the protection of other Muslims. One who rejected Islam when summoned to it became an infidel, devoid of faith, with possessions and blood lawful to the Muslims, from whom nothing could be accepted except entry into Islam or death, except for the People of the Book, whom God explicitly exempted, and who were to pay tribute.

Then the laws were revealed after this for the people who had affirmed Islam, and adoption of the laws became a work of faith. Thus God says in the Qur'ān, "Those who have faith, *and* do good works," and "One who has faith in God *and* does good works," and similar expressions. Thus loss as to works does not involve loss of faith, and faith may be attained without any other acts. If a loss as to works involved the loss of faith, one would be taken by a loss in works from the name of faith and its preservation just as those who lose faith are taken by its loss from the name of faith and its preservation and truth and revert to their former state of idolatry.

One of the ways that this may be known is the disagreement between act and faith. People do not disagree in faith and do not excel each other, but they do excel each other in acts, and their laws [*farā'id*] differ as well; yet the religion of those who go to Paradise and the religion of the prophets do not differ. Thus God says, "We have prescribed for you as religion what was enjoined on Noah, and what We have revealed to you, and what We enjoined on Abraham and Moses and Jesus" [Qur'ān 42:13].

Be aware that guidance in faith in God and His prophets is not like guidance in what is legislated as to works. How does this trouble you? You call people "faithful" for the faith they have, and God calls them so in His Book; but you call people "ignorant" for what they do not know of the laws. One needs only to learn that of which one is ignorant. Shall one who errs in knowledge of God and His prophets be like one who errs about what people learn when they already have faith?

God says in His teaching about the Law: "God explains it for you for you may err, and God is knowing of all things" [4:176], and "If one errs, the other will remember" [2:282], and "I [Moses] did it then, when I was among the erring" [26:20], that is, among the ignorant. The proof from the Book of God and the *sunna* for believing this is a matter too clear and too obvious to pose any problem for a man like yourself. Do you not say "a wicked believer," "a sinful believer," a "trespassing believer," "a cruel believer"? Shall one be rightly guided in wickedness and trespass as one is rightly guided in faith?

Or take the speech of the sons of Jacob to their prophet, their father, "By God, you are in your old error" [12:95]. Do you think they meant "You are in your old infidelity"? God forbid that you should so understand it, who are learned in the Qur'ān.

'Alī was called "Commander of the Faithful," and 'Umar as well: Commander of the Faithful. Now, would you say that meant "Commander of Those Who Obey All the Laws"? 'Alī referred to the Muslims of Syria with whom he was at war as "people of faith," in writing about it. Were they rightly guided when he fought them? The Companions of the Messenger of God fought each other, so both groups could not have been rightly guided in their acts. According to you, who were the wrongdoers?

As God is our Witness, I know of no sin that People of the Qibla [those who face Mecca in prayer] could commit that would be greater than fighting and shedding the blood of Muḥammad's Companions, may God bless him and give him peace. So what do you call the two factions? They were not both rightly guided; if you assert that, you are guilty of innovation. If you assert they were both in error, you have innovated. If you say one was rightly guided, then what was the other? But if you say, "God knows best," then you have hit the mark.

Understand well what I have written and know that I say the People of the Qibla are people of faith, and a loss as to act cannot remove them from their faith. One who obeys God in all the laws, according to us, will go to Paradise. One who leaves both faith and works is an infidel, who will go to the fire of Hell. But one who has faith and is guilty of some breach of the laws is a believing sinner, and God will do as He wishes about such a one: punish them if He wills, and forgive them if He wills.

And I say about the quarrels of the Companions of the Messenger of God, "God knows best." I do not think this is any different from your own opinion about the People of the Qibla, for their matter is just like that of the Companions of the Prophet: a thing that has been decided by tradition and insight.[2]

al-Māturīdī

The Mu'tazila whom I have mentioned called themselves ahl al-'adl wa al-tawḥīd, *the People of the Divine Justice and Unity. God's justice necessitated free will and moral choice, since if God as some Muslims said predestined sinners to sin and then punished them for it He would be guilty of injustice, punishing them for what He in fact had done. Clearly, He must give people the* qadar *or power to disobey him (hence the Mu'tazila were often given the name of Qadarīs, after an earlier movement). Equally, the divine attributes mentioned in the Qur'ān, such as being established on the Throne, seeing, having hands and face, or speaking, must all be created things, made at a moment in time for the purpose of revealing Himself. If the Word of God was not created, how was the Muslim teaching about the Qur'ān any different from the Christian teaching about Jesus, which Islam reproves? These rationalists, nearly all of the Ḥanafī school, studied Greek philosophy in translation and bolstered their position with logical arguments.*

Their arguments were not acceptable to people like Aḥmad b. Ḥanbal, who resented what they saw as an attempt to make God conform to human judgment. Reason is weak: surety is only in the Qur'ān and the sunna. *The attempt of three caliphs between 833 and 850 to make Mu'tazilism the official Islamic doctrine occasioned a reaction against it. Among other repellent things, Aḥmad b. Ḥanbal was flogged for his opposition, and those who shared it were persecuted.*

In the tenth century (the fourth century A.H.*), champions of traditional doctrine appeared who were willing to engage the Mu'tazila with their own weapons. Such a one was Abū Manṣūr al-Māturīdī (d. 944/*A.H. *333), leader of the Ḥanafīs of Samarqānd in Central Asia, who seems to have turned against the mainly Ḥanafī Mu'tazila of Iraq and Iran to affirm the position of "The People of the* Sunna *and the Collectivity" (i.e., the true Sunnīs). Not many of his original writings have survived, and this "creed" of his school was compiled after his death in the tenth century, though it represents his teaching.*

The Māturīdī school was an authentic Sunnī school of kalām, *preserved among the Ḥanafīs of Central Asia and India until modern times. And although located on the eastern peripheries of Islamic civilization, the Māturīdī theologians helped instruct the teachings of the intellectually less adept school of the Ash'arī theologians, who dominated the center of the Sunnī world. Again, in the eighteenth century, the Māturīdī school played a valuable role in the revivification of Islamic learning from Muslim academies in India.*

A Māturīdī Creedal Statement

1. There are three things in which knowledge [*'ilm*] occurs: sound perceptions, right intelligence, and information coming from truthful servants of God. The Sophists held that it does not occur at all, since the data furnished by these sources are self-contradicting: in perception, one who is squint-eyed will see one thing as two; reason's activity may hit or miss, and information may be true or false. We reply: we are dealing here with sound perception, so what you argue is not sound. By reason, we mean right reason, and by information we mean that of the infallible messengers of God, related by consecutive testimony.

2. The cosmos is originated [*muḥdath*], because it is divided into substances and accidents, and accidents are originated, since this is a name given to something that was not and then came to be. Cloud is such an occurrence. Substances are never free from accident, so they also are originated, due to their participation in existence with things that are originated. If it is established that the cosmos is originated, then it is clear that it is occasioned by the action of another than itself. If it is established that it has a maker, then the maker is eternal, since if he were not he would also have to have an originator, and similarly with the second and third events in a regressive causal series, and the causal series cannot be infinite.

According to the materialists, the world is originated from Primeval Stuff, that is to say from an eternal source which is matter, for they hold that creation from nothing is impossible.

3. The Maker must be one, since if there were two they would necessarily either concur or not concur in their creating. Agreement would be evidence of the weakness or both or either of them, since a free agent does not agree except by compulsion, and if they differed, then either both of them would attain their desire, which is absurd, or they would not attain it, which would mean their impotence, and a weakling is not suitable as a Lord. This is also taken from God's Word, exalted be He: "if there were other gods than God in heaven or on earth, they would both go to ruin" [Qur'ān 21:22]. The Zoroastrians have held that the cosmos had two creators: one was good and created good things; he is Yazdān. The other was evil and created evil things; he is Ahriman. This creator of evil is purposeless and not to be connected with Yazdān. We reply: the Creator of evil would only be purposeless if there was no wisdom in His creation of it, but there is; the least of it is that it brings down tyrants.

8. The Qur'ān, the Word of God, is an eternal attribute, subsisting in God's essence, though not in the form of letters and sounds, as one; not divided into sections and neither Arabic nor Syriac. Rather, His creatures express that one attribute with varying expressions as they do with the essence of God, exalted be He. In the same way, life, will, and eternal existence, among His eternal attributes, are expressed in varying ways. The Mu'tazila have held that the word of God is other than these expressions and that it is originated, for if it were eternal then God would eternally have been a Commander, a Prohibiter, and an Informer about things which did not exist, and that would be pointless.

We reply: it would only be pointless if when a command is given there had to be an immediate response, for priority and posteriority are dependent on time and space, and the Word of God is dependent on neither of these.

If it should be said that God, be He exalted, has said, "We have *made* it an Arabic Qur'ān" [43:3], and that making is creating, we reply that His Word, "They *make* the angels, the servants of the Merciful One, females" [43:19] does not support them.

The Ash'arī [theologians] have said that what is in the text is not the Word of God, but is only an expression of the Word of God, which is an attribute, and the attribute is not to be separated from that to which it is attributed. We say, it *is* the Word of God, but the letters and sounds are created, for we do not say that the Word of God inheres in the text so that there can be any talk of separation, for when a thing is known by God's knowledge, the attribute of knowledge is not thereby separated from Him.

14. The sins of humankind occur by God's wish [*irāda*], will [*mashī'a*], ordaining [*qaḍā'*], and power [*qadr*], but not by His good pleasure [*riḍā*], love [*maḥabba*], and command [*amr*], according to His Word, "One whom God wills to send astray, He makes the bosom close and narrow" [6:125], and His Word, "You wish nothing, unless God wishes it" [76:31]. If the creature were able to act by its own will, then it could prevail over the will of God, be He exalted. The Mu'tazila have held that God does not will to prevail over Humankind, according to His Word, "I have only created humans and Jinn that they might serve Me" [51:57]: meaning "I have not created them to reject Me," so that He does not will it. We reply, the meaning is: "He orders them to serve Him," and He has so ordered. The meaning is not: "God does not will injustice to His servants" [40:31]. That is true, but this is not the con-

text, and it does not apply here, nor does their saying that in causing sin God is doing what He Himself reproves: acting lightly. We say to this that it would only be light behavior if there occurred no proof that God is free of that. Also their statement that if God wills sin people are compelled to commit it does not apply. Just as humankind cannot escape God's will, it cannot escape God's omniscience, and it constitutes no excuse for sin. If they ask, "What does it mean then when God says, 'Whatever of ill befalls you is from yourself' [4:73]?" We reply: it means that evil cannot be attributed to God outrightly, for considerations of decency, just as one cannot invoke Him as "Creator of swine!" but must be attributed to him in a more general way, as He says, "Say, all comes from God" [4:78].

15. God created rejection and willed that it should exist, but He did not order people to commit it; rather, He ordered the rejecter to have faith, but He did not will that one must do it. If anyone asks, "Is God's will pleasing to Him or not?" we say, it is pleasing. If they then ask, "And why should He punish what pleases Him?" we reply: He punishes what is *not* pleasing. For His will and His providence, and all His attributes are pleasing to Him, but the act of the rejecter is *not* pleasing to Him. It is hateful to Him, and it is punished by Him.

17. Slain persons die in their due term; if they did not, then it would mean that God was unable to fulfill the due term or was ignorant of it. That is infidelity. The Mu'tazila say that it is clear they do not die in the due term, because the Qur'ān obliges retribution or payment of compensation on the slayer. We say these are necessitated by the act of killing, which is forbidden by God, and this is a part of the general question of who creates acts.

19. It is not incumbent on God to do what is most salutary for His creatures. We cite, "We give the infidels a respite, that they may increase their sins" [3:178]. A respite to the creature to increase its sin is not what is salutary for it. While if God chose to do what is most salutary it would be good and gracious, if He had to, it would invalidate His Word, "God disposes of grace abounding." The Mu'tazila have held that it is incumbent on God, and that He has given as much faith as possible to everyone, and as little infidelity, since if He did not He would be either unjust or ungenerous.

22. Some have said that faith and Islam are one, following God's Word, "If anyone desires a religion other than commitment [Islam] it

will not be accepted of him" [3:75]. Others say that faith and Islam are different, following His Word, "The Bedouins say, 'We believe.' Say, you have not believed; say rather, 'We became Muslims' [49:14]. The soundest thing is that which Abū Manṣūr al-Māturīdī said, God have mercy on him:

> Islam is knowledge of God without modality, and its locus is the breast [*ṣadr*]. Faith is knowledge of Him in His Godhood, and its locus is the heart [*qalb*], inside the breast. Gnosis is knowledge of God in His attributes, and its locus is the inner heart [*fu'ād*], inside the heart. Unitarianism is knowledge of God in His unity, and its locus is the innermost heart [*sirr*], within the inner heart. This is the analogy in God's Word, "The likeness of His light is like a niche in which there is a lamp" [24:35].

Hence this is a matter of four knots, not one, and there is no contradiction between them. When they are united, the sum is true service [*dīn*] of God.

If anyone says, "I do not know who created this world," or "I do not know if prayer is an obligation for me," or "I do not know what an infidel is," or "I do not know what happens to infidels," that one become an infidel, while anyone from the Land of the Turks who professes Islam in a general way, yet knows nothing of religious Laws and does not fulfill any part of them, would still have faith. This indicates the faith of the imitator [*muqallid*], who believes uncritically, *contra* the Mu'tazila and the Ash'arīs. What they have taught would imply that God was unwise in His sending the Prophet, for if uncritical faith were not enough God's intention would not have been fulfilled. Nonetheless, the stage where one seeks understanding is a higher one, for its faith is more enlightened.

27. The obligation to order to good and forbid wrong does not obtain for every individual in our times, because it is not an aspect of deterrence of evil. It is not permissible to rebel with the sword against an unjust ruler, because it leads to mischief and bloodshed.

28. The torments of the grave are a reality, we hold, in opposition to the Mu'tazila and the Jahmīya. They say, we see and observe that dead bodies do not undergo any suffering. Similarly they have denied that mineral bodies praise God, the Scales of Judgment, the Bridge, the Exit of the Faithful from the Fire, and the Ascending Stair to Paradise. We say: reason is weak. The Prophet said, "Reason about creatures, not

about the Creator," because of the weakness of the intellect. The proof is in the Word of God, "We shall chastise them [sinners] twice," that is, in the grave and at the Resurrection. He also says, "Punishments other than those," and "We shall make them taste the lower punishments before the greater" [32:21], that is, the torment of the grave. As to their other objections, we cite: "Nothing there is that does not chant His praise, yet you perceive not their hymns" [17:44], and "We have set a just balance for the Day of Resurrection" [21:47].

30. People who innovate in religion or do as they please about it go to the Fire of Hell, in accord with the *ḥadīth*.

34. It is not permissible to curse Yazīd the son of Mu'āwiya [responsible for the death of Ḥusayn, the Prophet's grandson] because he is a transgressor; God may forgive him.

36. The miracles [*karamāt*] of the saints are established. As to the objection of the Mu'tazila that, if they were possible, human weakness would be unable to distinguish between them and the wonders [*mu'jizāt*] of the prophets, we reply: a wonder occurs at the time of a specific prophetic claim, unlike a miracle. Their position would lead to denying God's Word, where Mary's miracle is mentioned, "Whenever Zachariah entered the sanctuary, he found food with her" [3:38].

37. The jinn and humankind are not preserved from grave sins, except for messengers and prophets. If they were not preserved, then prophets would not be free of lying. But they are not preserved from venial sins, so that their intercession will not be weakened, since those who are not tried cannot pity those who are. The Mu'tazila have held that prophets were preserved from all sins, because they do not recognize their intercession.

39. Errors of the prophets are in the things they did before the revelation, such as the marriage of David to the wife of Uriah the Hittite, or leaving the better for the good, such as Adam's failing to avoid what was prohibited out of respect for the name of God [according to one story, Adam ate the forbidden fruit believing it would keep him forever with God].

40. The elite of the Children of Adam, such as the prophets, are nobler than the elite among the angels, and the elite among the angels are nobler than ordinary humans, while ordinary humans are nobler than ordinary angels. The Rāfiḍī Shī'īs prefer 'Alī to Abū Bakr and the other

Companions of the Prophet, according to the *ḥadīth* that the Prophet prayed, "O God, bring me the creature dearest to You, to share this fowl with me," and 'Alī came. Also he is said to have been the bravest of the Companions, the one furthest from infidelity, and the one who learned most from the Prophet.

The Sunnīs quote the Prophet, "Abū Bakr does not surpass the rest of you by much fasting and prayer, but by something that is in his heart."

According to 'Umar's son, "We used to say when the Messenger of God was still living, the best of the Community is Abū Bakr, then 'Umar, then 'Uthmān, and then 'Alī." As to the *ḥadīth* of the fowl, if we were to give this due weight, God should have brought one of the prophets. As to their saying that 'Alī was braver and had learned more, such information would not be available to them. Still, some of the people of the *sunna* do prefer 'Alī to 'Uthmān.

'Ā'isha was nobler than Fāṭima, may God be satisfied with them both, because her position was higher with the Prophet. Others have held that Fāṭima was nobler, because 'Ā'isha's rank was only raised due to her closeness to the Prophet.[3]

al-Ash'arī

In Iraq, the scholar Abū al-Ḥasan al-Ash'arī (d. 935/A.H. 324) founded a school of theology which is named for him. He was one of the Baṣra Mu'tazila who became convinced around 912 that their arguments did not give sufficient weight to ḥadīths *which depict God as predestining all things and were opposed to the views of the People of the* sunna *and Collectivity. He has been claimed by both the Shāfi'īs (who for a long time made up the bulk of his followers) and the Ḥanafīs. While he preferred to argue from Qur'ān and* Ḥadīth *like the Ḥanbalīs, he was willing to use purely intellectual arguments if that was what it required to refute opponents, particularly the Mu'tazila. He was not the first to use reason to defend the Sunnī position; al-Muḥāsibī the Ṣūfī had attempted it and been attacked for it by Aḥmad b. Ḥanbal. Al-Ash'arī moved to Baghdad, and the school he founded later had tremendous success, due to official state backing. This was not in his time, however, because from 945 to 1055 the Shī'ī Būyī dictators dominated the caliphs, and the Būyīs favored the Mu'tazila, who sought a compromise with the Shī'īs. What al-Ash'arī seems to have done was forge weapons which could later be used to refute the Mu'tazila and finally drive them out of the Sunnī fold into Shī'ism. (The Zaydī*

Shīʿīs in particular have been reckoned among the Muʿtazila: see chapter 6.) This did not gain al-Ashʿarī or his school any credit with the fundamentalists, who disliked them quite as much as they did the Muʿtazila.

Al-Ashʿarī insisted that God's attributes could not be explained as created and that humans are not the creators of their acts, but bear moral responsibility for them, by kasb *or acquisition. Even the acquisition is God's act, but it seems to be "acquired" through human intention: cf. the* ḥadīth *"All acts are judged by their intentions." Hence God is not unjust in punishing them. Moreover, good and evil are only what God commands and prohibits: they are not standards that can be used to judge Him.*

The Māturīdī scholars differed from the Ashʿarī theologians most importantly on the rational basis of good and evil, the reality of free choice in human acts, the separation of faith and works, and the eternity of God's attributes of act, subsisting in His essence. In the eleventh-century restoration of Sunnism and later there were many opportunities for the two Sunni schools of theology to influence each other.

Acquisition

Question: Why do you assert that the acquisitions of God's servants are created by Him?
Answer: Because God has said: "God has created you and what you make" [Qur'ān 37:96].

The rational indication for the [divine] creation of people's acts is that we find that rejection [*kufr*] is repugnant, wrong, vain, inconsistent, and contrary, while faith is good, troublesome, and painful. If the matter is thus, rejection must have a producer who produces it intentionally as rejection, vain and repugnant. Its producer could never be the unbeliever, who desires that rejection be good, right, and reality, when it is the contrary of that. Similarly faith must have a producer who produces it as it really is, troublesome, painful, and vexatious, who is other than the person of faith, who, though he or she strives that faith be the contrary of its actual pain, trouble, and vexatiousness, has no way to effect it. So if the one who produces rejection as it really is cannot be the unbeliever, and the one who produces faith as it really is cannot be the faithful, then the intentional producer of both must be God Most High, Lord of the Worlds. For no body could produce these, since bodies can effect nothing in things distinct from themselves.
Question: Would you hold that evil is from God?

Answer: Some of our associates say that all things are from God, in totality, without specifically saying that evil is from God. This is like saying that all things belong to God. However, I hold that evil is from God in that He creates it for others, not for Himself.

There were twins in a desert, and it occurred to the heart of one of them that God is one: who cast it into his heart? God. Was what God cast into his heart true? Yes. It occurred to the heart of the other of them that God is the third of three: who cast it into his heart? God. Was what God cast into his heart false? Yes. Did God lie to him? It is wrong to say that God told him the truth, because the veracity of the Creator is one of His essential attributes, and He cannot lie. But it is not necessary when He creates falsehood for another, or creates falsehood in the heart of another, that He be lying.[4]

Question: Has God not charged the rejecter with the duty of faith?

Answer: Yes.

Question: Then the rejecter is capable of faith.

Answer: If one were capable of faith, one would have it.

Question: Then God charges one with what one cannot do.

Answer: This is a statement which involves two matters. If you want to say one is incapable of faith because of inability to have it, then no. But if you mean one is incapable of faith because one is preoccupied with its contrary, then yes.[5]

Question: Is God free to inflict pain on infants in the world to come?

Answer: God is free to do that, and in doing it would be just. In the same way, whenever He inflicts an infinite punishment for a finite sin, and subjects some living beings to others, and is gracious to some and not to others, and creates some knowing well that they will reject faith—all that is justice on His part. It would not be wrong on His part to create them in painful torments and make these everlasting. Nor would it be wrong on His part to punish the faithful and cause the rejecter to enter Paradise. We only say He will not do it because He has informed us that He will punish rejecters; and He cannot lie when He gives information. He is the Overwhelming Monarch, subject to no one. That being so, nothing can be wrong on God's part. For a thing is wrong on our part only when we go beyond the limit set for us and do what we have no right to do. But since the Creator is subject to no one, nothing can be wrong on His part.

Question: Then lying is wrong only because God has declared it to be wrong.

Answer: Quite so. And if He declared it good, it would be good; and if He commanded it, there could be no opposition to it.[6]

A Vindication of Theology

A certain sect have made ignorance their capital. They find reason and inquiry into religious matters burdensome and incline to ease and *taqlīd* [imitation, traditionalism]. They attack those who investigate the principles of religion and accuse them of error. They assert that if *kalām* were a matter of guidance and rectitude, the Prophet and his Companions would have discussed it, for the Prophet did not die until he had amply explained all that the Muslims needed in the matters of their religion.

There are three aspects of the answer to this argument. First, the Prophet also never said, "Whoever discusses it, regard as an erring innovator." So you must regard yourselves as erring innovators, since you have discussed something that the Prophet did not discuss and accused of error those whom the Prophet did not accuse.

The second answer is to say: Actually, the Prophet was not ignorant of the *kalām* you have mentioned. The basic principles of these things are present in the Qur'ān and the *sunna* in a general way, without details.

The third answer is that these questions did not occur in his days in a specific way that he should discuss or not discuss them, though the basic principles were present in the Qur'ān and the *sunna*. Whenever a question arose related to religion from the standpoint of the Law, people have discussed it, inquired, debated, and argued.

They may say: The *'ulamā'* cannot evade discussing new questions so that the ignorant may know how to judge. One may say: Why then do you forbid *kalām* [discussion]? You use it yourselves when you want to; but when you are silenced in discussion, you say, "We are forbidden to engage in *kalām*." And when you want to, you unquestioningly follow your predecessors without proof or exposition. This is concupiscence and arbitrary behavior![7]

al-Juwaynī

In the fifth Islamic century (the eleventh of the Common Era), mass migrations into Islamic territory of Central Asian Oghuzz Turks occurred. Fortunately, they had been converted by Ṣūfīs from Khurāsān and did not come as enemies, but as people for the most part eager to fit into the Islamic world. The 'Abbāsī caliph in Baghdad soon invited a family of their chiefs, the Saljūqs, to replace the Būyī dictators and uphold Sunnism as his delegated ruler, with the title of sultan. The Sal-

jūqs honored the caliphate and kept their tribesmen in check; those who wanted to live by raiding and plundering were sent to the Byzantine frontier, where they expanded into what is now Turkey and in time set up a Saljūq sultanate in Konya. Other Turks had already begun the conquest of northern India in the name of Islam.

The first Saljūq sultans were unable to read or write and were dependent on their Persian wazīrs *to administer the empire for them. At first they favored the Māturīdī school and made life in Khurāsān burdensome for the Ash'arī theologians. Some of them left Nishāpūr as a result. One of these was Abū al-Ma'ālī 'Abd al-Malik al-Juwaynī, a Shāfi'ī jurist and Ash'arī doctor who taught between 1058 and 1062 in Mecca and Madīna, so that he won the title* imām al-ḥaramayn, *the Imam of the Two Holy Places.*

Al-Juwaynī was brought back in triumph to Nishāpūr by a new wazīr, *the great statesman Niẓām al-Mulk (d. 1092/A.H. 485), who built for him a* madrasa *or academy where he taught until his death in 1085. Niẓām al-Mulk favored Shāfi'ism and Ash'arism as the broad middle way of Sunnism, with the best hope of producing unity, although he was not averse to founding madrasas for Māturīdī scholars in Ḥanafī territory. His policy was adopted by later rulers, and the success of Ash'arism was assured, even in areas where the people were mostly non-Shāfi'īs. While there were a few Ḥanbalīs willing to consider* Kalām, *the majority of that school stayed aloof from it.*

The following selection is from a work of Juwaynī's last years, a creed he dedicated to his patron, Niẓām al-Mulk.

From the Niẓāmī 'Aqīda: *Prophecy*

A group of people known as the Brahmans believe in the Creator, but they deny prophethood. We shall indicate the way in which they delude themselves and answer them briefly and clearly.

Among the things they mention is that if prophets brought things contrary to reason, they would have to be discarded, and if they brought what agrees with reason and is compatible with it, it would be absurd to send them.

We answer: They bring what reason cannot deny and would not be independently guided to: provisions of the Law, divine punishments, and threats on which judgments depend and which reason would not perceive unaided, even though it concurs with everything that is virtuous. Still, reason alone would not concur on all the particulars expounded by the Law. Hence there is no obstacle in what prophets bring to what reason clarifies; they confirm the data of reason and support it. When one speaks in accord with propositions of reason, the words may not be counted as nonsense, even when reason has already led to what one is saying. It is certain that there are satisfying proofs in some of the things the Creator has made as to His existence, and none of the wonders of creation may be accounted an absurd thing.

Among the things the Brahmans say is this: "In the laws of your prophets we find things permitted and even made obligatory which reason finds wrong, such as sacrificing animals who have done no harm, instructions of positions of prostration in prayer, running between Ṣafā and Marwa, the fast pace and the pointless throwing of stones."

We shall briefly mention what will cut off this whole argument. We say to the Brahmans: You assert that you have knowledge of the Creator, who acts as He chooses, and then you reject prophethood on the basis of what reason approves and disapproves. All that you call wrong is what He has commanded, and we shall show you the like about other things that God does. As for sacrificing animals, God lets them die, occasions their death, and permits what natural pains He will. What He Himself does in nature is not considered wrong and may not be considered wrong when He commands it. As to their disapproving the aspect of one performing the ritual prayer, we say: Even if God were to create some in the attitude of prostration and never enable them to find a rag with which to cover themselves, leaving them with pudenda exposed, still God's act could not be disapproved.

Whoever has come this far with us can refute such things as we have mentioned among all their objections, for they have based their whole position on criticizing the acts of God, and one can only criticize the acts of one who may be harmed or benefited by it.

Hence if anyone raises objections to prophethood depending on a position similar to theirs, we pay no attention to that person.[8]

al-Ghazālī

The greatest of the Ashʿarī theologians was al-Juwaynī's brilliant pupil and Niẓām al-Mulk's protégé, Abū Ḥāmid al-Ghazālī (d. 1111/A.H. 505). He also was in contact with Māturīdī theologians in Khurāsān and seems to show the evidence of this. At thirty-three he was chief professor of the Niẓāmīya Madrasa of Baghdad, teaching Law and kalām *and writing books attacking the Muslim philosophers and the adherents of the Ismāʿīlī Shīʿī caliphate of Cairo (see chapter 6). After the murder of Niẓām al-Mulk by Ismāʿīlī assassins in 1092, he entered a period of crisis and near breakdown which led him to quit the world in 1095 and become a wandering Ṣūfī. Until this time there had been great suspicion and hostility on the part of the* 'ulamā' *to the Ṣūfīs, but al-Ghazālī was a man whose ability and credentials they could scarcely reject. After eleven years of retirement, he was pressed by the ruling sultan to teach again at the Niẓāmīya Madrasa of Nishāpūr, where he once had been a student. He retired again and died among his disciples in a Ṣūfī retreat in his home city of Ṭūs.*

He has been called a mujaddid, *a renewer of Islam, and the greatest of the theologians. His great work* Iḥyā' 'Ulūm al-Dīn *(Revivification of the Sciences of Religion) restates Law and* kalām *with Ṣūfī emphasis on religious experience and purity of motive. Man's business is to seek to know God and love Him, and intellect's business is to know its own limitations in this supremely important task. Al-Ghazālī was responsible for a synthesis of Sunnism, scholasticism, and Ṣūfism that dominated Muslim learning until the modern age. He favored Aristotelian logic, but was strongly critical of the idea that one could study metaphysics by reason. His attack on philosophy put an end to its study by the Sunnīs—not the Shīʿīs—in the East. In Muslim Spain, Ibn Rushd (Averroës, d. 1198/A.H. 595) wrote an excellent refutation of his criticisms, but it was too late. Al-Ghazālī's victory over the study of philosophy had been won, and Ibn Rushd was chiefly studied by Western Christian scholastics. In his intellectual autobiography,* Deliverance from Error, *al-Ghazālī describes how he made a thorough study of Philosophy (he even wrote textbooks on it), and came to reject it.*

On the Philosophers

I observed that their sciences included several divisions. But to all of them, despite the multiplicity of their categories, cleaves the stigma of unbelief and Godlessness. They include six divisions: mathematical, logical, physical, metaphysical, political, and moral.

1. *Mathematical Sciences* deal with arithmetic, geometry and astronomy. They concern rigorously demonstrated facts which can in no wise be denied once they are known and understood. From them however two evils have been engendered: one is that whoever takes them up marvels at the fine precision of their details and the clarity of their proofs. He forms a high opinion of the philosophers and assumes that

all their sciences have the same lucidity. Thus when he learns through hearsay of their unbelief and rejection of religion, he concludes that it is right to reject and disavow it.

The second evil derives from the case of an ignorant friend of Islam who supposes that our religion must be championed by the rejection of every science ascribed to the philosophers. This is a great crime against religion.

2. Nothing in the *Logical Sciences* has anything to do with religion by way of negation and affirmation. They are the study of methods of proofs, of syllogisms, of the requisites for a sound definition. There is nothing here that must be rejected. It is the sort of thing mentioned by theologians and the partisans of reasoning in connection with the proofs they use. The philosopher's manner of discourse is exemplified by "If it is certain that every A is B, then it necessarily follows that some B is A," for instance: If it is certain that every man is an animal, then it necessarily follows that some animals are men. What has this to do with the important truths of our religion, that it should call for rejection and denial? The only effect of such a rejection in the minds of logicians is a low opinion of the rejecter's intelligence, and, what is worse, of his religion.

3. The *Physical Sciences* are a study of the world of the heavens and their stars, and of the sublunar world's simple bodies, such as water, air, earth and fire, and composite bodies, such as animals, plants and minerals. Just as Islam does not require the repudiation of the science of medicine, so also it does not require the repudiation of the physical sciences, except for certain specific questions which we have mentioned in our book *The Incoherence of the Philosophers*. The basic point regarding all of them is for you to know that nature is totally subject to God Most High: it does not act of itself but is used as an instrument by its Creator. The sun, moon, stars and elements are subject to God's command: none of them effects any act by and from itself.

4. It is in the *Metaphysical Sciences* that most of the philosophers' errors are found. Owing to the fact that they could not carry out [demonstrative proof] according to the conditions they had postulated in logic, they differed a great deal about metaphysical questions. Aristotle's doctrine on these matters, as transmitted by al-Farābī and Ibn Sīnā, approximates the teaching of the Islamic philosophers. But the sum of their errors comes down to twenty heads, in three of which they must be taxed with unbelief, and in seventeen with innovation. It was to refute their doctrine on these questions that we composed our book *The Incoherence*.

In the three questions first mentioned, they opposed the belief of all Muslims, viz. in affirming that people's bodies will not be assembled on the Last Day, but only disembodied spirits will be rewarded and punished, and the rewards and punishments will be spiritual, not corporal. They were right in affirming spiritual rewards and punishments, for these are certain, but they falsely denied the corporal rewards and punishments and blasphemed the revealed Law in their stated views.

The second question is their declaration: "God knows universals, but not particulars." This also is out-and-out unbelief. The truth is that "There does not escape Him the weight of an atom in the heavens or in the earth" [Qur'ān 34:3].

The third question is their maintaining the eternity of the world, past and future. No Muslim has ever professed any of their views on these questions.

On other matters their doctrine is close to that of the Mu'tazila. But there is no need to tax the Mu'tazila with unbelief because of such views. We have already mentioned in our book *The Clear Criterion* what shows the error of anyone who precipitously brands as unbelief everything that clashes with his own doctrine.

5. In the *Political Sciences* all the philosophers have to say comes down to administrative maxims concerned with secular affairs and the government of rulers.

6. All they have to say about the *Moral Sciences* comes down to listing the qualities and habits of the soul, and the way to cultivate the good ones and combat the bad. This they simply took over from the saying of the Ṣūfīs, godly people who applied themselves to invoking God Most High, resisting passions, and following the way to Him by shunning worldly pleasures.[9]

From the Iḥyā': *On the Love of God and Love for God*

Love for God is the furthest reach of all stages, the sum of the highest degrees, and there is no stage after that of love except its fruit and its consequences, nor is there any stage before love which is not a prelude to it, such as penitence, long-suffering, and asceticism.

Yet some of the *'ulamā'* deny the possibility of love for God and say that it means nothing more than persevering in obedience, while true love of God is impossible, except metaphorically. They also deny any intimacy with Him, or passionate longing for Him, or the delight of confiding in Him, and other consequences of love. Thus we must of necessity deal with this matter here.

Whoever loves God for other than God's sake does so from ignorance, for among those of insight there is no true beloved save God Most High, and none deserving of love save Him. To explain this we shall turn to the five causes of love and show that all of them unite in God's truth.

The first cause of love is one's love for oneself, and one's own permanency, perfection, and continued existence, and one's hatred of perishing and nonexistence. This is the natural disposition of every living thing, and it cannot be imagined that anyone would deviate from it.

It necessarily tends to the deepest love of God, for one who knows oneself and knows one's Lord knows absolutely that one has no existence of oneself, and that self-existence, continued existence, and perfection of existence are all from God and to God and for God who is the Creator and Sustainer and Perfecter. If one loves oneself, then of necessity one must love God. If one does not, then it is because of ignorance of one's self and one's Lord, for love is the fruit of knowledge.

The second cause is that it is human nature to love one who bestows benefits and possessions on one, is kind of speech to one, and gives evil to those who give one evil. If one has true knowledge, one will know that the Benefactor is God alone, whose benefits to all His servants are beyond number.

Benefits from human beings are not to be imagined, except in a metaphorical way, for the Benefactor is only God. Let us suppose that such and such a man has endowed you with all his treasures and empowered you to dispose of them as you will, and that you then think that these benefits came from that man. That would be a mistake, for his good action was only performed *by means* of himself and his possessions and his motivation to turn them over to you. But who was it that was gracious, and who created his possessions and his ability, and who created his will and motivation?

The third cause is the love of benefactors for his own sake, even when their benefits do not reach you. This love is natural, for if information reached you of a king in a far country who was pious, just, wise, gentle with people, and kindly to them, and word reached you of another king who was cruel, arrogant, corrupt, shameless, and wicked, you would find in your heart an inclination to the first which was love, and a repugnance to the second which was hate. The first emotion is love of the benefactor simply because he is good, and not because he is good *to you*. This also necessitates the love of God; in fact it necessitates loving none but God, for only He is truly good.

The fourth reason is to love every beautiful thing for its own beauty, and not for any satisfaction which can come from it. Beauty may be external and perceived with the eye of the head, or it may be interior and perceived with the eye of the heart. The first sort can be perceived even by children and beasts; to perceive the second sort is the special property of people of heart, and none may share in it who know only the life of the lower world. All beauty is beloved by a perceiver of beauty, and if one perceives it with the heart, it becomes the heart's beloved. What is beautiful is to be loved, and the Absolutely Beautiful is the One, who has no equal; the Unique, who has no opposite; the Eternal, who has no similitude; the Rich, who has no need; the Omnipotent, who does as He wishes and judges as He will.

The fifth cause is to love what is related and similar; for like inclines to like, as experience, report, and history all testify. This also necessitates loving God, because of the inner similarity, which goes back not to resemblances of feature and form, but to inner significance, some of whose meanings we may mention in books, and some of which it is not permissible to write, but which must rather be left under a covering of dust until the travelers stumble upon them in the path when they have completed the conditions of the journey.

What may be mentioned is the nearness of the servant to the Lord in attributes which call for imitation and patterning oneself on the character of the Lord: such attributes as knowledge, piety, goodness, kindness, and spreading mercy and good among God's creatures.

The things which may not be mentioned in books pertain to that special relationship of the human to which God has alluded in His Word, "They will ask you about the Spirit; say 'The Spirit is a matter for my Lord' "[Qur'ān 17:25]. He has revealed that this is a divine matter beyond the bound of created reason. Clearer than this is His Word, "When I have shaped humankind, and breathed my Spirit into it, fall you down and bow before it!" [15:29]. For that, the angels prostrated themselves before Adam. He indicates it again with His Word, "We have made you a successor in the earth" [38:29], which Adam would never have merited except for that relationship, and which the Prophet has hinted at in his saying, "God created humankind in His own image."

This is the greatest of the reasons of Love, the remotest and rarest of them all, and thus the reasonable and accepted view among people of insight is that God alone is worthy of true love. [10]

Al-Ghazālī wrote a creed designed to be taught to children at an early age, as a sort of catechism of basic articles of doctrine. It is a concise statement of what the 'ulamā' *thought the Sunnī faithful should commit to heart; al-Ghazālī himself states that they should learn by imitation and not dazzle their minds with theological discussions. The section on the last things follows.*

Eschatology

God will not accept the faith of any servants unless they believe what the Prophet narrated about the things after death. The first is the matter of Munkar and Nakīr. These are two awful and terrible angels who will cause one to sit up in the grave, with soul and body together, and will ask one, "Who is your Lord, what is your religion, and who is your Prophet?" They are the two examiners, and their questioning is the first examination after death.

One must believe in the punishment of the grave: that it is a reality and its judgment on body and soul is just, as God has willed. One must believe in the Balance: deeds are weighed in it by God's power, and it will weigh on that Day the weight of motes and mustard seeds. One must believe that the Bridge is a reality, a bridge stretched over Hell, sharper than a sword and finer than a hair. The feet of the infidels slip on it, by God's decree, and they fall into the fire of Hell. The feet of the faithful stand firm on it by God's grace, and so they pass over to the Everlasting Abode. And one must believe in the Pool, the Pool of the Prophet. The faithful shall drink from it after passing the Bridge and before entering Paradise. Whoever drinks one draught from it will never thirst again. It is wide as the journey of a month; its water is whiter than milk and sweeter than honey. Around it are pitchers like the stars of heaven in number and into it flow two channels from the Fountain of al-Kawthar. And one must believe in the Reckoning and the distinctions made between people in it: those with whom it will go hard in the Reckoning, those to whom compassion will be shown, and those who will enter Paradise without any reckoning. And one must believe that those who held faith in God's unity will be brought out of Hellfire, after their due punishment.

One must believe in the intercession of the prophets, then of the *'ulamā'*, then of the martyrs, then of the faithful, each according to their rank and station with God. One of the faithful who remains and has no intercessor will be brought forth by the grace of God. Thus not a single one of the faithful will abide eternally in the fire of Hell. One who has in one's heart the weight of a single grain of faith will be brought out of it.[11]

Ibn Taymīya

The Ḥanbalīs had for the most part remained outside the synthesis forged by al-Ghazālī and his followers. Taqī al-Dīn Ibn Taymīya of Damascus (d. 1328/A.H. 728), was a member of a Ḥanbalī family, educated in his father's Ḥanbalī madrasa, who became embroiled in such vigorous disputes with the religious establishment of his day that his sojourns in prison were guaranteed. The Mamlūk sultanate was a military dictatorship, regarded as necessary in the face of the Mongol threat from Iraq and Iran. It maintained the puppet 'Abbāsī caliphate in power in Cairo and relied on the assistance of the 'ulamā' *for its legitimacy. It therefore gave the* 'ulamā' *wide discretion in the religious domain, and they felt threatened by Ibn Taymīya. He was hostile to Ash'arism and* kalām *and any sort of innovation. Although like many fundamentalists he was a Ṣūfī and believed in the possibility of a personal relationship with God, he was hostile to the cult of saints, the cult of the Prophet, the idea of intercession, antinomianism, and Ṣūfī pantheism, and he preached* jihāds *against Christians and Shī'īs. In this period after the destruction of Baghdad, when most* 'ulamā' *believed that* Ijtihād *or independent interpretation of the Law was no longer possible or necessary, he insisted on the fundamentalist's right to return to the sources of Qur'ān and* Ḥadīth *and make fresh judgments, and he was regarded by his following as a* mujtahid *or interpreter. He spent years in the prisons of Damascus, Cairo, and Alexandria, but it did not stop him from turning out more works attacking and refuting all those with whom he disagreed.*

Ibn Taymīya is the Islamic Martin Luther, unafraid to say that the doctrine of ijmā' *or consensus—that when the Community "joins together" on something it is always right—is wrong; willing to break with history, tradition, and religious authority to insist that anything that cannot be justified by Qur'ān or* Ḥadīth *has no place in Islam. He is undoubtedly a theologian, despite his attacks on theology, and we find in his work a genuine neo-Ḥanbalī* kalām. *Along with al-Ghazālī, he is a theologian of decisive importance in Islam.*

Religion and princes must join hands, Ibn Taymīya holds: Islam requires the state's coercive power to implement the Law, and whatever government rules Islamically is the Prophet's successor. Hence there is place for several contemporary caliphs in Islam.

He died in the citadel of Damascus—according to tradition due to frustration because he had been deprived of paper, pens, and ink to keep writing—and he was buried in the Cemetery of the Ṣūfīs in a funeral attended by great numbers of people. Ironically, a cult promptly grew up around his tomb and is still flourishing.

Although he was attacked, ignored, and regarded as a crackpot by many in his own time, his memory was kept alive by the Ḥanbalīs. In 1744, in the weakening Ottoman Empire, a Ḥanbalī scholar, Ibn 'Abd al-Wahhāb, made a pact with Muḥammad b. Su'ūd, prince of the oasis market-town of Dar'īya in Arabia, to create a theocracy where Ibn Taymīya's doctrines would be enforced. This was the beginning of the Wahhābī Sa'ūdī Arabian Kingdom, which was soon in rebellion against the "innovating" Ottomans. Sa'ūdī Arabia has been a source of backing for Ibn Taymīya's doctrines in the modern world, and today his doctrines are the inspiration of many fundamentalist reformers and radical activists. The Muslim Brotherhood and Maududi of Pakistan are two conspicuous examples, but the influence of Ibn Taymīya's teaching has ranged quite extensively, because it gives Muslims intellectual justification for a radical break with the past, the rejection of "innovations," and a return to fundamentals.

Ijmā' [*Consensus*]

The Ṣūfīs have built their doctrine on desire [*irāda*], and it is indispensable, but on the condition that it is desire to serve God alone, in what He has commanded. The exponents of *kalām* have built their doctrine on reason conducing to knowledge, and it is also indispensable, on condition that it is knowledge of what the Messenger has informed us of, and reasoning about the sure things which he indicated: Divine Revelation. Both these conditions are indispensable [to right use of desire and knowledge].

Whoever seeks knowledge without desire or desire without knowledge is in error, and whoever seeks them both without following the Prophet is also in error. It is as some of the early Muslims said: religion and faith consist of speech, act, and following the *sunna*. One cannot dispense with knowledge of the One to be worshiped and how He is to be worshiped. Erring heathens, Christians, and suchlike have rites of religion and acts of asceticism, but for someone other than God, or by other than God's command. The goal and the desire may only be to serve God alone, and He may only be served by doing what He has laid down, without innovation. The religion of Islam turns on these two principles: worshiping God alone and worshiping Him by what He prescribed. He is not served by innovation.

As for the Qur'ān, it is independent of others, and its people have no need to look into other scriptures. Rather, it comprises all the good qualities that are in those scriptures and has many additional ones not found in them. For this reason it affirmed and protected what was before it in the way of scriptures, reinforcing the truth that was in them, annulling what had been altered in them, and abrogating what God abrogated.[12]

Many *mujtahids* early and late have held or practiced what was innovation, not knowing that it was so, because of weak *ḥadīths* they thought were sound, or understanding from a Qur'ānic verse what does not follow, or for some personal view held in ignorance of definitive texts on the matter.

What we mean here is that the Messenger of God has clearly shown all of religion in the Book and in his *sunna*. *Ijmāʿ* of the Community is a reality, and it cannot unite on error. Sound analogical reasoning is a reality as well, and it is based on the Book and the *sunna*.

The verse cited as a proof-text for *ijmāʿ* is Qur'ān 4:115: "But one who breaks with the Messenger after guidance has become clear, and follows other than the way of the Faithful, we shall consign to what he turned to, and roast in Hell: an evil homecoming."

[Possible exegeses of this are:] Blame attaches to those who break with the Messenger only, or those who follow another way than that of the faithful only, or else blame does not attach to one of these but to both, either because they are the same, or both although they are separate, or both because they are closely connected. The first two positions are false, because if only one of the two actions is affected, there would be no point in mentioning the other. It is quite untenable that blame should not attach to one of the two actions. Breaking with the Messenger clearly entails the divine threat, apart from anything else. Attaching blame to both actions but treating them as separate is not indicated by the verse: it concerns both together. There remains the last position, that all those thus described incur the divine threat, because they are closely connected, just as the like is said of those who rebel against God and His messenger.

It is similar with those who part with the Prophet and follow a way other than that of the faithful. Whoever parts with him is not following their way: that is obvious. Those who follow another way than the way of the faithful have broken with him and exposed themselves to the divine threat. Those who depart from their consensus have followed another way absolutely and exposed themselves to the divine threat. If anyone says they are only blamed because they broke with the Messenger, we reply, "Yes, because the two acts are intimately connected, for the reason that whatever the Muslims join together on must be based on texts from the Messenger of God."

Hence whoever opposes them has opposed the Messenger also, and whoever opposes him opposes God. It necessarily follows that everything on which they join together should have been demonstrated by the Messenger; that is the correct conclusion.

There is absolutely no question on which they are joined together that has not been thus demonstrated. That has escaped some people, who know what the *ijmāʿ* or consensus is, and they try to use it as a proof, just as one would use a text. However, *ijmāʿ* is a second proof, to be added to the text, like an example. Whatever it indicates has also been indicated by the Book and the *sunna.* All that the Qur'ān indicates has come by way of the Messenger, since both the Qur'an and the *sunna* came through him, so there cannot be any question on which *ijmāʿ* has occurred, unless it was based on a text.

Many *'ulamā'* have not known the texts and still have concurred with the Collectivity, just as they have used logic on a matter where consensus had occurred and still agreed with the consensus.

Any modern person who says that *ijmāʿ* is the basis for the greater part of the Law has given himself away, for it is lack of knowledge of the Book and the *sunna* that drives him to say it. Similarly when one says that most new events require use of logical analogy, because there is no indication in the texts: that is only the statement of one who has no knowledge of the Book and the *sunna* with their clear rules for making judgments.

It is often, or even usually, impossible to know what is consensus, for who can encompass all the opinions of all the interpreters of the Law? It is quite the contrary with the texts, for knowledge of these is possible, and easy by comparison.

The *sunna* cannot abrogate the Book. If there is anything abrogated in the Qur'ān, then the abrogation is written there, since nothing can take precedence over it. If one does not find something in the Book, one may look in the *sunna,* and nothing can abrogate a *ḥadīth* except another *ḥadīth:* the *sunna* cannot be abrogated by "joining together" or anything else, for the *ijmāʿ* cannot contradict the Book or the *sunna.*[13]

Ḥisba

To order good and forbid wrong is not obligatory on every individual in its essence, but is to be carried out as far as possible. Since the *jihād* is its completion, it is exactly like *jihād*. If it is not performed by those whose duty it is, then there is fault in those who are able, for it is a collective duty. Yet each must act according to ability, as the Prophet said: "Whoever sees something rejected by God, let them change it with their own hand, and if it is impossible, with their tongue, and if they are unable to do that, then in their heart, though that is the weakest of faith."

This being so, it is known that ordering good and forbidding wrong, together with its completion, *jihād*, is one of the most important things we are commanded to perform.[14]

The Necessity of the Legal Punishments [Ḥudūd]

It is not permissible when guilt has been established by proof or by witness to suspend the legal punishment, whether by remitting it or by substituting a fine or any other thing: the hand of a thief must be cut off, for the application of the punishments is one of the acts of religion, like the *jihād* in the Way of God. It must be kept in mind that the application of legal sanctions is one of the acts of God's mercy. Thus the ruler must be strict in applying it and let no compassion deter or delay him in the observance of God's religion. Let his goal be to have mercy on God's creatures by deterring people from things rejected by God, and not to discharge his anger or gratify a desire for power.[15]

On Pantheist Ṣūfīs

God, praise be to Him, is not His creation, not a part of His creation, nor an attribute of it. He is the Praised and Exalted, set apart in His holy existence, aloof in His glorious Selfhood from all the things that He has created. That is what the four divine books of the prophets have brought, the Torah, the Gospel, the Psalms, and the Qur'ān, and thus God has created His servants, and thus reason attests.

I have often thought that the appearance of such people as these Ṣūfīs is the main cause for the appearance of the Mongols and the disappearance of the Law of Islam, and that they are the vanguard of the one-eyed Antichrist, the great liar who will declare that he is God.[16]

Ibn Taymīya clearly states that the goal of human life is not to know God, as philosophy or theology derived from the Greeks might say, nor to love Him, as the Ṣūfīs would hold: it is to serve Him, individually and communally. Hence al-Ghazālī, as an Ash'arī theologian, is no better than the philosophers whom he condemned. The goal of the Islamic state is no more nor less than the worship/service of God.

Philosophers and al-Ghazālī

The self-styled philosophers opine that worldly delights are of three sorts: sensual, imaginative, and intellectual. The true delight is intellectual, which is knowledge. Thus they came to make knowledge a goal in itself, erring on several points, among which is that the goal cannot be knowledge itself, but that which is known. Because of this they have held that the happiness of the soul consists in the knowledge of eternal things. Then they imagine that the heavenly spheres, their intellects, and the spirits are eternal, and that through knowing them happiness reaches the soul.

Al-Ghazālī in his works like the *Mi'rāj al-Sālikīn* also indicates this. His statements are an intermediary stage between the doctrines of Muslims and philosophers: in them philosophy is mingled with Islam, and Islam mingled with philosophy. Hence in his books like the *Iḥyā' 'Ulūm al-Dīn* he makes the goal of all action only knowledge. This is also the essence of the doctrine of the philosophers. He greatly magnifies renunciation of the world and is more proccupied with it than with *tawḥīd,* which God's messengers brought and which is the service of God alone, Who has no peer, abandoning the service of any instead of Him. Such *tawḥīd* comprises loving God alone and absolutely abandoning the love of created things unless God loves them too.

The self-styled philosophers magnify separating the soul form "the material," which means renunciation of physical desires and of the world. But this only leads to an emptiness of the soul which Satan then fills, causing them to imagine that this is knowledge of hidden things and essences, whose end is "absolute being": a purely mental construction devoid of real existence.

In this way, al-Ghazālī has divided the path to God into three stages, like stages of the way to Mecca, with elaborate comparisons. One who does not understand his real purpose will be awed by such statements, for their author speaks as from full experience and knowledge, not like one who follows another's authority. The question, however, is whether what he says is right. What he has made the goal of human life, the knowledge of God, His attributes, His actions, and of angels, in his *al-Maḍnūn*—which is pure philosophy—is worse than the beliefs of the idolatrous Arabs, let alone of Jews and Christians.[17]

VI
SECTARIAN MOVEMENTS

About 86 percent of the world's Muslims are Sunnīs, those who believe that the majority of the Community has been rightly guided. The selections offered up to here have been virtually all from Sunnī sources. However, there are also groups who believe the majority has been fallible and can go wrong and that infallibility has to be sought elsewhere. At times they have regarded the Sunnī majority as infidels, and this has put them outside the main Community, on the basis of the ḥadīth: *"When any Muslim says to another 'You infidel!' one of the two deserves that name."*

The divisions of the Community all began as political, although they have with time become sectarian and theological. Most of them center around the position and actions of 'Alī, the Prophet's first cousin, husband of his daughter Fāṭima, and father of his only two surviving grandsons, Ḥasan and Ḥusayn.

It is generally conceded that on the way home from his last or "Farewell" Pilgrimage the Prophet made a pronouncement about 'Alī. Many Sunnī Ḥadīth *collections do not include this, because they find it controversial and embarrassing. Sunnīs who deal with it say that the Prophet was only showing his affection for a not too popular son-in-law. The Shī'a, or Partisans of 'Alī believe however that it was Muḥammad's appointment of his successor. The particular* ḥadīth *here included is taken from the important seventeenth-century Twelver Shī'ī source, Majlisī's* Biḥār al-Anwār.

The Ḥadīth *of the Ghadīr of Khumm*

Ḥamūya b. 'Alī, from Muḥammad b. Muḥammad b. Bakr, from al-Faḍl b. Ḥubāb, from Makkī b. Mardak al-Ahwazī, from 'Alī b. Baḥr, from

Ḥātim b. Ismāʿīl, from Jaʿfar b. Muḥammad [sixth Imam of the Twelvers], from his father Muḥammad b. ʿAlī b. Ḥusayn b. ʿAlī [fifth Imam], from Jābir b. ʿAbdallāh: When the Messenger of God had completed the rites of the Ḥajj and made ʿAlī his partner in the sacrifice after, they set out together with many of the Muslims in the caravan until they came to the place known as the Ghadīr or Deceiver [because it was a salty pool unfit to drink] of Khumm. Because of the lack of water and pasturage there, it was not a convenient place for a caravan-stop. However, he halted there, and the Muslims halted with him. The reason he halted was that verses of the Qur'ān were revealed to him concerning ʿAlī b. Abī Ṭālib as his Successor in the Community. This revelation had come to him earlier without an instruction to publish it immediately, and he had postponed it until a time when he would be secure from opposition to it from his followers. After passing the Ghadīr, many of the people would split off to go to their homelands and dwellings. Now he received the revelation, "O Messenger, make known what has been sent down to you from your Lord, for if you do not, you will not have delivered His message. God will preserve you from the people; God guides not a faithless folk" [Qur'ān 5: 74].

Being ordered now to reveal the designation of ʿAlī as his successor and appoint him as the Imam, the Messenger of God dismounted, and the people dismounted around him. Since it was a day of intense heat, he ordered them to clear the area under some trees that were there and gather the camel saddles at that place. They were piled one upon the other, and then he told his herald to call the people to collective prayer. When they had gathered around him, he climbed up to the top of [the platform of] saddles and called ʿAlī, who climbed up to him and stood at his right. He then praised and lauded God and called to the people, "I have been called and am soon to answer; the time of my passing from among you is at hand; yet surely I leave among you such that, if you hold fast to it, you will never stray: the Book of God and my family, the People of my House, who will never be separated until both join me at the Pool of Paradise." Then he called to them at the top of his voice, "Am I not nearer to you than your own selves?" They answered, "O God, it is so!" Thereupon without any pause he said, raising ʿAlī's arms until the light skin of his armpits appeared, "Then if I was near to anyone, this ʿAlī is near them [*mawlāhu*]! O God, befriend those who befriend him, and oppose those who oppose him! Assist those who assist him, and forsake those who forsake him!"

He then came down, and, since the sun was at its height, they prayed two prostrations. The sun then began to decline, and his prayer-caller proclaimed the noon-prayer. He then sat in his tent and ordered 'Alī to sit in a tent next to him. Then he ordered the Muslims to visit 'Alī in groups, to congratulate him on his station and salute him as Commander of the Faithful. All of the men then did this. He then ordered his wives and the wives of the faithful there with him to visit 'Alī and salute him as Commander of the Faithful, and they did so. One of those most profuse in congratulations was 'Umar b. al-Khaṭṭāb, showing much pleasure in the occasion. One of the things he said was, "Bravo, bravo for you, 'Alī! You have become my master [*mawlāy*], and the master of every faithful man or woman!"[1]

Khārijīs and Ibāḍīs

As we have seen, 'Umar was instrumental in having Abū Bakr acclaimed successor of the Prophet, and Abū Bakr then appointed 'Umar as his own successor. At his death in the year 644 (A.H. 23), 'Umar appointed the six most prominent Companions of the Prophet still living to choose one of themselves as his successor. The choice soon narrowed to the Prophet's two sons-in-law, the aristocratic early convert 'Uthmān of the Clan of Umayya, married to two daughters of the Prophet in succession but without living issue from them, and 'Alī. 'Alī was known to be critical of many arrangements 'Umar and Abū Bakr had made in the growing Arab empire and would not promise to perpetuate these, while 'Uthman offered to do so and was chosen as the next caliph.

'Uthmān was personally pious, but was felt to be too partial to his clan, the very family which had led opposition to the Prophet until it seemed more profitable to join him. When they behaved corruptly as his appointees, he refused to correct them. Discontent grew until the twelfth year of his reign, when there was a mutiny in the army. Blockaded in his mansion, 'Uthmān refused to abdicate. At last murderers, including a son of Abū Bakr, burst into the house and killed him. The Companions of the Prophet then in Madīna, including Ṭalḥa and Zubayr, who had been electors of 'Uthmān, persuaded 'Alī that only he could save the day by becoming caliph. Zubayr and Ṭalḥa then seem to have been persuaded by their kinswoman 'Ā'isha, daughter of Abū Bakr, to accuse 'Alī of an illegal election and to fight him. The result was the Battle of the Camel near Baṣra in Iraq, the first pitched battle between Muslims, so-called for the camel 'Ā'isha rode on, crying en-

couragement to her side. Ṭalḥa and Zubayr were killed, while ʿĀʾisha was sent home honorably to Madīna.

The governor of Syria, ʿUthmān's cousin Muʿāwiya, brother of the Prophet's wife Umm Ḥabība, then claimed vengeance for ʿUthmān's death and made war on ʿAlī, who had moved his capital to Kūfa in Iraq. Muʿāwiya was a diplomat of considerable skill, who now maneuvered ʿAlī into a situation where he accepted arbitration in order to avoid further bloodshed among Muslims. At this, many of ʿAlī's supporters deserted his camp, on the grounds that ʿUthmān had deserved death and that ʿAlī had committed apostasy by accepting arbitration with Muʿāwiya, who was clearly in the wrong. The position of these deserters, or Khārijīs, was that anyone committing a major sin rejects Islam and is outside the protection of the Muslim Community. This led to fighting between ʿAlī's supporters and the Khārijīs. In the end a Khārijī murdered ʿAlī in revenge, and Muʿāwiya founded the Umawī dynasty, which ruled the Muslim empire until 750.

The Khārijīs thus formed a third party in Islam, neither Shīʿī nor Sunnī. They found followers in South Arabia and among Arab tribes, but it was in North Africa among the Berber tribes that these Muslim Puritans found their Scotland. From the first, they were people who could not compromise, and they soon split into quarrelling sects, which often felt called upon to "trade their lives for Paradise," in religious wars. The only one of these to survive into modern times is the most moderate, the Ibāḍī sect, which can accept a situation of truce with other Muslims. Today they survive in the Sultanate of Oman and small enclaves in North Africa and on the East African coast. They prefer not to be called Khārijīs and live in the state of kitmān or concealment (i.e., they have no Imam to rule them now and take direction from their religious leaders). This is permissible in their sect unless the conditions are ripe for an Imamate, at which point kitmān is no longer acceptable. There are probably no more than a million Ibāḍīs in the world today. They look upon other Muslims as unfaithful to the true religion, but not as apostates whose blood must be shed, and cooperate with them in many ways. Unlike some Khārijī sects, they did not hold that hijra, or moving away from other Muslims they could not dominate, was a religious necessity. The Ibāḍīs were among the first Muslim sects to produce theologians, have a distinctive school of Law and have fostered literacy and scholarship among their adherents. They were known for their fair and generous treatment of People of the Book, Jews and Christians, under their protection. They are *also known as industrious and honest traders, who are fiercely independent.*

The following selections are the Friday sermons of an Ibāḍī rebel who in 747 briefly took Mecca and Madīna from the Umawī dynasty on behalf of an Ibāḍī Imam in the Yemen. They have been preserved in collections of early Arabic rhetoric and were admired for their eloquence and moral fervor. In them one finds the Khārijī view of early Muslim history and what had gone awry in the Muslim Community, as well as their religious hatred of their opponents.

The Sermons of Abū Ḥamza the Khārijī

Al-Ṭabarī the Historian, from his authorities: Abū Ḥamza the Khārijī entered Madīna in the year 130 [747 C.E.]. He mounted the minbar of the Mosque of the Prophet and preached as follows:

People of Madīna, we have asked you about these rulers of yours, and, as God lives, what you had to say of them was bad. We asked you, "Did they put people to death on suspicion?" You told us, "Yes." We asked you, "Did they take as lawful wealth and women forbidden to them?" You answered, "Yes." So we said to you, "Come, let us go together and ask them in God's name to turn away from you and from us." You said, "They will not do it." We said, "Then come, let us go and fight them together, and if we prevail, we shall bring you rulers who will establish the Book of God among us and the practice of His prophet Muḥammad, God's blessing and peace be upon him." You said, "We are not strong." So we told you, "Then leave us and them to ourselves. If we are victorious, we shall judge you fairly, relying with you on the practice of our Prophet, and divide the revenue of properties taken in conquest fairly with you." Yet you refused, and fought us without them [at the Battle of Qudayd]. May God keep you from good and from prosperity! [2]

Mālik b. Anas the Jurist said: Abū Ḥamza preached us a sermon that would have thrown doubt into the most perceptive and refuted a skeptic. He said:

I counsel you in fear of God and obedience to Him; to act according to His Book and the *sunna* of His Prophet, to observe the ties of kinship, and to magnify the truth which tyrants have diminished, and to diminish the falsehood that they have magnified, to put to death the injustice they have brought to life, and to revivify the just laws they have let die:

to obey God. Those who obey Him disobey others in obedience to Him, for there is no obedience to a creature who disobeys its Creator.

We call you to the Book of God and the *sunna* of His prophet, to equal sharing, to justice for the subject peoples, and to putting the fifths of the booty of battle where God ordained.

We did not become Khārijīs lightly or frivolously, in license or for play, or to overthrow the empire wishing to immerse ourselves in government, or in revenge for what had been taken from us. We did it when we saw that the earth had been darkened and the markers of tyranny had appeared, and propagandists in religion increased, but people did as they pleased, laws were neglected, the just were slain, and the speaker for truth was treated violently.

Then we heard a herald, calling us to Truth and to the Straight Path. We answered the summoner of God; we came forward from scattered tribes, little people, the oppressed of the earth. And God received us and aided us by His succor, so that by His grace we became brothers and assistants of religion.

O people of Madīna, your beginning was the best of beginnings, and your end is the worst of endings, for you hearkened to your readers and your lawyers, and they severed you from the Book that has no crookedness with the exegesis of ignorant people and the pretension of triflers, so that you became strayers from the Truth, dead, not alive, and unfeeling.

O people of Madīna, children of the *Muhājirīn* and the *Anṣār* and those who followed them in goodness! How sound were your roots, and how rotten are your branches! Your forefathers were people of certainty and knowledge in religion, with minds effective and hearts aware, but you are people of error and ignorance. God opened the door of religion for you, and you corrupted it; He closed the door of this world for you, and you forced it open; hasters to temptation and laggards in the *sunna* of the Prophet; blind to demonstrations of truth and deaf to religious knowledge; slaves of greed and allies of affliction!

How excellent was the legacy your forefathers left you, had you preserved it, and how miserable will be that of your children, if you cling to it! Them God aided to the Truth; you He abandons to vanity. They were few and pious; you are many and pernicious. The preachers of the Qur'ān chide you, and you are not abashed; they warn you, and you do not ponder! [3]

People of Madīna, it has reached me that you belittle my comrades. You say they are callow young men, barefoot Bedouins. What were the followers of the Messenger of God, God bless him and give him peace, but callow young men? Youths, by God, who were fully mature in their youth: youths whose eyes were closed to evil and whose feet were slow to approach wrongdoing, trading God the life that dies for the life that dies not. They mingled all they had with their fatigue and rose at night to watch and pray, after fasting all the day. They bent their backs over portions of the Qur'ān, and so oft as they came upon a verse of fear, they were racked with terror of the Fire, and when they came upon a verse of desire, they were racked with longing for Paradise. When they looked to swords drawn against them, lances pointed at them, arrows notched for them, when a detachment of cavalry thundered at them with bolts of death, they made little acount of the threat of that detachment beside the threat of God. They did not take God's threat lightly in the threat of a detachment; so blessed were they, and fair the place where they returned! And how many an eye which had overflowed long in the depth of night from fear of God met the beak of a bird! How many a hand left its wrist whereon its owner had supported himself long in prostration to God! How many an excellent cheek and fine forehead was cleft by maces of iron! God have mercy on those bodies and make their souls to enter His gardens! I have said my say, and I ask God to forgive our deficiencies, for there is no success for me but in God; in Him have I put my trust, and unto Him I shall repair.[4]

Abū Ḥamza entered Mecca. He was one of the Khārijī pietists and preachers, and his name was Yaḥyā b. Mukhtār. He went up into the pulpit there and supported himself on his Arab bow. He praised and lauded God, and said:

O people, the blessing of God and peace be upon our Prophet, who neither delayed nor hastened save by God's leave, command, and revelation. God sent down on him a book, revealing to him in it what is to come and what is to be feared, and there was no doubt about His religion, no ambiguity about His command. Then God took him after he had taught the Muslims the waymarks of their religion and entrusted Abū Bakr with their prayers. The Muslims entrusted Abū Bakr with the rule of their world, since the Messenger of God had entrusted him with the matter of their religion. He fought the people of apostasy and acted in accord with the Book and the *sunna,* and he passed his way: God have mercy on him!

Then 'Umar b. al-Khaṭṭāb ruled, and he walked in the path of his friend and acted in accord with the Book and the *sunna*. He collected the tribute of the conquests and distributed the Muslims' allowances, gathered the people in the month of Ramaḍān, gave eighty lashes for drinking wine, and raided the enemy in their homelands. Then he passed his way: God have mercy on him!

Then 'Uthmān b. 'Affān ruled. For six years he followed the way of his two friends, but he was less than they. In his last six years he rendered to no avail what he had done in the first six, and then he passed his way.

Then 'Alī b. Abī Ṭālib ruled. He did not attain the goal in truth, and no beacon was raised for his guidance, and he passed his way.

Then ruled Mu'āwiya, son of Abū Sufyān, cursed by God's messenger and son of one accursed. He made gardeners of God's servants, possessions of God's property, and a briar patch of God's religion, so curse him with God's curse!

Then Yazīd b. Mu'āwiya ruled: Yazīd of the wines, Yazīd of the apes, Yazīd of the hunting-panthers! He of the sinful belly and the effeminate arse, and God and his angels curse him!

One by one he spoke of the caliphs, but when he came to 'Umar, the righteous son of 'Abd al-'Azīz, he passed over him without mentioning him. He went on:

Then Yazīd, the son of 'Abd al-Malik, ruled, a libertine in religion and unmanly in behavior, in whom was never perceived right guidance. God has said about the property of orphans, "If you perceive right guidance in them, then deliver their property to them" [Qur'ān 4:6], and the rule of Muḥammad's Community was greater than a property! He would eat forbidden food and drink wine and wear a robe worth a thousand gold-pieces, through which you could see his flesh, so that the veil of modesty was torn: an unpardonable disrobe. With Ḥabāba the singing-girl on his right, and Sallāma the singing-girl on his left, and if you had taken drink from him, he would have rent his garments! He turned to one of them, and said, "Will I not fly? Will I not fly?" Aye, he flew: to God's damnation and burning fire and painful torment!

The Sons of Umayya [the ruling dynasty] are a party of error, and their strength is the strength of tyrants. They seize people on suspicion, judge by caprice, and put them to death in anger. They rule by mediation, take the Law out of its context, and give the *zakāt* money to those who are not entitled to it. God has made clear those who are entitled to it, and they are eight classes of people, for He says, "The freewill offerings are for the poor and the needy, for those who work to collect them, those whose hearts are to be reconciled, and slaves and debtors, and those on the way of God, and travelers" [Qur'ān 9:60]. They make themselves the ninth, and take it all! Such are a party ruling by other than God's revelation.

As for this Faction [*Shī'a:* of 'Alī], they are a faction which has repudiated the Book of God to promulgate lies about Him. They have not parted ways with people because of their penetrating insight into religion or their penetrating understanding of the Qur'ān. They punish crime in those who commit it and commit it themselves when they have the chance. Determined upon discord, they know not the way out of it. Crude in the Qur'ān, followers of soothsayers, teaching people to hope in the resurrection of the dead yet believing in the return [of the Imam] to this world, entrusting their religion to a man invisible to them! God smite them! How perverse they are![5]

From 777 to 909 C.E., the town of Tāhart in Algeria was the seat of an Ibāḍī Imamate in North Africa whose influence radiated to most Berber tribes and reached below the Sahara to black Africa. Today there are surviving Berber Ibāḍī communities in the oasis towns of the Mzāb in the Algerian Sahara, in the island of Jarba of Tunisia, and in the Jabal Nafūsa of western Libya.

The creed which follows was originally written in Berber (using the Arabic alphabet), probably in the ninth to tenth century, and was translated into Arabic by Ibn Jumay', a shaykh of the island of Jarba, who lived in the first half of the fourteenth century. It is still regarded by Ibāḍīs as an authoritative statement of their doctrine, and was recommended to me for this book by leading Ibāḍī scholars of the Sultanate of Oman in southeastern Arabia.

It seems originally to have been intended as a sort of catechism or compendium of the doctrine that people could memorize and bear in mind. Its convenient and comprehensive character still recommends it as it did in the fourteenth century, when Ibn Jumay' says that an important Ibāḍī personage asked him to translate it to Arabic for the convenience of Ibāḍīs who no longer read Berber. The source states that one may not hold that the Qur'ān is uncreated. Other Ibāḍī sources state that God does not predestine one's acts and their punishment.

Especially notable are the doctrines of "solidarity" and "avoidance" in this treatise.

The Doctrine of Monotheism
Translated by the Very Learned Shaykh 'Amr b. Jumay'

Praise be to God, who pitched the heavens without supports, who is without beginning or end or limit in His existence, Knower of all things visible and invisible, who decrees election to some and reprobation to others. He is the Living God; there is no divinity save He, so call upon Him in pure and sincere worship.

Praise be to God, Lord of the Universe!

I discovered this little work treating of the Unity of the Creator of All written in the Berber language. One whose word I cannot reject, and of whose virtue I am not ignorant, requested me to translate it into the Arabic language to clarify its expression and facilitate its memorization. I acceded to his request and hasten to present him with what he desired, hoping to perform a good deed, for in God is our assistance; in Him have I put my trust, for He is my sufficiency, and how good a support He is!

Should anyone ask you "What is the basis of the true faith?" tell them, "It is that there is no god but God alone, according to His Word, exalted be He: 'The true service of God is Commitment [Islam]' [Qur'ān 13:17], and Commitment is not complete without both word and act. Verbal profession is to confess that there is no god but God alone, without partner, without emulator, without rival, without peer, without resemblance, without similitude. It is to confess that Muḥammad is His servant and His messenger and that what he brought is a reality from his Lord. Active profession is to perform all the divine ordinances. Whoever undertakes these three precepts without diminishing any part of them has achieved monotheism in all that is between them and other creatures.

In that which is between one and God, one must observe ten precepts of faith, in: (1) all the angels (2) all the prophets and the messengers (3) all the scriptures which were revealed through them (4) death, (5) resurrection (6) the Day of Judgment (7) accountability (8) punishment (9) Paradise and Hellfire, and (10) that God is the Creator of all that has been, is, and shall be. Whoever has faith in these ten precepts without diminishing any part of them has achieved monotheism in what is between one and God, be He exalted, and other creatures. Whoever omits any one of them has committed polytheism [i.e., has ascribed a partner to God: the greatest sin]; one who doubts it is a polytheist; and one who doubts about the doubter is also a polytheist until the Day of Judgment.

If people bear faith in all these precepts, it is forbidden to shed their blood or take their possessions or enslave their children, because of their monotheism.

If anyone should ask you, "What are the bases of Commitment [Islam]?" say, "They are four: knowledge, practice, intention, and fear of

God; its cornerstones are four: submission to God's command, contentment with His decree, trust in God, and delegation of all matters to His authority."

The bases of infidelity [*kufr*] are also four: ignorance, denial, arrogance, and envy; and its cornerstones are four as well: love of the world, intimidation, lust, and anger.

The arrows of Islam are eight: (l) [liturgical] prayer, (2) the poor-tax, (3) fasting, (4) Pilgrimage to Mecca, (5) Visitation of the Ka'ba, (6) *jihād,* (7) ordering the good, and (8) forbidding the reprehensible.

True religion [*dīn*] is perfected in three things: revelation, tradition, and sound view. From revelation are derived many prescriptions, for example, four: [liturgical] prayer, the poor-tax, the fast, and the Pilgrimage of those who are able. From tradition are derived many prescriptions, for example, four: purification after excretion, circumcision, night-prayer [*witr*], and stoning the adulterous. From sound opinion are derived many prescriptions, for example, four: the laws of absence [when one has disappeared so that it is not known if one is dead or living], the Imamate, the penalty for fermented drinks [eighty lashes], and the inheritance-portion of the grandfathers and grandmothers [one-sixth].

Three groups emerge in religion: the committed Muslim, professing the truth and performing what one professes; the hypocrite, professing but betraying what one professes; and the polytheist, who rejects the truth.

Three things safeguard our religion: (1) solidarity with the faithful [*walāya*] (2) avoidance [*barā'a*] of those of whom evil is known, and 3) quitting sin altogether; or as some say, suspending judgment of unknown persons until they are known.

The bulwarks of our religion are three: knowledge of that which is not permissible for humankind to ignore for the blink of an eye, that is, monotheism; performance of that which is not permissible for humankind to ignore, that is, all the religious obligations; and abandoning what is not permissible for humankind to do, that is, all sins.

The paths of our religion are four: Manifestation [of the Imamate]; defense [under an Imam of defense given supreme power]; purchase [of Paradise, in fighting to the death], and secrecy [outward conformity with the existing order]. Manifestation is the way of Abū Bakr and 'Umar, defense is the way of 'Abdallāh b. Wahb al-Rāsibī, purchase is the way of Abū Bilāl Mirdās b. Judayr, and secrecy is the way of Abū 'Ubayda Muslim b. Abī Karīma and Abū al-Sha'tha Jābir b. Zayd, may God be pleased with all of them.

Six obligations become incumbent on a child of Adam with six others: (l) legal responsibility along with puberty. (2) ordering the good with forbidding the reprehensible (3) knowing God with knowing His messenger (4) acknowledging God's goodness with the proofs for His existence (5) fear of God with hope for mercy, and (6) solidarity with true believers with enmity to enemies.

We worship God Most High with twenty prayers, of which eight are legal obligations and twelve are traditional obligations. The legal obligations are (1–5) the daily prayers (6), the night prayer [*witr*] (7) the Friday prayer, and (8) the Pilgrimage prayer, for those able to make the Great Pilgrimage. The traditional obligations are (9–10) two prostrations before the dawn-prayer (11–12) the prayers of the Two Feast Days [Fast-breaking and Sacrifice], (13) funeral prayers, (14) prayers of the nights of Ramaḍān, (15) the prayer of the lunar eclipse, (16) the prayer of the solar eclipse, (17) the prayer on the occasion of an earthquake, (18) the prayer at the Station of Abraham [in Mecca], upon him be peace (19) thc prostration [on special occasions], and (20) benediction of the Prophet, which is a request for divine mercy.

Humankind are of three categories: the committed Muslim, the hypocrite, and the polytheist. Solidarity has four aspects, or some say seven: solidarity with all committed Muslims, whether we know them or do not; living, dead, humankind and jinn; solidarity with these preserved from sin, whom God has mentioned in His Book and praised, assuring them of Paradise. We are obligated to solidarity with these and testify that they are in Paradise. They are ten men and ten women. The men are (1) the prophets (2) the messengers (3) the priests (4) the monks (5) the Seven Sleepers (6) the Martyrs of Najrān (7) the people warned by Jonah (8) the Sorcerers of Pharaoh [converted by Moses and Aaron] (9) Ḥabīb the Carpenter [believed to be a martyr of Antioch] and (10) the believer from the family of Pharaoh. The women are (1) our mother Eve, (2) Sarah, wife of Abraham, (3) Raḥma wife of Job, (4) Āsiya, wife of Pharaoh (5) Qinna, the hairdresser of Pharaoh's daughter (6) Ḥinna [Elizabeth, wife of Zachariah], (7) Minna [Anna, mother of Mary], (8) Zulaykhā, wife of Joseph on whom be peace, (9) Mary, daughter of 'Imrān [mother of Jesus] and (10) 'Ā'isha, Mother of the Believers [the wife of Muḥammad], God be pleased with all of them.

Solidarity in itself consists of affection of the heart and praise of the tongue. Should anyone ask, "By what is it made due?" answer, "By righteous deeds." By whom? "By those of good appearance, and is due only for those of whom good is known, who are deserving of it." Should any ask, "Who is rewarded for it?" say, "The one who gives it to the aforementioned." It is also said, "To both parties." Whoever gives solidarity to one not due it commits infidelity; whoever delays it when it is due commits infidelity.

The opposite of solidarity is avoidance [*barā'a*], and the opposite of avoidance is solidarity. Once solidarity is due, it does not cease except for avoidance. Once avoidance is due, it does not cease except for solidarity. We must also exercise solidarity with ourselves, by repentance and shunning sins [*dhunūb*].

Solidarity is due to Muslims who fulfill their religion. God's solidarity with His servants is His knowledge of them, their return to Him, and the stations they will occupy in Paradise. The solidarity of His servants with Him is their acceptance of His commands.

Solidarity with individuals is due under four conditions: (1) the ear accepts what it hears (2) the eye accepts what it sees (3) the heart agrees with both and (4) the religious law is followed. Whoever does not give it after these conditions are fulfilled commits the infidelity of hypocrisy.

Solidarity of the heart [*bayḍa*] is due to a just sovereign. Solidarity is due from us to his secretary, his minister, his treasurer and all Muslims under his banners.

It is said that it is due to all who turn from polytheism to Islam and from dissidence to correct behavior if they are pious in their service of God. It is due to the children of the Muslims; as for the children of polytheists and hypocrites, one should suspend judgment. As to the children of the slaves of the Muslims, there are two opinions.

Avoidance has four categories or, according to others, six: exemption toward all infidels, whether we know them or not, living or dead, humankind or jinn. (1) Avoidance of the people of the divine threat, whom God has mentioned in His Book and assigned to Hellfire. It is obligatory for us to regard them as exempt from our concern and recognize that they are going to Hell. The people of the divine threat are Hāman, Qārūn [Korah], Pharaoh, Nimrod, the wife of Noah, and the wife of Lot. (2) Avoidance of all whom we see commit evil. It is obligatory for us to hold them in avoidance and act accordingly. (3) Avoidance of the unjust sovereign, his secretary, his minister, and his treasurer, but not all those under his banners, for they may include some Muslims who act from fear for their lives. (4) Avoidance of all those who turn from Islam to polytheism, or from correct behavior to dissidence.

Whoever knows the six religious groupings and does not know the rules for them is as one who does not know them at all. They are those whom God has mentioned in His Book. He says, Lord is He who speaks, "The faithful, and those of Jewry, the Ṣābi'ans, the Christians, the Zoroastrians, and the polytheists: God will judge between them on the Day of Judgment" [Qur'ān 22:17]. As for the faithful, the poor-tax is taken from their wealth and given to the poor among them. If some of them are rebels, they are called upon to renounce the error leading them from the right way. If they reject it, they are left in peace; if they do not, their blood may be spilled, and the Community is absolved of responsibility for them. If a group of [true] Muslims prevail over them and they flee to a refuge where they may regroup, the fugitives may be pursued and the wounded be put to death. If they have no place of refuge where they may regroup, their fugitives are not pursued and their wounded not put to death. As for the weapons of the rebels, they may be given back to them. It is said they may be buried or they may be sold and the price given to the poor among those who had to fight them. They are to be treated with avoidance, because of their rebellion.

As to the People of Scriptures [Jews, Christians, and Ṣābi'ans]; they are summoned to monotheism. If they comply, then they are due all that is due to Muslims. If they do not, they are asked to pay tribute in constraint and humiliation. If they submit and pay it, it becomes illegal to shed their blood, take their property, or enslave their children. Muslims are allowed to eat the animals they slaughter and marry the free women among them. If they do not submit and pay tribute, their blood, their property, and the enslaving of their children are lawful, and the eating of the animals they slaughter and marriage with their women is forbidden. [If they pay], each individual who has attained puberty and is of sound mind must pay ten *dirhams;* the Christians must pay an extra two *dirhams.*

The regulation for the Zoroastrians is: they are summoned to monotheism. If they comply, all that is due a Muslim is due to them. If they do not, then they are asked to pay tribute in constraint and humiliation. If they submit and pay, their blood, their property, and the enslaving of their children are forbidden to Muslims, but Muslims are forbidden to eat animals they slaughter or marry their free women whether they pay tribute or not.

As for idolators, they are fought, and nothing is acceptable from them but monotheism or death. Their blood, their property, and the enslaving of their children are lawful, except for those of the tribe of Quraysh, whom it is not permissible to enslave, due to their kinship with the Prophet, peace be upon him.

The number of books revealed by God to His prophets is one hundred and four; of these fifty were revealed to Seth, son of Adam, thirty to Enoch [*Idrīs*], ten to Abraham, and ten to Moses before the Torah. Four books were most precious: the Torah, to Moses; the Psalms, to David; the Good News, to Jesus; and the Qur'ān, to Muḥammad; may God bless him and all of them. The number of the prophets is one hundred and twenty four thousand, and the number of the messengers among them is three hundred and thirteen. The ones of universal jurisdiction among them were seven: Adam, Noah, Abraham, Moses, David, Jesus, and Muḥammad, God bless him and all of them. There were four Arab messengers: Hūd, Ṣāliḥ, Shu'ayb, and Muḥammad, God bless him and bless them all. Four were sent with the sword: David, Joshua, Moses, and Muḥammad, God bless him and all of them. Four of them have not yet died: Jesus and Enoch in heaven, and Khiḍr and Elijah on earth. Those with two names among the prophets are four: Jacob, who is Israel; Jesus, who is the Messiah; Jonah, who is Dhū al-Nūn [He of the Fish]; and Muḥammad, who is Aḥmad, God bless him and bless them all. Three were Syrians: Adam, Seth and Enoch; three were ancestors: Adam, Noah, and Abraham; the men of resolution among them were five, as the verse says:

Those of resolution are Noah and Abraham both,
And Moses and Jesus and the Prophet Muḥammad.

The Prophetic tradition has two aspects, that which the Prophet, peace be upon him, did but did not order us to do, which is supererogatory. Performance of it is a virtue, but failure to perform it entails no punishment. The second sort is that which he did and ordered us to do, which is religious obligation. Abandoning it entails infidelity, of two sorts: infidelity of hypocrisy and infidelity of polytheism. Polytheism is of two sorts: polytheism of negation and polytheism of association. There are two sorts of hypocrisy: the hypocrisy of treason and that of making lawful and unlawful what is not.

Faith is of two sorts: monotheism and nonmonotheism. Monotheism is of two sorts: profession and practice. It is not permissible to be ignorant of monotheism or to abandon it; it is not permissible to be ignorant of polytheism or to practice it.

Accomplishment of religious duties is of two sorts: with latitude and straitened: with latitude at the beginning of the time for it, and straitened at the end of the stipulated time.

In things ordered, there are two aspects: what has to do with monotheism and what does not.

It is said, "God befriends the Muslims, and they befriend Him." The meaning of "God befriends the Muslims" is that He has appointed great rewards for them, and that of "they befriend Him" is that they do what He has commanded them. One does not say that God befriends Himself or that He does not.

We must recognize that God's are all the angels, and we especially mean Gabriel. We feel solidarity with him and recognize that he was the messenger of the Lord of the Universe to Muḥammad, may God bless him and give him peace. He brought him the service of God and the Qur'ān and Islam. We feel solidarity with the angels and invoke God's mercy on them, but without asking Him to pardon them: we desire for them what is conformable to their nature. Some of the shaykhs opine that what conforms to their nature is to transmit guidance to the Muslims and punishments to the infidels. If one prays that God may give Paradise to the angels or that they will have Paradise as their reward one commits infidelity, and whoever says they are male or female is a polytheist. Can one say they are men? According to some, this is improper; according to others, it is permissible, since God says, "There will be a veil between them, and on the battlements will stand the *men* . . . who will call to the inhabitants of Paradise "Peace be upon you!" without having entered it themselves" [Qur'ān 7:46]. Some opine that these "men" are angels, yet others say they are those whose good works were exactly the sum of their bad deeds, or those who contracted debts without lavishness, or that they are people who went out to a *jihād* without their parents' consent.

We must recognize that God's are all the Muslims and feel solidarity with them. Yūnus b. Abī Zakarīya said, "We must recognise that each species is different from the other: the angels are one species, the jinn are another, and the Children of Adam still another. Whoever has not recognized that is a polytheist."

We must recognize that the prophets were all of humankind, descendants of Adam, on whom be peace. If anyone asks, "Must we believe that their religious laws were all the same or different?" the answer is: that is not for us to know.

If one says, "I do not know Adam," one is a polytheist. If one says, "It is not for me to know anything of him," let that one alone. If one says, "I do not know Muḥammad," one is a polytheist, and if one says, "It is not for me to know anything of him," then one commits infidelity and hypocrisy.

Adam was named Adam because he was made of dust of the earth; Eve was named Eve [inclination] because she was made of the crooked left rib of Adam.

It is recommended that we know of twenty-one angels. (1–4) four who visit the children of Adam during the day and the night (5–6) two who record the acts of Adam's children (7–14) eight who support the throne of God (15) Riḍwān, Keeper of Paradise (16) Mālik, Keeper of Hellfire (17) Gabriel (18) Michael (19) Israfel (20) Azrael (21) the Preserved Tablet and the angel of divine inspiration [*sic*] yet God knows best.

The sacred months are four; one of them stands alone, and three are consecutive. The isolated month is Rajab; the three consecutive are Dhū al-Qaʿda, Dhū al-Ḥijja, and Muḥarram.

The months of the period [for armistice with polytheists] are four: twenty-four days from Dhū al-Ḥijja, Muḥarram, Ṣafar, Rabīʿ I, and ten days of Rabīʿ II.

The months of the Pilgrimage are Shawwāl, Dhū al-Qaʿda, and ten days of Dhū al-Ḥijja. Some opine that it is twenty and others that it is all of the month.

The "known days" [mentioned in the Qur'ān] are the ten days before the Day of Sacrifice [10 Dhū al-Ḥijja]. The "counted days" are the three days after the Day of Sacrifice, and there is a difference of opinion about the day itself as to whether it is of the "known" or the "counted" days; some say one, others the other, while still others say it is both.

We must recognize grave sins, those that lead to the state of polytheism and those that lead to hypocrisy. One who lies to God is a hypocrite, while one who calls God a liar is a polytheist. A liar to God is one who says that God has sent a prophet He has not sent or revealed something He has not revealed. One who calls God a liar is one who says that God did not send a prophet whom He sent or denies one of the revelations He sent down by His prophets. Whoever denies one prophet or one letter of the scriptures is a polytheist, but one who doubts that person is a polytheist is not one, except in the cases of Adam and Muḥammad: ignorance of them is not permissible. One who does not recognize them is a polytheist. One who denies all the prophets is a polytheist, one who doubts that is a polytheist, and one who doubts about the doubter is one as well, to the Day of Judgment.

Not of us is one who says that the names of God are created.

Nor one who says that the Qur'ān is uncreated.

Nor one who says that all those who turn to Mecca in prayer are entitled to solidarity.

Nor one who says that Abū Bakr and ʿUmar were prophets.

Nor one who says two sovereigns may rule jointly.

Nor one who says that the obligation to emigrate for religion continued after the conquest of Mecca.

Nor one who says that it is permitted to take the property of all whose blood it is permitted to shed.

Nor one who asserts that knowledge of religion can be gained without learning.

Nor one who says the Imamate is not obligatory, if the conditions for instituting it are present.

Solidarity with Muslims is part of monotheism, and so is ordering it, practicing it, and legitimizing it. It is polytheism to deny it, consider it a mistake, or ignore it.

Truly an infidel is one who ignores the following five precepts: (1) recognize God the Adored; (2) be content with what one has; (3) institute Qur'ānic punishments; (4) be patient about what one does not have; (5) perform what one promises.[6]

Zaydī Shī'īs

The Shī'a of 'Alī received its greatest impetus from the violent death of his younger son, al-Ḥusayn. His elder brother, al-Ḥasan, had been proclaimed caliph in Kūfa after 'Alī's death by the Shī'a, but was persuaded by Mu'āwiya to give up his claim in return for a large pension and retirement in Madīna. He died in 660 after an illness, poisoned according to many sources by one of his wives. Most Shī'īs believe the murder was instigated by Mu'āwiya, rather than motivated by jealousy, as Sunnīs allege.

Headship of the family of 'Alī now passed to Ḥusayn, and when he refused to give allegiance to Mu'āwiya's son Yazīd in 680 the people of Kūfa offered to make him caliph. He crossed the desert from Madīna to Kūfa with his family, but in the meantime Yazīd's viceroy in Iraq found out about the plot and put patrols on all the approaches to the city from the direction of Madīna. Ḥusayn's caravan fell into the trap at Karbalā', about twenty five miles from Kūfa on the Euphrates. After ten days of being cut off from water and food, Ḥusayn still refused to give allegiance to Yazīd, and the little band was cut down to the last adult male. The day was the tenth ('Ashūra) of Muḥarram, a day of obligatory fasting in early Islam for the atonement of sins which originally seems to have coincided with the tenth of Tishri in the Jewish calendar, the Day of Atonement or Yom Kippur. It is still a day of voluntary fasting for pious Muslims. Ḥusayn's head was cut off and sent to Yazīd in Syria, who seems to have been genuinely shocked. Pious Muslims were horrified, and the martyrdom of Karbalā' served as a rallying point for everyone who distrusted the Umawī family.

The tale soon spread: Ḥusayn had died as a willing atonement for the sins of his grandfather's umma, *he is the Prince of Martyrs, and those who weep for him will be consoled. With moving and heartrending details, it is dramatized at 'Ashūra by Shī'īs. Sunnī dervishes also organize processions of mourning on the day. Ḥusayn's murderers are cursed, a special pudding is eaten to recall his last meal, and poems recalling his sufferings are recited.*

Although at first they were an Arab political faction, the Shī'īs soon came to differ doctrinally from the Sunnīs and to divide into sects following different leaders from the 'Alawīs (the family of 'Alī). Of the three divisions of the Shī'a, that of the Zaydīs most preserves its old Arab character and seems to form a bridge between Sunnīs and other Shī'īs. According to their doctrine there can be more than one Imam at the same time in widely separated areas if the welfare of the faithful demands it, and they founded states at various times in the Caspian region of Iran, northern Morocco, and the Yemenī highlands. They have survived in the Yemen until modern times. The following exposition is by a Zaydī scholar who was Imam in the Yemen, al-Mahdī lī-Dīn Allāh Aḥmad b. Yaḥyā b. al-Murtaḍā, who died in 1436 (A.H. 840).

On the Sects of the Shī'a

The Shī'īs fall into three divisions: the Zaydīs, the Imāmīs [Twelvers] and the Bāṭinīs [Seveners]. The Zaydīs trace their name to Zayd b. 'Alī b. Ḥusayn b. 'Alī, peace be upon him. Their school unites on giving preference to 'Alī, on his being most worthy of the Imamate, on restricting it to the two lineages [of Ḥasan and Ḥusayn], and on its being derived through merit and laying claim to it, not through inheritance, on the necessity of rebelling against tyrants, on professing the Unity and Justice of God [i.e., theologically they are Mu'tazila: Ed.], and on the divine threat. After that, however, they divide into the schools of the Jārūdīya and the Butrīya. The Jārūdīya trace their origin to Abū al-Jārūd Ziyād b. Munqidh al-'Abdī. They hold that 'Alī, peace be upon him, was designated as Imam by description though not explicitly, and call infidels all who hold otherwise. They accord the Imamate to one from the two lineages who lays claim to it and has religious knowledge and merit. Some have been said to hold that one may be Imam while in absence [*ghayba*], but it is not true.

As for the Butrīya and the followers of Ḥasan b. Ṣāliḥ, they went so far as to state that the Imamate comes through electors [*shūra*] and is made sound by contract, even when there is a better qualified candidate. They thus hold that the Two Shaykhs [Abū Bakr and 'Umar] were Imams, even though 'Alī, on whom be peace, was more worthy. They were called al-Butrīya [dock-tailed] because they left off pronouncing out loud the invocation "In the name of God" between two *sūra*s of the Qur'ān. It is also said that when Sulaymān b. Jarīr denied the designation of 'Alī, on whom be peace, Mughīra b. Sa'īd dubbed him Abtar [cut-tail]. They were opposed by others falling between these two sects, who held that 'Ali had received an absolute designation for the Imamate in secrecy. They held that the Shaykhs were in error for opposing him, but refused to take sides about calling them sinners and differed as to whether one should call them pleasing to God. Those among the pious forebears [*salaf*] who belonged to their Shī'a were Ḥasan b. Ṣāliḥ of Kūfa [d. 785/A.H. 168] and his brother 'Alī, both sons of Ṣāliḥ b. Ḥāyy, as well as Waqī' b. Yaḥyā b. Adam and al-Faḍl b. Dhukayn. Among the Mu'tazila were al-Iskāfī, Ibn al-Mu'tamar, and others. Among the jurists were Sulaymān b. Jarīr [mentioned above] and many sympathizers.

Later the Butrīya divided into the Qāsimīya and the Nāṣirīya and held each other to be in error until the [Imam] al-Mahdī Abu 'Abdallāh al-Dā'ī rose and silenced them by stating that every interpreter hits the target [*kull mujtahid muṣīb*]. Their Imams are well-known in the histories for their virtues and good conduct, and those who most took their part were the Mu'tazila.[7]

The Zaydī doctrine of the Imamate is notably different from that of the Twelvers and the Seveners, since they believe that the Imam is not infallible and can be deposed if he fails in rectitude. He must also be a mature interpreter of the Law, who rises to enforce his claim to the Imamate.

The Imamate

The Qāsimīya and the Shāfi'īs said that the Prophet did not designate any Imam to follow him, but the Zaydīs say that he did designate 'Alī, Ḥasan, and Ḥusayn. (*Text Commentary:* this is known from the well-known *ḥadīth* of the Ghadīr and from the *ḥadīth* "Ḥasan and Ḥusayn are both Imams whether standing or sitting, and their father is better than they are," related by scholars from acceptable authorities.) The Twelvers say he designated twelve Imams, the Bakrīya that he designated Abū Bakr. We say that both 'Alī's sons were worthy of acceptance as Imams, and no other families are acceptable.

We say the Imamate should go to the two lineages, because all agree that it is correct when they exercise it, and there is no indication for giving it to another. The Twelvers say it should go to the descendants of al-Ḥusayn, and the Ash'arīs say it should go to the Quraysh, because of the *ijmā'*, the joining together of the Companions on Abū Bakr. We say, there was no *ijmā'*.

We say the Imam after the Prophet was 'Alī, then Ḥasan, then Ḥusayn. The majority of the Muslims have said, no: first Abū Bakr, then 'Umar, then 'Uthmān, then 'Alī, by *ijmā'*. We say there was no *ijmā'* because 'Alī opposed it, and the position of the Bakrīya and Ḥasan of Baṣra that the Prophet had designated Abū Bakr as his successor is worthless, because Abū Bakr himself said, "Choose one of these two, 'Umar or Abū 'Ubayda."

The Mu'tazila and most of the Zaydīs say that there cannot legally be two Imams in the same place and time. The Karrāmīs and some Zaydīs say it is permissible. We adduce the united opinion of the Companions when the Madīnans said, "Let us have one commander and you have another."

Ṭalḥa, Zubayr, and 'Ā'isha were absolutely wrong to rebel against 'Alī, since he was the true Imam. Some have held that it is excusable. Our argument is that rebellion against the Imam is a serious transgression. Ibn Jarīr held that it was apostasy, but we say there is no indication for that.

Most hold that the decision of 'Alī to allow arbitration was not an error. The Khārijīs say it was apostasy. Some have held that 'Alī was forced. We say, it was a question of *ijtihād* [legal interpretation] and cannot be faulted.

Most hold that Ḥasan was not deposed as Imam by his agreement with Mu'āwiya. The Ḥashwīya say he was. We say that the Imamate cannot be invalidated except by wrongdoing of the Imam.

The Imam after Ḥusayn was Ḥasan b. Ḥasan, then Zayd b. 'Alī, then Yaḥyā b. Zayd, then Muḥammad b. 'Abdallāh al-Nafs al-Zakīya, and then all of the family who rose up and fulfilled the qualifications of the Imamate. This is counter to the position of the Imāmīs, who say the Imamate is conferred by designation from the previous Imam, and the Ḥashwīya, who say by the allegiance of the majority.

No one was impeccable after the Prophet [as the Twelvers assert that the twelve Imams were] except 'Alī, Ḥasan, Ḥusayn, and Fāṭima. Al-Jubbā'ī, following the Baṣra Mu'tazila, says that the ten close Companions of the Prophet were impeccable. I reply, one must give due regard to the statements of 'Alī that 'Uthmān had openly transgressed and the opinion of learned men that Ṭalḥa and Zubayr transgressed.[8]

The following excerpts are from one of the earliest Ḥisba *manuals to be preserved, written by the Zaydī Imam al-Nāṣir li'l-Ḥaqq, who ruled the Caspian area of Iran and died in 917 (A.H. 304). It contains a very early prohibition of pictures and dolls, which would be picked up by some Sunnī jurists much later, as well as a prohibition against building shrines over the graves of holy persons, of the sort later enforced by the Ḥanbalīs. The society it depicts would have been very puritanical by the Muslim standards of its time.*

An Early Zaydī Ḥisba *Manual*

The *muḥtasib* must give orders that the doors of mosques not be locked, or any pictures painted on them, and they may not be decorated with gold, be appointed like churches or synagogues, have curtains hung in them, or be decorated with stucco or the like. All that is objectionable. Minarets of mosques may be no higher than their roofs, and cresting raised above people's houses must be suppressed. It is related that the Commander of the Faithful, 'Alī—God's blessing be upon him and his family, and peace—said, "Minarets of a mosque shall not be raised above its walls."

The *muḥtasib* must forbid using burial places as mosques, according to the word of the Prophet, "God cursed the Jews for taking the tombs of their prophets as mosques." Ja'far b. Muḥammad relates from his ancestors, from 'Alī, peace be upon him, "If you see story-tellers [*qaṣṣāṣ*] in the mosques, then say good-bye to Islam."

No Jew, Christian, or Zoroastrian should enter a mosque, even if the governor is holding audience there. Menstruating women should not enter, and punishments should not be administered there. The *muḥtasib* should know the insignia of the People of the House of the Prophet, see to it that the people of his district perform their prayers, and say "There is no god but God" twice at the end of the call to prayer. They should say it once at the beginning of the prayer and leave off saying "Amen." They should add "Hasten to the best of works" to the prayer-call [all Shī'īs do this: Ed.] and once at the beginning of prayer. He should make them say "In the name of God the Merciful, the Compassionate" out loud, and forbid them the *masḥ 'alā al-khuffayn* [wiping the socks instead of washing the feet at ablutions, permitted by some schools: Ed.], and he should order them to say "God is greater" five times at funerals instead of four.

The *muḥtasib* must forbid carpenters and turners to make backgammon and chess sets and sets for "fourteen," as it is a game of chance. It is mentioned that the Commander of the Faithful 'Alī would say "Peace be upon you" to all who passed by him, even boys and Abyssinians wearing necklaces, but he would not greet anyone with a backgammon or chess set. He once passed some people playing chess and said, "What are these images to which you are applying yourselves?" He then ordered the chess set broken and burned the board on which they were playing.

He shall see to it that they do not make idols, images, or dolls for children and break whatever he finds of such things.

The people should not adopt hand-drums, pipes, lutes, tambourines, mandolins, timbals, or other musical instruments. Whatever he confiscates of this nature is to be broken. The makers shall be instructed in this, according to the instruction of the Prophet to 'Alī, peace be upon them and their family, "I send you as God sent me, to break flutes and lutes and to level heaped-up graves."

Similarly he shall order anything with pictures on it it such as glass or other things to be rubbed out—and if the pictures cannot be rubbed out without breaking them, then break them. Likewise with pictures on doors and garments: he shall cut off the heads of the pictures. In the same manner he shall break coins minted by foreigners with pictures on them. And he shall forbid men to mix with women in the streets.[9]

Twelver Shī'īs: Ithnā'asharīs

The Ithnā 'asharīya or Twelver Shī'a are the largest and best known of the Shī'ī sects which have survived. Like the Zaydīs, they follow the theology of the Mu'tazila. They believe that the Qur'ān is the created Word of God, and that since God is essentially good He cannot *do evil. He desires the welfare of humankind and has created it with free will so that it might know Him. Not only does He reveal the books of the prophets, but He sends an infallible guide in religious matters to interpret their true meaning. This guide is the Imam, divinely appointed from birth, whose identity is revealed to the previous Imam.*

*They also believe in the doctrines of occultation (*ghayba*) and return (*raj'a*). The Twelfth Imam was not murdered by his enemies, but, like the Qur'ānic Jesus, was taken by God from human sight and will re-*

turn with Jesus as the promised mahdī *(Guided One), to usher in the triumph of true Islam and the last days of Earth.*

In Law, they do not accept ḥadīths *transmitted by enemies of the Imams such as ʿĀʾisha, Abū Bakr, ʿUmar, and Muʿāwiya, but they do accept pronouncements of the Imams, who being sinless like the Prophet himself also give guidance about the Law. They admit the necessity of* taqīya, *permissible concealment of one's true beliefs when among nonbelievers, and retain the peculiar practice of* mutʿa, *temporary marriage for pleasure, which they assert that ʿUmar had no right to abolish since the Prophet considered it lawful. They hope for the intercession of descendants of the holy family of the Prophet left by him as a blessing to his Community and make pious visitations to their tombs.*

Following the disappearance of the Twelfth Imam in 874 (A.H. 260), they follow the teachings of the living Twelver mujtahids, *interpreters of the Law, who include the* ayatullāhs *of Iran. Writings from past interpreters must be reinterpreted in every generation.*

Shīʿīs were persecuted and forced to hide their sympathies except in the Zaydī enclaves in Morocco, the Yemen, and the Caspian during the first centuries of Islam, but when the ʿAbbāsī caliphate in Baghdad was under the control of the Shīʿī Persian dictators of the Būyī family from 945 to 1055, the Twelver doctrine could be openly elaborated. An important systematizer of this period was Ibn Babūya, Shaykh Ṣadūq, who died in 991 (A.H. 381). These selections on the Imamate are from his treatise on doctrine.

On the Prophets and the Imams

(35) Our belief is that there have been one hundred and twenty-four thousand prophets and a like number of plenipotentiaries (*awṣiyāʾ*). Each prophet had a plenipotentiary to whom he gave instructions by the command of God. Concerning the prophets we believe that they brought the truth from God and their word is the word of God, their command God's command, and obedience to them is obedience to God.

The leaders of the prophets are five, on whom all depends: Noah, Abraham, Moses, Jesus, and Muḥammad. Muḥammad is their leader; he confirmed all other messengers.

It is legally necessary to believe that God did not create anything more excellent than Muḥammad and the Imams. After His prophet, the proofs of God for the people are the Twelve Imams.

We believe that the Proof of God in his earth and His viceregent (*khalīfa*) among His slaves in this age of ours is the Upholder (*al-Qā'im*), The Expected One, Muḥammad ibn al-Ḥasan al-'Askarī, the Twelfth Imam. It is he concerning whose name and descent the Prophet was informed by God, and it is he who WILL FILL THE EARTH WITH JUSTICE AND EQUITY JUST AS IT IS NOW FULL OF OPPRESSION AND WRONG. It is he whom God will make victorious over the whole world until from every place the call to prayer is heard, and religion will belong entirely to God, exalted be He. He is the rightly guided *Mahdī* about whom the Prophet gave information that when he appears, Jesus Son of Mary will descend upon the earth and pray behind him. We believe that there can be no other *Qā'im* than he; he may live in the state of occultation (*ghayba*) as long as God wishes; were it the space of the existence of the world, there would be no other *Qā'im* than he.

(36) Our belief concerning prophets, messengers, Imams and angels is that they are infallible and impeccable (*ma'ṣūm*), and do not commit any sin minor or major. He who denies this to them in any matter is an infidel.

(37) Our belief concerning those who exceed the bounds of faith, the *ghulāt* [such as those who ascribe divinity to an Imam], and those who believe in delegation, *mufawwiḍa* [that after creating Muḥammad and 'Alī, God rested and delegated administration of His creation to their hands], is that they are rejecters and deniers of God. They are more wicked than Jews, Christians, Fire-Worshippers, or any heretics. None have belittled God more.

Our belief concerning the Prophet is that he was poisoned [by a Jewish woman] during his expedition to Khaybar. The poison continued to be noxious and shorten his life until he died of its effects.

Imam I: The Commander of the Faithful 'Alī, on whom be peace, was murdered by Ibn Muljam al-Murādī, may God curse him, and was buried in Ghārī.

Imam II: Ḥasan b. 'Alī, peace be upon him, was poisoned by his wife Ja'da bint Ash'ath of Kinda, may God curse her and her father.

Imam III: Ḥusayn b. 'Alī was slain at Karbalā'. His murderer was Sinān b. Anas al-Nakhā'ī, may God curse him and his father.

Imam IV: 'Alī b. Ḥusayn the Sayyid Zayn al-'Ābidīn was poisoned by al-Walīd b. 'Abd al-Malik [Umawī caliph], may God curse him.

Imam V: Muḥammad Bāqir b. 'Alī was poisoned by Ibrāhīm b. al-Walīd [Umawī caliph], may God curse him.

Imam VI: Ja'far al-Ṣādiq was poisoned by Abū Ja'far al-Mansūr al-Dawāniqī ['Abbāsī caliph], may God curse him.

Imam VII: Mūsā al-Kāẓim b. Ja'far was poisoned by Hārūn al-Rashīd ['Abbāsī caliph], may God curse him.
Imam VIII: 'Alī al-Riḍā b. Mūsā was poisoned by Ma'mūn b. Hārūn al-Rashīd ['Abbāsī caliph], may God curse him.
Imam IX: Abū Ja'far Muḥammad al-Tāqī b. 'Alī was poisoned by al-Mu'taṣim ['Abbāsī caliph], may God curse him.
Imam X: 'Alī al-Naqī b. Muḥammad was poisoned by al-Mutawakkil ['Abbāsī caliph], may God curse him.
Imam XI: Ḥasan al-'Askarī was poisoned by al-Mu'tamid ['Abbāsī caliph], may God curse him. The Prophets and the Imams, on all of whom be peace, had informed people that they would be murdered. One who says that they were not has given them the lie and has imputed falsehood to God the Mighty and Glorious.
[*Imam XII* is his son, Muḥammad b. Ḥasan, who disappeared at Samarrā as a child around 874 C.E.]
(39) Our doctrine concerning *taqīya* [hiding Shī'ī faith] is that it is obligatory, and one who forsakes it is in the same position as one who forsakes prayer [i.e., an apostate]. Until the time the Imam al-Qā'im appears, *taqīya* is obligatory and one is not allowed to dispense with it. One who does has gone out of the religion of God. God has described the showing of friendship to unbelievers as being possible only in *taqīya*.

The Imam Ja'far said, "Mix with enemies openly but oppose them inwardly, so long as the authority is a matter of question." He also said, "Diplomacy (*al-ri'ā'*) with a person of faith is a form of polytheism, but with hypocrites in their own house, it is worship." He also said, "One who prays with hypocrites [i.e., non-Shī'ī Muslims] standing in the first row is as one who prayed with the Prophet standing in the first row." He also said, "Visit their sick, attend their funerals, and pray in their mosques."
(40) Our belief concerning the ancestors of the Prophet, contrary to that of the Sunnīs, is that they were Muslims from Adam down to 'Abdallāh, father of the Prophet.
(41) Our belief concerning the descendants of 'Alī and Fāṭima is that they are the progeny of the Messenger of God, and devotion to them is obligatory in requital of his mission.[10]

Observing the instructions of their sixth Imam, Twelvers formed a generally quietist community living among Sunnīs and maintaining its faith discreetly. Another period of relative toleration for Twelverism came under the Mongols who destroyed Baghdad in 1258 and put an end to the 'Abbāsī caliphate there. These selections are from a doctrinal statement of 'Allāma al-Ḥillī, Ḥasan b. Yūsuf (d. 1326/A.H. 726), who taught in Iraq as perhaps the most eminent mujtahid *of this period, with its commentary by a later scholar, Miqdād-i Fāḍil (here in italics). It is still a basic text for study in Twelver academies.*

Knowledge of God, the Prophet, and the Imam

Our learned men agree in considering as a legal duty the knowledge of God, what is proper for Him and impossible for Him, and Prophecy, the Imamate, and the Return.

Knowledge of God: God Most High is a Speaker [*mutakallim*], as all agree. By speech [*kalām*] we mean audible and orderly letters and sounds. The meaning of His being a Speaker is that He brings speech into existence in some sort of body [*jism*]. The explanation of the Ash'arīs is contrary to reason. They say that God's speech inheres in the divine essence [hence is uncreated]. The Ḥanbalīs and the Karrāmīs also say it inheres in His essence. The Mu'tazila and the Imāmī Shī'īs say the reality: it inheres in something else, for example, the burning bush of Moses, not in His essence. The meaning of His being a Speaker is that He makes speech, not that He is One in whom speech inheres. As to the priority of His speech, the Ash'arīs have said that the idea was prior, and the Ḥanbalīs said that the letters were prior. The Mu'tazila have said that speech was an originated thing, and that is the reality, for several reasons.

On the Nature of God: God is truthful, for a lie is necessarily evil, and He is far removed from evil, since it is impossible for Him to have any imperfections.

It is not possible for Him to be in a place, for then He would have need of it, nor in a direction, for then He would have need of it. *These are both negative qualities. Contrary to the Christians and some Ṣūfīs, He is not in a place* [*e.g., the person of Jesus*]. *What is understood by Incarnation is the inhering of one entity in another, and if they intend this, then it is false, for then the Necessary would have to be in need, which cannot be.*

Pleasure and pain are not valid attributes for Him, since it is not possible for God to have a constitution.

Ocular vision of God is impossible, because what can be seen has direction. Then He would be a body, and that is impossible. There is also the word of God to Moses, "You shall never see Me" [Qur'ān 7:139]. *On the Day of Resurrection, perfect knowledge will be necessary, but it will be without ocular vision.*

Our acts occur by free choice, and reason requires this. *The doctrine of the Ash'arīs is that all actions take place by the power of the Most High, and no action whatever belongs to the creature. But if the creature did not bring its actions into being, then the Creator would be most unjust to punish it, and all agree that God does punish* [*sin*].

Evil is not possible for God, because He has what deters Him from it, the knowledge of evil. Also He has no motive, for the motive would be either the need or the wisdom of evil, both of which are ruled out.

The will to do evil is impossible for Him, for that will is evil.

Kindness, *luṭf,* is necessary in God Most High. *Luṭf* is what brings the creature near to obedience and keeps it far from disobedience. If God wills that humankind perform the Law, and gives it no possibility of attainment without His assistance, then not to give it would frustrate His own aim—and reason knows that it would be repugnant behavior. God is far above that.

On the Imamate:

(1) The Imamate is a general authority in religious and worldly matters for a specific person, *derived from the Prophet.* It is necessary [*wājib*], according to reason. For the Imamate is a kindness from God, and we know beyond question that when people have a chief who avenges the oppressed and restrains the oppressor, they come closer to sound behavior and are further from corruption.

(2) It is necessary that the Imam be *ma'ṣūm,* divinely preserved from sin and error, otherwise, he would need an Imam himself. Also, if he committed sin, he would lose his place in people's hearts. Also, he is the guardian of the Law, so he must be immune from sin to preserve it from addition or loss. Finally there is the Word of God: "My Covenant embraces not the doers of evil" [Qur'ān 2:118].

(3) It is necessary that the Imam be specified [*manṣūṣ*] for the office, for immunity from sin is one of the hidden matters. Thus there is no escaping a specification made by one who knows that he has immunity [i.e., the Prophet or the previous Imam]. *All agree that the Imam may be designated by a prophet or previous Imam, but the Sunnīs go on to say that he is established by the acknowledgment of "those with power to loose and bind," and some of the righteous Zaydī Mu'tazila have agreed with them. The Jārūdī Zaydīs add that any learned courageous Fāṭimī* [*from the line of Ḥasan or Ḥusayn*] *who rises with the sword to summon people to right becomes the Imam. The objection to this is that then there would be contention among those fitted for the Imamate.*

(4) It is necessary for the Imam to be better than any of his subjects. *Otherwise the worse would take precedence over the better.*

(5) The Imam after the Messenger of God is ʿAlī b. Abī Ṭālib, and then his eleven [named] descendants. *The Twelfth Imam, the lord of our age, Muḥammad b. al-Ḥasan al-ʿAskarī, is alive and existent since the time of his birth in 870 (A.H. 256), for there must be an Imam in every age, so long as there are people to obey the Law. The cause of his staying absent is the strength of his opponents and the weakness of his helpers, or a benefit on which the faithful depend, or wisdom known to God alone. O God, let his advent shine upon us, and enlighten our eyes with his beauty, for the sake of Muḥammad, his following and his family!*[11]

Sevener Shīʿīs: Ismāʿīlism and Developments

The third major division of the Shīʿīs which has survived is that of the Seveners, who trace their line of Imams through Ismāʿīl, the eldest son of Imam Jaʿfar. According to his followers, he had already been given the naṣṣ, *the designation to be next Imam, by his father, and so it could not be revoked to give it to his younger brother as the Twelvers claim: that was only an example of* taqīya, *designed to draw the trail from the real Imam so that the true line of Imams could go underground and work for the triumph of their religion.*

*Sevener Shīʿism is esoteric (*bāṭinī*) Islam: nothing is what it seems to be; all has hidden meanings, into which one must be initiated (originally in seven degrees) by the Imam or a master designated and trained by him. The following selection is a good example of early Sevener teaching,* taʾwīl al-bāṭin, *or interpretation of the esoteric meaning of Qurʾān verses, ascribed to a very important early* dāʿī *or summoner, Ibn Ḥawshab al-Kūfī (d. 880/A.H. 266), who established a base of power for the doctrine in the Yemenī mountains, out of the reach of the ʿAbbāsī caliphs. Ismāʿīlī Shīʿism in all its known forms owes much to Neoplatonism and the physics of Ptolemy: it was a radical reinterpretation of Islam in the light of Hellenistic philosophy and science. This appeal as a "scientific" religion explains some of its medieval attraction for Muslim intellectuals and mystics.*

Esoteric Interpretation

The first words of the Qurʾān are "In the name of God, the Merciful, the Compassionate." *In the name of God* is written with seven Arabic letters, from which twelve others can be derived, and then the twelve letters of *the Merciful, the Compassionate* follow. The *sūra* is "The *Sūra* of Praise" [*ḥamd*], and is seven verses. The seven letters of *In the Name of God* refer to the seven *nāṭiqs* or major spokesmen [of the Universal Reason] and the twelve derived letters indicate the fact that every *nāṭiq* has twelve intendants [*naqībs*]. From the twelve letters of *the Merciful, the Compassionate* are derived nineteen letters, indicating the fact that from each *nāṭiq* are derived seven Imams and twelve *ḥujja*s, making nineteen altogether.

The seven verses of the *sūra* symbolize the seven degrees of religion. The *Sūra* of Praise opens the Book of God, and similarly the degrees of religion open the door of knowledge in God's religion.[12]

The letter *yā* in *mahdī* has the numerical value of ten, and the seventh *nāṭiq* will be the tenth after Muḥammad and 'Alī and the seven Imams of their line. He is the tenth, and will be the seventh *nāṭiq,* and he is the eighth after the seven Imams.

God says, glory be to Him, "Then We cleft the earth in fissures"—the earth is the *wāṣī,* 'Alī—"and caused to grow therein grain and the grape, reeds, olives, palms, and dense-treed gardens, fruits, and pasture: an enjoyment for you and your flocks" [Qur'ān, 80:26–32]. The meaning of "pasture," *āb,* which also means "father," is 'Alī, and referred to here are his descendants the seven Imams, and the eighth, who is the *mahdī,* the seventh *nāṭiq.*[13]

From the Yemen, the doctrine was spread to the Kutāma Berber tribe of North Africa by another dā'ī, *and 'Ubaydallāh, a man claiming to be the promised* mahdī, *set up the "Caliphate of the Fāṭimī Imams" of the Ismā'īlī line in Qayrawān, North Africa, in 909. Here the doctrine could be openly preached, and in 969 a Fāṭimī army conquered Egypt and built a new capital, al-Qāhira—"The Overwhelming"—origin of the name of Cairo. Briefly the Fāṭimī Empire reached across North Africa and included Sicily, Palestine, the Yemen, and the Holy Cities of Arabia.*

Ismā'īlī Law was systematized in the North African period by their chief justice and chief dā'ī, *al-Nu'mān b. Muḥammad, an Arab who began as a Sunnī in North Africa and converted to the Ismā'īlī doctrine. He moved with his Imam, Caliph al-Mu'izz, to Cairo and died there in 974.*

The following section on the Ismā'īlī doctrine of the Imamate is from Qāḍī al-Nu'mān's Da'ā'im al-Islām, *once the major law work of the Ismā'īlīs and still used by the Sevener Bohoras of the Yemen, India, Pakistan, and East Africa. All Shī'īs add to the profession of faith "There is no god but God and Muḥammad is the Messenger of God" the words "and 'Alī is the* walī *of God." Here the idea of solidarity* [walāya] *with the Imams is developed in one of the earliest systematic Sevener treatises on the Imamate.* Walāya *is first of the Sevener "Seven Pillars of Islam," followed by Purity, Ritual Prayer,* Zakāt, *Fasting, Pilgrimage, and* Jihād, *or striving in the way of God.*

Walāya *with the Commander of the Faithful 'Alī and with the Imams*

Imam Abū Ja'far Muḥammad b. 'Alī b. Ḥusayn, God's blessing be on him, stated: God revealed the law of ritual prayer when the people still did not know what that was, and the Messenger of God, may God bless him and give him peace, made it clear to them by his example. Similarly with the *Zakāt,* the Fast, and the Pilgrimage. Then God revealed the law of solidarity: "Your *walī* is only God, and His messenger, and those who have faith, who establish the ritual prayer and pay the *zakāt,* bowing down to God" [Qur'ān 5:55] and ordered His prophet to explain to the people what *walāya* is. The Messenger of God hesitated at this, fearing that people would apostatize from his religion and call him an impostor, but God commanded him to do it. He did it on the day of the Ghadīr of Khumm and ordered those present to inform those absent. The laws of God were revealed one by one, and the law of *walāya* was the last revealed.

'Alī b. Abī Ṭālib, God's blessing be on him, said: When God revealed the words, "And warn your relations, your next of kin" [Qur'ān 6:217], the Messenger of God invited all the male descendants of his grandfather 'Abd al-Muṭṭalib to a leg of mutton and a cup of milk, for they were sociable at that time. Every one of them could eat a sheep and drink a firkin, and there were some forty of them. They ate until they were stuffed and drank until they were quenched, and that day Abū Lahab [later enemy of the Prophet] was among them. Then the Messenger of God said, "Sons of 'Abd al-Muṭṭalib, obey me and you will be kings and rulers of the earth. God never sends a prophet without appointing for him a lieutenant, an assistant, an heir, a brother, and a *walī.* And which of you will be my lieutenant, my heir, my *walī,* my brother, and my assistant?" They were still, and he began to offer it to them one by one, no one accepting it, until none remained but I, the youngest of them all that day. He turned to me, and I said, "I will do it, Messenger of God!" Then he said, "Yes, you will do it, 'Alī!"

'Alī said: Two pontiffs [*ḥabarān*] of the Christians visited the Messenger of God and spoke long with him about the matter of Jesus. Then God revealed to him the verse, "The likeness of Jesus with God is as the likeness of Adam: He created him of dust, and said to him 'Be,' and he was" [Qur'ān 3:59]. Then the Messenger of God came into our house and took me, Ḥasan, Ḥusayn and Fāṭima by the hand, went out, and challenged them to imprecation [i.e., to pray with him that God would curse those who were in the wrong: Ed.]. He raised his palm to heaven, spread his fingers wide, and invited them to the ordeal. When the two pontiffs saw this, one said to the other, 'As God is my witness, if he is a prophet, we shall perish, and if he's not, his own people will do for him,' so they both gave up and went home.

Imam Ja'far said: This is the interpretation of the verse, "And what of him who is on a clear proof from his Lord, and a witness from Him recites it, and before him there was the Book of Moses as an Imam and a mercy? Those have faith in it, but whoever rejects it among the parties, the Fire is their destination. So be not in doubt about it; it is the truth from your Lord, but most of the people do not have faith" [Qur'ān 11:17]. The one on clear proof from his Lord here is the Messenger of God, God bless him and give him peace, and the one who comes after him here is 'Ali, who follows him as Imam and as proof to all who come after him in his Community.

Imam Ja'far also said: This is the meaning of the verse, "You are only a warner, and for every people there is a guide" [Qur'ān 13:7]: The warner is the Messenger of God, God bless him and give him peace, and in every age there is an Imam from among us to guide people to what the Messenger of God brought. The first of the guides after him was 'Ali, God bless him, then the legatees who came after him one after the other, may peace be on them all.[14]

The Durūz Faith

A remarkable episode of the Cairo caliphate is the rule of the Fāṭimī caliph al-Ḥākim bi Amr Allāh from 996 to 1021. As Imam, he was in the esoteric Sevener view the earthly manifestation of the Universal Intelligence, an emanation from the transcendent One, who can only be approached through His emanations. In the latter part of his rule, al-Ḥākim was willing to be considered God on earth. This movement was at first led by the Dā'ī *al-Darazī (hence the name* Durūz*), but al-Ḥākim rejected him and turned to the Persian* Dā'ī *Ḥamza b. 'Alī, for whom al-Ḥākim was the embodiment of the One, beyond good and evil, from whom the Universal Intellect (*Ḥamza *himself) and four other cosmic principles called* ḥudūd *emanated. These were the Universal Soul, the Word, the Preceder, and the Follower, each represented by a hierarch.*

The new doctrine was greeted with outrage in Cairo, and in the middle of great disorders, al-Ḥākim vanished: killed, some have said, at the instigation of his family, in 1021 (A.H. 411). However, this new version of Sevener religion found followers, called the Unitarians (Muwaḥḥidūn) in the mountains of geographical Syria, where the Durūz are still found today in tightly knit communities. When al-Ḥākim disappeared in Egypt, they taught that the One had appeared on earth, but now had returned to transcendence. Only those who had accepted Him would be given immortal souls, and these would be reborn as Durūz until He chose to manifest Himself again. Among Muslims, Durūz will often pray with Muslims. In predominantly Christian countries such as the United States they usually join a Christian church, without giving up their identity.

They are divided into the initiates ('Uqqāl*), both men and women, from whom the male elders—the shaykhs—are chosen, and the uninitiated or* Juhhāl. *The latter know the doctrine of Unity through al-Ḥākim, but often little more. The following selection on the Durūz interpretation of* Walāya *shows how they diverge from Shī'ī Muslims and suggests the esoteric nature of their doctrine, though it is not an esoteric text. They number perhaps half a million, but their number is also kept secret. Members are born: converts are not accepted, and marriage outside the sect is not recognized.*

Walāya

We come to the seventh of the pillars: allegiance to the Imam (*walāya*). Relying on the Qur'ān, the Sunnīs believe that every Muslim should pay allegiance to the head of the Muslim Community, the Caliph or Imam. They believe that he must be chosen by the Community as successor of the Prophet's temporal powers, and succeeds him in implementing the religious law, defending Islam, and spreading the faith. He is not the recipient of new revelation.

The people of allegorical interpretation [Sevener Shī'īs] believe he is more than that: he has divine illumination and continues the task of the Prophet. The Prophet conveyed the outer meaning of the divine message, and the Imam conveys its inner meaning. Thus they considered allegiance to him the (first) pillar of Islam. Al-Mu'ayyad fī'l-Dīn al-Shīrāzī (d. 1077) says this:

"If *walāya* to the Legatee (*wāṣī*) stops, then Purification, Zakāt, Fasting, Pilgrimage, and Jihād will go to paganism. It is the mainstay of Religion."

The Unitarians understand by this seventh pillar submission to the Universal Intelligence (*'Aql*) and the Soul, i.e. to the two sources of creation that caused the emergence of all things created. Since they and the other cosmic principles are embodied in human forms, the true believer accepts submission to the human embodiments of the luminary cosmic principles. This is the true meaning of *walāya*. In one of his epistles, Ḥamza b. 'Alī says,

"Hold fast to the Embodiments of the cosmic luminaries; persist in their cause and beware of disobeying them; adhere strongly to them and be joyfully gratified with whatever they accord to you."

Addressing his followers, Ḥamza b. 'Alī says:

"O concourse of the Faithful, who profess the unity of our Lord, you must know that our Lord is the One who has no associates. Then you must know the luminary principles, and you must endeavor to know God's existence."[15]

Ismā'īlī Metaphysics

Typical Ismā'īlī systems see God as pure Unity, the One, inaccessible to human thought. He may therefore only be reached through His emanations. The Universal Intellect, the nous *of the philosophers, receives the divine knowledge, which it imparts to the Universal Soul or Spirit, the* pneuma. *At the bottom of a scale of emanations through the spheres of being is the sublunary material world, but even it bears the stamp of the divine. Here the emanation of the Universal Intellect, the* 'aql kullī, *is manifested in the* nāṭiqs *or great spokesmen in seven cycles. The current cycle runs Adam, Noah, Abraham, Moses, Jesus, Muḥammad (the sixth). Each* nāṭiq *is accompanied by a* wāṣī *or legatee, who is the emanation of the Universal Spirit. This is the Imam, who may be incarnated in many bodies. As Ibn Ḥawshab's treatise states, the seventh* nāṭiq *will come from the line of Imamic manifestations. There will be no new Law after Muḥammad; the seventh* nāṭiq *will manifest the true (i.e., esoteric) meanings of religion.*

The following is from a treatise by a great Persian dā'ī, *Nāṣir-i Khusraw, who was active among the Ismā'īlīs in Persian enemy Sunnī territory and visited Cairo in the mid-eleventh century, the period of Imam Mustanṣir, the grandson of al-Ḥākim.*

On the Word of God

The Creator is the Cause of all causes, and the Word (*Kalima*) uttered by God in the beginning was "*Be!*" This Word was perfect, because

God did not create it from anything. Thus the First Cause was the Word of God, and the first caused, the *'aql,* came into being through it. Yet it would be futile to divide them one from the other, and so we say that the *'aql* is both Cause and Caused, both Reasoning [*'āqil*] and Reasoned [*ma'qūl*]. It is the first entity brought into existence by God. As [human] reason cannot be found unaccompanied by the [human] spirit, and the spirit unaccompanied by reason is incomplete, we realize that God has made them a pair from all eternity. The Universal Spirit [*nafs-i kull*] was like seed sown in the essence of the Universal Reason. It emanated through the *'aql* instantaneously, before time. Time itself was produced by the action of the *nafs*.

As explained, the *'aql* is the first, but it is also bound to be the last. God says, "He is the first and the last, the manifest and the hidden, and has knowledge of all things." [Qur'ān 57:3]. The Chosen one [Muḥammad], God bless him and give him peace, said, "The first that God created was Reason [*'aql*]. He said to it, "Draw nigh!" and it drew near, and "Go back!" and it went back. Then He said, "By My glory and majesty, I never created anything nobler or more sublime than you! By you I shall reward, and by you punish!"[16]

Ṭayyibī Ismā'īlīs

At the death of Imām al-Mustanṣir in Cairo in 1094 (A.H. 487), the Sevener Ismā'īlīs divided. The chief dā'ī, wazīr, and chief commander of armies, al-Afḍal Shāhānshāh, son of Badr al-Jamālī, stated that the elder son had not really received the naṣṣ *or designation, as was supposed: it had only been allowed to appear so. In reality, the new Imam would be a younger son, his protégé al-Musta'lī, whom he enthroned in Cairo.*

The followers of the older son, al-Nizār, refused to accept this, and al-Musta'lī's son al-Āmir was assassinated in Cairo by emissaries of the Nizārīs in 1130. A relative was made ruler, and thus Fāṭimī Ismā'īlīs (the now defunct Ḥāfizī Da'wa) ruled in Cairo until 1171, when the last caliph died.

Followers of the Musta'lī Imams maintain that al-Āmir's posthumous son al-Ṭayyib was smuggled into hiding, and since then the identity of the Imams has been kept secret. The sect is led in the meantime by the dā'ī muṭlaq, *the absolute* dā'ī, *held to be in touch with the Imam, and like him to be* ma'ṣūm *or impeccable. The sect made*

Hindu converts in western India, where they form a merchant community called the Bohoras, from a Gujarati word meaning "trader." In 1539, the chief dā'ī *moved from the Yemen to India, and in 1588 the Ṭayyibīs split over the claims of two* dā'īs *into the majority Dā'ūdīs with their headquarters in Surat and with adherents in East Africa and the Yemen and the minority Sulaymānīs, whose leader resides in the Yemen.*

Ṭayyibī Ismā'īlism is a gnostic system. It concerns a hierarchy of spiritual emanations from their Source. Humankind is at the lowest rank. After some billions of years, in which the souls of each rank may rise higher, the parousia, *the Resurrection of Resurrections, will be achieved. All the sect's history and writings are supposed to be esoteric and thus forbidden to outsiders, though something is known of them.*

The following selection is from a doctrinal statement, the Tāj al-'Aqā'id, *written by the fifth* dā'ī muṭlaq, *'Alī b. Muḥammad b. al-Walīd (d. 1215/A.H. 612) in the Yemen. It argues against the "absence" of the Imam from his people held by the Twelvers.*

On Refutation of the Absence [Ghayba] *of the Imam from the Earth*

The Imam cannot be absent from the Community in any way for any reason. Even for an interval, the elite of his Shī'a are in contact with him, knowing his whereabouts, directing those of pure intention and action toward him, and attaining his abode, the place of the blessing of his prayer and general guidance. Absence would have to be attained by one of three means: (1) through God, (2) through himself, (3) through other people, in fear of his enemies. Absence could not be through God Most High, for that would be a command not to be obeyed. God would not order us to obey a man and then cause him to be absent from us.

We find that it cannot be through himself, for he is divinely preserved from sin, and solidarity with him is ordered on the basis of his presence. Nor can it be said that he is veiled after his appearing, because absenting himself or veiling himself would be the suppression of that virtue and guidance for which he came and was set apart.

If it was through fear of other people, then there would be grave doubt of God's religion, since it was God who set him up and made guidance of the Community necessary through him, and informed him that he would not leave the world until a guide like him had inherited his position. Thus it cannot be in any way due to his fear of others or any doubt about what he was ordered to do. The Imams of the ages have abstained from any such infamous statement.

If anyone should object: But flight was necessary for him as it was for Moses, according to God's Word: 'So I fled from you when I feared you, yet my Lord endowed me with wisdom and appointed me one of the Envoys" [Qur'ān 27:21], we reply: There is the very truth of it. Do you think when Moses fled it was from the world at one swoop? And did he hide himself when God's command came while he was among the Children of Israel, his place known and his situation divulged? While he was sought for, his position was not yet established. When that was done, he said what God has him say in that verse. When that rank [of envoy] came to him, he did not return to hiding. The Imam gives judgment among God's servants endowed with wisdom from the All-Wise, the Aware. He is His deputy in His successorship in creation, inheritor of the earth, governing it in judgment, as God Most High indicates: "When your Lord said to the angels, 'I am placing in the earth a Successor," they said, 'Will you place there one to do mischief therein and shed blood, while we give glory with Your praise and call you Holy?' He said, 'Assuredly I know what you know not.' [2:30]. He does not have to be suppressed, nor is his absence necessary in any way.[17]

Nizārī Ismā'īlīs

Those Ismā'īlīs loyal to the line of Nizār claimed that it was continued at the Castle of Alamūt, in Daylam—old Shī'ī mountain country in northern Iran. This Nizārī "New Da'wa" owed much to the activity of the Ḥujja or leading dā'ī, *Ḥasan b. al-Ṣabbāḥ. It was he who organized it at Alamūt and at other strongholds as far west as Syria, where the Nizārīs came in contact with the Crusaders. The Nizārīs were accused by their enemies of the immoderate use of Indian hemp or* ḥashīsh, *hence the name* ḥashīshiyīn. *Their well-known practice of sending* fidā'īs—*"self-sacrificers"—to stalk and murder the enemies of the sect was justifiable on the ground that opponents of the Imam were manifestations of the material world of nonexistence. This has given us the word "assassin."*

The following selection is from a treatise probably written by Ḥasan b. al-Ṣabbāḥ. It was intended to appeal to nonbelievers and would have been attractive to Christians. Here the Imams are the Logos, the universe is divinized, and God wears a human face.

The Great and Exalted has a manifestation in His own form for all eternity in this world. He has made a man noble with that form, and all the prophets and friends of God have indicated a man who would be the Great and Exalted among people in the form of a man.

Those who speak the truth call him Mawlānā, Our Lord, and they consider this the greatest name of God. Further Mawlānā has been called Imam. The Shī'īs call Mawlānā the *Qā'im* of the *Qiyāma* (Upriser of the Resurrection); some hold to the name Malik al-Salām [King of Salem; Prince of Peace]; some say Muḥammad the Mahdī; some say Muḥammad b. Ḥasan al-'Askarī [Twelfth Imam]; some are sure it is 'Alī's son Muḥammad b. al-Ḥanafīya.

It is known at large and among the elite that the Prophet indicated Mawlānā 'Alī b. Abī Ṭālib as Qā'im of the Qiyāma. He is above all the Imams and has no end or beginning. But relatively to the people he appears now as a son, now as a grandson, now aged, now young, now a king, now a beggar. He appears in the form of the Imam of the age, now and tomorrow.

Haḍrat Bābā Sayyidnā Ḥasan b. Ṣabbāḥ was the greatest *ḥujja* [proof] of the Qā'im of the Qiyāma.

This whole world from the core of the earth to the zenith of the heaven of heavens is one body (*shakhs*). The same power that appears in the sun and moon and stars is in the black stone [of the Ka'ba] and in darkness. But it is necessary to see, and one must treat all opposites analogously.

The Divine light first shines from the heavens, and also rises from the core of the earth. The (Ptolemaic) heavens are called "fathers" and the four humours (hot, cold, dry and moist) are called "mothers"; minerals, plants and animals are called "offspring." Then the power of the Divine light causes whatever is subtly alive in fathers, mothers and offspring to be gathered into the body of a man, and in this special form to arrive at Godhead.

In the realm of *sharī'a* its people imagine God conjecturally. But one must know that in this form of Man, the Lord has manifested Himself. The Lord has made man great and ennobled; regarded relatively He has brought Himself into this special form.[18]

After the destruction of Alamūt in 1258 by the Mongols, the Nizārīs were forced to conceal their identity and that of the Imam, who took the guise of a Ṣūfī leader in southern Iran. In 1817, the Nizārī Imam was given the honorary title Aghā Khān by the Qajar shah of Iran, and the Imams continue to use it today as a secular title. The Aghā Khān is the living sharīʿa *for his followers, an inerrant and impeccable source of guidance.*

The Daʿwa had many adherents in western India, where a Vaishnava caste of Hindus, the Khojas, identified the Imam as the avatar of their supreme god, Vishnu. Other, non-Khoja, Nizārīs resided in Syria, Persia, and Central Asia. The Daʿwa necessarily changed from place to place, according to who was involved, and where, and when. What really mattered was that one be devoted to the sinless Imam.

The following is taken from a revered manual of the Nizārīs of Badakhshān in Central Asia, wrongly attributed to Nāṣir-i Khusraw and much esteemed by them. Here the central doctrines of Islam are made part of an allegory and the Law is an exterior form for those who do not have the gnosis imparted by the Ḥujja.

Bāṭin *in Religion*

In human nature are diabolical as well as angelic and human elements. It is necessary for the prophet to explain the demonic and brutal in physical imagery; thus he tells people that the place for evildoers is Hell, full of fire with snakes, scorpions, and the Zaqqūm Tree. He also explains the meaning of the angelic qualities in people in physical imagery, telling them that the place for good-doers is Paradise: a garden full of delicious foods and drinks and charming girls and boys. A prophet must explain his teachings in such palpable similes, devised for the understanding of both strong and weak minds. The weak intelligence will not understand anything but physical imagery, but the strong intelligence will quickly grasp the simile.

Since in every period the conditions of humankind are changing, due to the influences of the stars and the peculiarities of the age, the Law must also change. If the prophet is the bringer of a scripture, then his words in scripture must be allegorical and expressed in similes. Primitive people who are on the sensual level, like animals, understand nothing beyond the outer meaning, the *ẓāhir;* hence they should follow the outer side of the prophet's words, similar to straw or bark. Those who can understand the reality of things, the *bāṭin,* and are on the level of intelligence and understanding will perceive the meaning of his words. The *ẓāhir* must be continually changing, while the *bāṭin* is concerned with the world of reality or divinity, and does not change.[19]

Prayer, *ṣalāt,* comes from *waṣala,* to be in contact with or arrive. This is arriving at knowledge of the Imam and the true religion.

The meaning of the fast is observing *taqīya* or dissimulation. The Feast of Fast-breaking is the Day of the Great Qiyāma [the triumph of the true religion].

The meaning of the *zakāt* tax is teaching the religion and making it reach the faithful according to their ability to understand it. The distributor is the Ḥujja, who distributes to each their due portion.

The meaning of the Ḥajj is leaving the beliefs one once held, advancing stage by stage from neophyte to Ḥujja. Running in the Pilgrimage means hastening toward the Imam.

The meaning of prostration in error is, when a fully licensed initiate [*ma'dhūn*] or a *dā'ī* commits an error, he must return to the knowledge of the *bāṭin* which is with the Ḥujja, because *sajda* or prostration indicates the *nāṭiq* or the Ḥujja.[20]

The following selection was apparently written for a small, isolated community of Nizārīs in Badakhshān early in the sixteenth century. The Imam was concealed, and connection with the Ḥujja was the best one could hope for. It was a gloomy time, and the author, not a very learned man, seems to have been driven by the circumstances into mysticism. Yet it is still an authentic presentation of Sevener Islam, looking forward to the promised time of the great deliverance and based on a particular interpretation of the revelation given to Muḥammad.

The Recognition of the Imam

This is a section on the recognition of the Imam, who is the manifestation of the divine creative act [*amr*]; on his Ḥujja, who is the manifestation of the Universal Reason, on the *dā'ī,* or summoner to truth; on the *ma'dhūn akbar,* or senior initiate licensed to teach; on the *ma'dhūn asghar,* or junior licensee, and on the *mustajīb*, the questioner-neophyte, who are all a manifestation of the Universal Soul. It also deals with the People of Opposition, who are manifestations of the Universal Material Body.

I begin with the recognition of the Imam. He may be known at one time directly in his own person, and at other times through his Ḥujja. It is possible to recognize him directly only in the "Sabbath of Faith." Every Day of Faith is equal to a thousand years [each belongs to a *nāṭiq* or major prophet: the thousand years after the Hijra, near the end of which this was written, was the Day of Muḥammad]. On the Seventh Day, the Sun of Faith, the Imam, is manifested. In the other six days, called the "Night of Faith," the *sharī'a* acts as a veil for for the Imam.

As there is a moon to take the place of the sun at night, so the Ḥujja takes the place of the Imam when he is not manifest.

In the six thousand years of the "Night of Faith," the Imam occasionally becomes manifest, but these manifestations are not in his full glory. Yet it would be absurd to think that he would leave his elite without the possibility of recognizing him: it is for the purpose of their acquiring this knowledge that the world was created. Therefore the moon must exist in this night of faith.[21]

AFTERWORD: ISLAM TODAY

Since the 1970s, Islam has been undergoing a tremendous resurgence all over the world. This is a major fact of late twentieth century religious and political history.

Islam has been at least three things: it is a religion, pointing the way to human salvation; it was one of the world's great civilizations, producing art, architecture, literature, and material culture which have been the envy and admiration of the world; and it is a community which seeks for governance: a polity. Thus a resurgence in Islamic religion will necessarily be a political fact as well.

Today Islam is reasserted in the public and personal lives of Muslims in a way it has not been for many years. Their dress—especially that of women—reflects this, whether in the streets of Cairo, Istanbul, or Jakarta. Islamic banking, taxes, laws, and punishments are being introduced in many Muslim lands. Islam is reflected in politics from Morocco to Mindanao. The revival of Islamic practice involves an increased emphasis on religious identity; more faithful attendance at mosques; increased avoidance of alcohol, dancing, and gambling; the growth of new Islamic associations; and the proliferation of Islamic literature and media programs. There is also renewed vitality in Ṣūfism.

Cultural authenticity in Islam today is seen as involving religious orthopraxy, and it is seen as normal to mix religion and politics, even though this may at times seem to observers to involve manipulating and controlling people. Rulers in Muslim lands increasingly use Islam to bolster their legitimacy and justify their policies, and their opponents use it to impugn them for not being Islamic enough.

The Western world, particularly the United States, has been slow to grasp how much the world has changed. When North America was colonized in the seventeenth century, Europeans had been in direct and continuous contact with the civilization of Islam for nearly a thousand years since Muslims invaded and conquered Spain in 711. During all that time, the Muslims had usually demonstrated an easy sort of superiority over the West, in terms of seapower, productivity, trade, gracious living, science, and intellectual achievements. Western Europe could usually hold its own militarily, but it frequently lagged behind culturally. Islam was always the great challenger.

The seventeenth century knew something about Islam. In 1658, Muslims had invaded Hungary from Turkish-controlled Transylvania; in 1669, they conquered Crete. In 1672, Muslims invaded Poland; by 1678, they had defeated the Russian Empire and invaded the Ukraine. In 1683, a Muslim army marched to the gates of imperial Vienna and besieged it. Europe trembled. At the same time, Islam was spreading deep into Africa and Asia. Southeast Asia was being Islamized just when the Europeans appeared, and it was Islam that offered the peoples of that region the best hope of organizing resistance. Islam had penetrated to Subsaharan Africa from North Africa in the eleventh century, and it continued to spread among local peoples.

With the eighteenth century, however, Europeans began to demonstrate a growing technological and organizational edge over the Muslims. That gave Europe a great sense of confidence and optimism. The United States was born in a world in which the power of Islamic civilization appeared to be breaking down. For two hundred years, the United States was isolated from the Islamic sphere and buffered by great oceans from the world that its ancestors in Europe, Asia, and Africa knew. Islam appeared to be a spent force, politically speaking. Today no rational person could hold that view. However, U.S. leaders have been poorly prepared to deal with the Islamic resurgence of the late twentieth century.

When one looks at the map of the Middle Eastern states, one sees what appear to be a number of nations, often with borders that look as if they were drawn with a ruler, in neat straight lines—and they were, with British and French rulers. Few states in the Middle East have any history as nations, and the loyalty of their citizens to them is weak. Exceptions include Egypt, a country with 5,000 years' continuous history—Egyptian nationhood is a reality. So is Iranian nationhood, Turkish nationhood, and most recently Palestinian nationhood, which has been forged by the ordeal of European Jews taking over the Palestinian homeland and the need to resist that takeover. Most of the other states were put together from pieces of the Ottoman Empire, carved up by England and France after World War I. Hence Middle Easterners have little sentiment for their states as such. While they may have deep affection for their homelands, that is not the same thing as nationalism.

The nation all the Arabs (except Egyptians) will most easily recognize is the Arab nation. Arab nationalism only appeared at the beginning of the twentieth century and is based on the idea that all Arabs—Christians, Muslims, and other sects—from every land are products of a common family and history. It is a strong tie, but it results from Western cultural influences in the Middle East, and its roots are rather weak. For those Arabs who are Muslims, Islam today seems a stronger tie, though it involves seeing Indian, Turkish, or Malay Muslims as more closely related than the Arab Christians next door.

But Arabs are only a small portion of the world's Muslims. During the period of Western colonialism, which began in Indonesia/Malaysia in the eighteenth century, in India and North Africa in the nineteenth, and in the Asian Arab countries only after World War I, Muslim decision makers for the most part became convinced that their best hope was to modernize by imitating the West; to introduce secular law (independent of religion), parliamentary systems, Western dress, Western architecture, and Western institutions; and to emphasize nationalism rather than Islam. After World War II, this was varied occasionally with imitation of East European socialist states, because these states seemed to be successful in achieving progress and independence from Western control. In all cases, it was essentially a period of imitation, in which inspiration came from outside Muslim society.

This period came to an end in the 1967 Middle East War, in which the state of Israel, created in 1948, backed morally by the West and materially by the United States, quickly and decisively defeated its Arab neighbors (who had taken up threatening positions) in a carefully planned preemptive attack. Old Jerusalem with its shrines, third holiest city of Islam, was lost to Israel. The West Bank, the Gaza Strip, the Jawlān (or Golan) of Syria, and Egypt's Sinai Peninsula also fell under Israel's control.

One-seventh of Egypt's landmass was occupied by Israel, and the Suez Canal became impassable. To add insult to the injury, the West exulted at the victory and jeered at the losers. This was something that not just Arabs but Muslims everywhere felt keenly. The result was an identity crisis. Something seemed very wrong, something which called for a critical reordering of national and individual life. "The liberation of Jerusalem" became a worldwide Muslim slogan. Imitation of the West now began to seem to Muslims only the road to destruction; perhaps inspiration must be sought in their own distinctive heritage.

Western-oriented elites and individuals felt particularly damaged. They had based their hopes of modernization on borrowing from the West, and these hopes had been shattered. They had not strengthened their societies, nor had they built secure ties with their Western or East European models and allies.

That year, 1967, was when disillusionment with imitating the West or socialism began. It picked up speed, particularly in the 1970s. One of the events that gave the Muslim world the sense that new hope was on the horizon was the 1973 war, in which Egypt demonstrated the ability of a Muslim government to wage a modern war. It did not win, because the United States was aiding Israel politically and materially, and Israel had one of the best armies in the world in any case. But the war at least demonstrated that Muslims could fight a war with modern weapons. It was something that the world, and not least the Muslim world, needed to learn. Moreover, the war was fought in the holy month of Ramaḍān, when the Muslims of the world were fasting, and it was accompanied by a great outpouring of prayer and religious devotion. Egypt's president, Anwar Sadat, portrayed the war as a Muslim struggle against oppression. Its gains seemed the answer to prayer.

Along with this went the success of the Arab oil embargo. To prevent the West from backing Israel completely in the war, the other Arab states managed successfully to deny a critical part of their oil resources to the industrialized world, dependent on these oil imports. After the war, they managed with the help of the shah of Iran to hold out for better prices for their undervalued product. This too suggested new power, new hope.

The second major event was the 1978 overthrow of the shah of Iran, a man widely regarded by the Iranian people as a cruel tyrant. The shah was backed by the American presidency, by the CIA, by the U.S. military establishment—backed, in fact, by the United States, wholly and uncritically.

Against the shah and his well-armed military and police unarmed civilians demonstrated, chanting the old battle-cry of the Muslims, *Allāhu akbar,* God is greater. Many of these people were Iranian women who had abandoned modern costume for the *chador,* the outer covering which veiled traditional women. In the end, the shah was forced to abdicate, and a revolutionary government came into power. Regardless of whether one liked what happened to that revolutionary government afterward, whether one approved of Ayatullāh Khomeini or not, the fact remained that here was a historic Muslim people that had grasped its ancient Muslim identity and proclaimed it successfully to face down a high-tech, U.S.-backed tyrant. It seemed an enormous accomplishment and was a source of great enthusiasm from one end of the Muslim world to the other. Perhaps other tyrants too, and other unjust situations, could now be addressed by a reaffirmation of Islamic identity.

The Gulf War of 1991, with its terrifying revelation of what Arabs were willing to do to "brother Arabs," was very damaging to the idea of Arab nationalism and, to some degree, nationalism in all Muslim lands. Islamic solidarity then appears as the correct alternative.

A part of the Islamic resurgence today is the rejection of the idea that Muslims can find any satisfactory model in the Western world. Muslim attitudes toward the United States are ambivalent: they admire its material well-being and ease of existence as well as its professed ideals, but they regard it and most of the West today as a violent and bedeviled society which deserves to be pitied, not emulated; one whose people are prey to crime, promiscuity, addiction, and deep sexual confusion. They watch American television serials and know that they do not wish to be the sort of society depicted in them. Certainly economic frustration and urban alienation play their roles, attractive for neo-Marxist observers' analysis. Muslims also resent the hypocrisy and manipulation that the West has used on them, symbolized in such matters as the forcible colonization of Palestine by Europeans with the aid of the United States.

Muslims are also deeply apprehensive at the threatening and fearful image that they and their religion are often given in Western media. They fear that now that the Soviet empire no longer exists, Islam will be cast in the role of a demon by aggressive Western leaders who want an enemy in order to socially manipulate their own people.

Attitudes common to all the Islamic revivalists today include the following:

1. Both Western-style liberal nationalism and Marxist socialism are failures; they are failed systems which cannot make their people happy, and Islam is the correct option.

2. Islam is a total way of life. Muslim societies have failed because they tried to isolate religion from society and follow Western materialism, hedonism, and secularism.

3. Islamization, the reinstitution of an Islamic way of life, involves reinstating the reign of Islamic Law. The *sharī'a,* based on the Word of God in the Qur'ān and the practice of His messenger and the Companions, contains the plan for Muslim society.

4. Modernization, science, and technology are all acceptable and desirable things, provided that they are not seen as autonomous, but as subject to divine Law.

5. The re-Islamization of society demands Muslims who are dedicated, repentant, and ready to struggle against corruption and injustice.

A minority of revivalists go beyond this program. Professor John Esposito has aptly called them the *radical activists*.[1] Still a fairly small group, these militants would agree with all the statements above and add the following:

1. A state of war already exists between Islam and the West, Islam and Marxist power, Islam and Zionist Israel. All these forces seek to dominate, colonize, and exploit the Muslims. It is not necessary to declare war against them; the war is there. It is only necessary to recognize that war exists.

2. Islamic government is not simply an option, it is an imperative from God. Islamic government means one based on *sharīʿa* (almost never do activists spell out what system of *sharīʿa* is to be the constitution of the Islamic state—this is left vague). Any other form of government is illegitimate and must be struggled against.

3. A holy struggle against the enemies of Islam is not just a collective obligation (*fard kifāya*). It is essential individual religious obligation (*fard ʿayn*).

4. Here there is a changed attitude toward Christians and Jews. Islam has always been very tolerant of these other religions. The radical activists tend to say that, wherever they look, those groups stand on the side of evil. Therefore Islam can no longer treat them with tolerance: they are part of the conspiracy against it.

Women's rights had made significant progress in the period of rapid Westernization of the Islamic world. Today many Muslim women fear that an uncritical return to tradition is endangering their grains. Christians and other minority groups in Islamic societies often feel threatened and isolated in the current Islamization of society. They see a society developing which will have no place, or only a secondary citizenship role, for them. But to many Muslims Islamization seems the last and best hope against an aggressive external world that wishes them harm.

The press has done a considerable disservice to the English language by lumping revivalists and radical activists all together, never distinguishing between them, and usually calling them "fundamentalists." There is a fundamentalist position in Sunnī Islam: it is that of the Ḥanbalīs, who admit only the texts of Qur'ān and *Ḥadīth,* without interpretation, without any consensus but that of the first generation of Muslims, "without asking how or why," as the basis of Islamic Law. Revivalists may or may not be fundamentalists. Certainly the Wahhābī movement which began in the eighteenth century has been a major inspiration for revivalist thought, but so too was the teaching of the Naqshbandī Ṣūfī order, which often organized resistance to foreign imperialism, including Russian and Chinese, when it threatened Muslims. Accurately speaking, it is impossible for Twelver Shīʿīs, with their emphasis on the *ḥadīths* of the Imams and the interpretation of the *mujtahids*, to be fundamentalists—though they may well be radical activists. We may also note that radical activists among the Shīʿīs are led by the *ʿulamāʾ*, but in Sunnī Islam this is rarely the case: the leaders are usually educated in secular universities, including those of the United States, the United Kingdom, France, and Germany. Fundamentalism has a meaning, but it is not easily applicable to the phenomena indicated here. It may be as well to avoid it as a label when discussing Islamic resurgence.

Revivalists may be Ṣūfīs and often are. In fact, it can be observed that where there is a revival of the ideal of *sharīʿa* in the modern Muslim world there is also a revival of Ṣūfism. The two are not necessarily in conflict with each other; they are the two sides of the traditional Islamic coin.

Islam in politics takes on the color of the local sociopolitical issues. The ideology of the political Muslim is the local interpretation of the religious worldview reflected and applied in the specific context of a region or country.

The moderate revivalists want to transform Muslim society by participating in government and transforming society. Many of them have been put on guard by the excesses of the Iranian Islamic Revolution: they would say that it made mistakes and that they wish to avoid these and improve upon them. Organizations like the Muslim Brotherhood in the Arab World, the Jamaat-i Islami of Pakistan and India, and ABIM (the Malaysian Islamic Youth Movement) take part in student and national elections (their members have participated in cabinets) and organize schools, camps, hospitals and infirmaries, legal aid societies, and youth centers.

Radical activists such as al-Jihād al-Islāmī (Islamic Jihad), Takfīr wa Hijra (Recognition of Infidelity and Emigration from it), and Hizballāh (the Party of God) believe that existing governments try to co-opt and manipulate Islam. For example, President Anwar Sadat of Egypt secured a *fatwā* from the Azhar ratifying what they see as the corrupt Camp David accords (wrong because they gave far too much to Israel), failed to implement the *sharīʿa,* and imprisoned Muslim dissenters, so the Jihād group assassinated him. In their eyes, violence is permissible and necessary to attack such governments, along with the corrupt *'ulamā'* who cooperate with them.

It is deeply irritating to the revivalists as well as the radicals to raise the questions "What Islam are we talking about? Whose interpretation? Which system of *sharī'a?*" Yet these questions are profoundly important. There is no pope in Islam, and no synod of bishops, no central authority that all can recognize except the Qur'ān, since Muslims have never recognized all the same *Ḥadīths*. The Shī'is of Iran currently endeavor to get around this difficulty by having a *mujtahid* who has the right to pass on the legality of all governmental acts: the doctrine of *vilāyat-i faqīh*. Even for them however, the question arises of what happens if another *mujtahid* does not agree with him. The pluralism of the past does not lend itself easily to the ideology of the activists. And how can there be a generally acceptable system of *sharī'a* for Sunnīs if the *ḥadīths* and interpretations on which such a system is based are not generally accepted?

The answer which seems to follow necessarily is: the one that is enforced. But it is an answer which must deeply disturb many moderate spirits, in Islam and outside of it, particularly those who live as minorities within Muslim societies. For example, most Christians and Jews cannot practice their religions without drinking sacramental wine. What happens if a Muslim government enforces the prohibition of all wine? And that is a relatively trivial example. Failure to make clear what system of law is to apply is not rule by law as most people understand it: it is like having a government which refuses to say what constitution it is going to use.

Secularism used to be quite common in Muslim societies. It is the doctrine, borrowed from the West, that religion is a private matter. Secularism is not necessarily irreligious, as some Muslims would claim. It does insist that religion is not a public affair and that attempts to mix it with politics are usually for manipulation rather than for sincere religious goals, since all that sincerely religious people desire can be privately accomplished within a secular society. Today secularists are on the defensive in almost all Muslim societies. Certainly they are not found among the wing of modern Muslims I have called the revivalists.

Among those who call for a "return to Islam," we can find three major positions. These positions may be classified as conservative, neofundamentalist, and neoreformist. These are descriptive classifications rather than denominations; since it is quite possible for an individual or an association to use aspects of each position, they are not mutually exclusive.

1. Conservatives are characterized by *traditionalism.* They accept that the formulations of the medieval thinkers are normative for today's community. It is not Islam which needs to be altered, but modern society. For the traditionalists, return to Islam means a return to established rules which are not in any need of reinterpretation. Most of the *'ulamā'* in countries like Morocco, Tunisia, Egypt,and Pakistan, with their followers, could be classified as belonging to this grouping.

2. Neofundamentalists, inspired chiefly by Ibn Taymīya and the Wahhābīs, claim the right to go back to first principles, to Qur'ān and *Ḥadīth,* to derive Islamic Law for today. They reject the *ijmā'* of the past and refuse to be bound by the classical interpretations, even though they may have great respect for them. By and large, the Muslim Brothers (al-Ikhwān al-Muslimīn) and the Jamaat-i Islami of Pakistan/India fall into this grouping, as well as the Jam'īyat al-Iṣlāḥ (Reform Grouping) of Kuwait. They ordinarily emphasize the need for Islamic law in such matters as cutting off the hands of thieves, stoning adulterers, flogging for drinking, and segregation of the sexes in order to purify society and tend to speak of Islam as being an "ideology." They wish to modernize society in accordance with their neofundamentalist interpretations, tend to reject modern nationalism (for them Islam is the true "nation"), and see no problem with science and technology, so long as they do not lead to ignoring Islamic values.

3. Neoreformists wish to go beyond Qur'ān and *Ḥadīth* to reinterpret Islam. They revere the Islamic past, particularly the first generation of Muslims, and look to them for inspiration, but hold that historically conditioned practices can and should be changed with no damage to true Islam. They believe that human society has been changed profoundly by the technological age and that Islam can and should "respond" to these changes. This it should do not by imitating the West, from whose mistakes it can learn, but by seeking authenticity of the principles of change. Traditionalist *'ulamā'* attack them for their "deviations" and point out that they are completely unqualified to be *mujtahids*.

There are deep divisions of contemporary Muslim society caused by what Esposito has called the "bifurcation of education." This exists in most Islamic societies, between the traditional religious learning and the more secularized modern instruction prevailing in foreign institutions and in the national school systems and universities.[2] The graduates of the first system have little understanding of any need for change, and those of the second system lack the solid knowledge of the cultural and religious tradition that they should have in order to effect enlightened and sensitive changes in the society. There is also no doubt that this division creates a cleft stick in which many of the younger generation find themselves caught. In this situation, the appeal of those who see Islam as an ideology and political program is necessarily very strong.

The resurgence of Islam as religion in our time is well established. At the same time, Islam as polity appears to contain the seeds of troubling instability for itself and for the rest of the world. It behooves non-Muslims to understand the terms in which Islam thinks and to communicate with Muslims today. The matter concerns us all.

NOTES

Introduction

1. A. J. Arberry, *The Koran Interpreted* (London: Allen and Unwin, 1955).

2. Mohammed Marmaduke Pickthall, *The Meaning of the Glorious Koran* (London: Allen and Unwin, 1930, and many subsequent editions); A. Yusuf Ali, *The Holy Qur'ān: English Interpretation with Arabic Text* (Lahore: Muhammad Ashraf Press, 1938 and 1969, with many subsequent editions).

1. The Word of God: The Qur'ān

1. H. A. R. Gibb, *Mohammedanism* (Oxford: Oxford University Press, 1949, and many subsequent editions), 37.

2. The News of God's Messenger: The *Ḥadīth*

1. Ibn Isḥāq, found in Ibn Hishām: *Sīrat al-Nabī,* 4 bks. (Cairo, 1963), bk. 1:153–156, and al-Ṭabarī, *Tā'rīkh,* 3 series (Leiden: Brill, 1879–1901) series 1:1150–1152, abridged (my translation and abridgments throughout unless otherwise noted).

2 Ibn Isḥāq, from Ibn Hishām, *Sīrat,* 1:158–165, abridged.

3. Ibid., 221–225, abridged.

4. There is a difficulty here. Al-Ḥasan of Baṣra had not been born at this time, so if it is true, it was his source who was lifted up as a child to see this.

5. Ibid., 2:268–276, abridged.

6. Ibid., 282–283.

7. Ibid., 292.

8. Ibid., 320–321.

9. Ibid., 330–344, abridged.

10. Ibid. 354–355, abridged.

11. Ibid., 4:1057–1071, abridged.

12. Ibid., 1071–1074, abridged.
13. al-Ṭabarī, *Tā'rīkh,* 1:1817–1819, abridged.
14. Ibn Isḥāq, in Ibn Hishām, *Sīrat,* 4:1074–1075, abridged.
15. al-Bukhārī, *Jāmi' al-Ṣaḥīḥ* (Leiden: Brill, 1868–1908), 4:431.
16. al-Nawawī, *al-Arba'īn* (*Forty Ḥadīths*, in many editions), no.3.
17. al-Bukhārī, *Ṣaḥīḥ,* 4:115.
18. Ibid., 139.
19. Ibid., 300.
20. Ibid., 302.
21. Ibid., 308.
22. Ibid., 298.
23. Ibid., 3:413.
24. al-Nawawī, *Arba'īn,* no. 5.
25. Ibid., no. 14.
26. Ibid., no. 22.
27. Ibid., no. 17.
28. Ibid., no. 34.
29. al-Bukhārī, *Ṣaḥīḥ,* 3:402–403.
30. Ibid., 410–411.
31. Ibid., 4:179.
32. Ibid., 114.
33. Ibid., 431.
34. Ibid., 139.
35. Ibid., 507–508.
36. Ibid., 448.
37. Ibid., 2:435–436.
38. Ibid., 4:43.
39. Ibid., 121.
40. Ibid., 3:410–411.
41. al-Nawawī, *Arba'īn,* no. 25.
42. Ibid., no. 35.
43. Ibid., no. 13.
44. Ibid., no. 24.
45. Ibn Khaldūn, *al-Muqaddima* (Beirut, 1988), 280–282, abridged.

3. The Law of God: *Sharī'a* and *Fiqh*

1. Cf. Ibn Manẓūr, *Lisān al-'Arab* (Beirut, n.d.), s.v. "sh-r-'."
2. Muwaffaq al-Dīn b. Qudāma, *Kitāb al-'Umda fī al-Fiqh al-Ḥanbalī* (Damascus, 1990), 21–26, abridged.
3. Ibid., 29–32, abridged.
4. Ibid., 33–38, abridged.
5. Ibid., 38–39, abridged.

6. Ibid., 43–44.
7. Ibid., 47–52. abridged.
8. Ibn Abī Zayd al-Qayrawānī, *al-Risāla,* 4th ed. (Algiers, 1952), 56–68, abridged.
9. Mālik b. Anas, *al-Muwaṭṭā',* ed. M. F. 'Abd al-Bāqī, 2 vols. (Cairo, 1951) 1:222–232, abridged.
10. Abū Isḥāq al-Shīrāzī, "Zakāt," in *Kitāb al-Tanbīh* (Beirut, n.d.), abridged.
11. Muḥyī al-Dīn al-Nawawī, *Minhāj al-Ṭalibīn* (Batavia, 1882), 279–291, abridged.
12. al-Qayrawānī, *al-Risāla,* 141–147.
13. Burhān al-Dīn al-Marghinānī, *al-Hidāya* (Beirut, n.d.), 1:189–227, abridged.
14. Ibid., 4:231–236, abridged.
15. al-Māwardī, *al-Aḥkām al-Sulṭānīya* (Cairo 1909), 3–14, abridged.
16. Ibn Khaldūn, *al-Muqaddima* (Beirut, 1988), 130–32, abridged. The passages in brackets were suppressed in this edition, but occur in others.
17. Al-Marghinānī, *al-Hidāya,* 4:62–63.
18. Ibid., 70–78, abridged.
19. Ibid., 78–87, abridged.
20. Ibid., 90.
21. Ibid., 87–90, abridged.
22. Ibid., 108–111, abridged.
23. Ibn al-Ukhūwa, *Ma'ālim al-Qurba,* ed. by R. Levy (London: Gibb Memorial Series, 1938), Arabic text, 79.
24. Ibid., 143.
25. Ibid., 163–164.
26. Ibid., 195–198, abridged.
27. In Paul Horster, *Zur Anwendung des islamischen Rechts im 16en Jahrhundert* (Stuttgart, 1935), 67.
28. Ibid., 70–71, abridged.
29. Ibid., 78.

4. Interior Religion: Ṣūfism

1. Abū Ṭālib al-Makki, *Qūt al-Qulūb,* 2 vols. (Cairo, A.H. 1310), 1:149.
2. Abū Nu'aym al-Iṣbahānī, *Ḥilyat al-Awliyā',* 10 vols. (Beirut, 1985), 2:132–33, abridged.
3. Ibid., 144.
4. Ibid., 140.
5. Ibid., 134–137, abridged.
6. Abū 'Abd al-Raḥmān al-Sulamī, *Ṭabaqāt al-Ṣūfīya,* ed. N. Shurayba (Cairo, 1953) 30.

7. al-Iṣbahānī, *Ḥilyat*, 8:29–30.
8. Farīd al-Dīn al-ʿAṭṭār, *Tadhkirāt al-Awliyā'*, 2 vols. (London and Leiden, 1905 and 1907), 1:93.
9. al-Iṣbahānī, *Ḥilyat*, 8:35.
10. Abū Jaʿfar b. Yazdānyār, *Rawḍat al-Murīdīn*, ed. and trans. J. A. Williams (Ann Arbor: University Microfilms, 1959), translation, 83.
11. Abū al-Qasim al-Qushayrī, *al-Risāla* (Cairo, 1966), 624.
12. Margaret Smith, *Rābiʿa the Mystic* (Cambridge: Cambridge University Press, 1928), 27. I first encountered the prayers of Rābiʿa in this ground-breaking study, and though I have elected to make fresh translations in this section I wish to acknowledge my debt to Smith and direct readers to her works on the Ṣūfīs.
13. al-ʿAṭṭār, *Tadhkirāt al-Awliyā'*, 73.
14. Al-Hurayfish, *al-Rawḍ al-Fā'iq*, quoted by M. Smith in *Rābiʿa the Mystic*, 11.
15. al-ʿAṭṭar, *Tadhkirāt al-Awliyā'*, 67.
16. Ibid., 69.
17. *Adab al-Nufūs*, trans. by M. Smith in *Readings from the Mystics of Islam* (London: Luzac, 1972), 15, 16. Every effort has been made to contact the copyright holder for permission to use this quotation. We will gladly request the permission if the copyright holder contacts us.
18. al-Iṣbahānī, *Ḥilyat*, 10:79.
19. Abū al-Faḍl al-Sahlajī, *Kitāb al-Nūr fi Shaṭaḥāt Abī Yazīd*, in *Shaṭaḥāt al-Ṣūfīya I*, ed. ʿAbd al-Raḥmān Badawi (Cairo, 1949), 119, abridged.
20. al-Iṣbahānī, *Ḥilyat*, 10:35.
21. al-Sulamī, *Ṭabaqāt*, 70.
22. al-Sahlajī, in *Shaṭaḥāt al-Ṣūfīya*, ed., Badawi, 138.
23. al-Junayd, *Risāla*, no. 4, quoted by ʿAli Abdel Kader, "The Doctrine of al-Junayd," *The Islamic Quarterly* 1:3, (London: Islamic Cultural Centre, 1954), 174.
24. Quoted by M. Smith, *Readings from the Mystics of Islam*, 36. This famous *ḥadīth* is given in Bukhārī and is the thirty-eighth in the *Forty Ḥadīths* of al-Nawawī. It is a *ḥadīth qudsī*, or quotation from God given by a prophet, in this case Muḥammad, but not occurring in the Qur'ān or Bible. I have given the full text here, although Junayd in the text quoted did not.
25. Ibn Yazdānyār, *Rawḍat*, 83.
26. al-Iṣbahānī, *Ḥilyat*, 10:74.
27. Ibn Yazdānyār, *Rawḍat*, translation, 111–112.
28. Abū Naṣr al-Sarrāj, *Kitāb al-Lumaʿ* (Leiden: Brill, 1914), 210.
29. M. Smith, translator, *Readings from the Mystics of Islam*, 34.
30. *Kitāb al-Tāwasīn*, ed. L. Massignon (Paris, 1913), Arabic text, 25.
31. Ibid., 11, 13, 19–20. No one who wishes to study al-Ḥallāj can ignore Professor Massignon's works on him, but Massignon read somewhat more into the texts than others can locate there.

32. *Akhbār al-Ḥallāj,* ed. L. Massignon and P. Kraus (Paris, 1936), Arabic text, 7–8, abridged.

33. See *Encyc. Islam* 2, article by H. Ritter: "Abū Sa'īd b. Abī 'l-Khayr." R. A. Nicholson has translated most of his biography in *Studies in Islamic Mysticism* (Cambridge: Cambridge University Press, 1921), 1–76.

34. Abū Sa'īd's quatrains have been edited by R. Ethe.

35. Smith, *Readings from the Mystics of Islam,* 53, 54.

36. Ibid., 49.

37. *Tarjumān al-Ashwāq,* ed. and trans. R. A. Nicholson (London: Luzac, 1911).

38. 'Afīfī edition (Cairo, 1946) 48–50, abridged.

39. Ibid., 61–64, abridged.

40. Ibid., 214–217, abridged.

41. A. J. Arberry, *Islamic Culture* (Hyderabad, 1936): 370–389 (here changed from second person singular to second person plural).

42. Edward Fitzgerald, *Manṭiq al-Tayr.* Reprinted by permission of the publishers from *Fitzgerald: Collected Works,* edited by Joanne Richardson, Cambridge, Mass.: Harvard University Press, introduction and editorial material © Joanne Anderson, 1962.

43. al-'Aṭṭār, *Diwān,* trans. by A. J. Arberry, *Immortal Rose* (London: Luzac, 1948), 32–33 (here second person singular changed to plural). Every effort has been made to contact the copyright holder for permission to use this quotation. We will gladly request the permission if the copyright holder contacts us.

44. Ibn al-Fāriḍ, *Diwān,* "Tih Dalālan" (Beirut, 1962), 157–158.

45. Odes of Ibn al-Fāriḍ, trans. by R. A. Nicholson, in *Studies in Islamic Mysticism* (Cambridge: Cambridge University Press, 1921), 176.

46. Ibid., 173–74.

47. R. A. Nicholson, ed., *Selected Poems from the Divani Shamsi Tabriz* (Cambridge: Cambridge University Press, 1898/1977), 125.

48. *Masnavī Ma'navī,* ed. R. A. Nicholson, 3 bks. (Tehran, n.d.), bk. 1, lines 1–19.

49. Ibid., lines 2433–2437.

50. E. G. Browne, *A Year amongst the Persians* (London: A. and C. Black, 1926 and 1950) 137f.

51. I have chosen the Persian word, since *khānqāh* was widely employed as a term even in the Arab world. However, *tekke* is often used in Turkey, and *zāwiya* or *ribāṭ* in North Africa.

52. *Ihyā',* bk. 9, trans. K. Nakamura (Cambridge: Islamic Texts Society, 1990), 5, 9, 23.

53. Constance C. Padwick, *Muslim Devotions* (London: SPCK, 1961), 242.

54. Ibid., 280.

55. Ibid., 257.

56. From the *Ihyā'*, bk. 9, trans. K. Nakamura, 62–63.
57. Padwick, *Muslim Devotions*, 219.

5. The Statements of Theologians: *Kalām*

1. *al-Fiqh al-Akbar I*, found in no. 1, *Majmū'at Shurūḥ al-Fiqh al-Akbar* (Hyderabad, A.H. 1321), my comments.
2. *Kitāb al-'Ālim wa al-Mut'allim* (Cairo, 1949), abridged.
3. Arabic text in *Islām Dair Eski Metinler* (Istanbul, 1953), abridged.
4. al-Ash'arī, *Kitāb al-Luma'*, ed. R. J. McCarthy, S.J., in *The Theology of al-Ash'arī* (Beirut: Imprimerie Catholique, 1953), Arabic text, propositions 82, 85, 107, 119, abridged.
5. Ibid., proposition 135, abridged.
6. Ibid., propositions 169–70, abridged.
7. *Risāla fī Istiḥsān al-Khawḍ fī 'Ilm al-Kalām*, ed. McCarthy, in *The Theology of al-Ash'arī*, Arabic text, propositions 2–6, 21, 27; abridged.
8. al-Juwaynī, *al-'Aqīda al-Niẓāmīya* (Cairo, 1948), 47–48, abridged.
9. al-Ghazālī: *al-Munqidh min al-Dalāl*, trans. Richard J. McCarthy, in *Freedom and Fulfillment* (Boston: Twayne, 1983), 70–77, somewhat abridged.
10. *Iḥyā' 'Ulūm al-Dīn*, 5 vols. (Beirut, 1989), 4:318–325, abridged.
11. Ibid., 1:110–112, abridged.
12. *Ma'ārij al-Wuṣūl*, in *Majmū' al-Rasā'il al-Kubrā* (Cairo, 1905), 1:193, 202–203, abridged.
13. Ibid., 208–17, abridged.
14. "al-Ḥisba fī al-Islām," in *Majmū' al-Rasā'il* (Cairo, A.H. 1323), 66f., abridged.
15. Ibn Taymīya, *al-Siyāsa al-Shar'īya* (Cairo, 1955), 98, abridged.
16. Ibn Taymīya, *Majmū' al-Rasā'il wa al-Masā'il*, 2 vols. (Cairo, 1922), 1:179–180.
17. *Kitāb al-Nubūwwāt* (Cairo, A.H. 1346), 79–81, abridged

6. Sectarian Movements

1. Muḥammad Bāqir Majlisī, *Biḥār al-Anwār*, 110 vols. (Beirut, 1983), 21:386–388.
2. al-Ṭabarī, *Tā'rīkh*, 3 series (Leiden: Brill, 1879–1901), series 2:2008.
3. Ibn 'Abd Rabbihi, *al-'Iqd al-Farīd*, 6 vols. (Cairo 1944), 4:144–146.
4. al-Ṭabarī, *Tā'rīkh*, 2:2010–2011 (the Cairo edition supplies lacunae present in the Leiden edition for this address).
5. al-Jāḥiẓ, *al-Bayān wa al-Tabyīn* (Cairo, 1961), 2:122–124.
6. Ibn Jumay', *Muqaddamat al-Tawḥīd wa Shurūḥuhā*, treatise translated from Berber, with commentaries by Badr al-Dīn al-Shammākhī and Abū Sulaymān al-Tilātī al-Jarbī (Masqāt, 1989) 17–164.

7. al-Mahdī lī-Dīn Allāh Aḥmad b. Yaḥyā b. al-Murtaḍā, *al-Baḥr al-Zakhkhār* (Beirut, 1975), 1:40.
8. Ibid., 91–96, abridged.
9. "A Zaydī Manual of Ḥisba of the 3rd Century," ed. R. Serjeant, in *Rivista degli Studi Orientali* 28 (1953): 16–17, abridged.
10. A. A. A. Fyzee, Ed. and trans., *A Shī'ite Creed* (Bombay: Islamic Research Association, 1942), somewhat abridged, by permission of Oxford University Press.
11. 'Allāma Ḥasan b. Yūsuf al-Ḥillī, *al-Bāb al-Hādī 'Ashar* (Tehran, A.H. 1365), 150–205, abridged.
12. Arabic text, ed. by Kamil Hussein, in *Collectanea of the Ismā'īlī Society* (Leiden: Brill, 1948), 1:189.
13. Ibid., 199, abridged.
14. Qāḍī al-Nu'mān, Abū Ḥanīfa al-Tamīmī al-Maghribī, *Da'ā'im al-Islām,* ed. Asaf b. 'Alī Asghar Fayḍī (A. A. A. Fyzee) Cairo, 1963), 1:14–22, my selections.
15. Sami Makarem, *The Druze Faith* (Delmar, N.Y.: Caravan Books, 1974), 108–111, abridged.
16. Nāṣir-i Khusraw, *Shīsh Faṣl,* ed. W. Iwanow (Bombay, 1949), Persian text, 10–15, abridged.
17. 'Alī b. Muḥammad al-Walīd, *Tāj al-'Aqā'id,* ed. Aref Tamer (Beirut, 1967), 69–70.
18. Trans. Marshall Hodgson, in his *The Order of the Assassins* (New York: AMS Press, 1980), 284–313, abridged.
19. *Kalām-ī Pīr,* ed. W. Iwanow (Bombay, 1934), Persian text, 54–55, abridged.
20. Ibid., 95–97, abridged.
21. *Faṣl dar Bayān-i Shinākht-ī Imām* (Bombay, 1949), abridged.

Afterword: Islam Today

1. John Esposito, *Islam, the Straight Path* (Oxford: Oxford University Press, 1988), 170.
2. Ibid., 197.

INDEX